McDougal, Littell
Wordskills

Red Level

James E. Coomber
Concordia College
Moorhead, Minnesota

Howard D. Peet
North Dakota State University
Fargo, North Dakota

 McDougal, Littell & Company
Evanston, Illinois
New York   Dallas   Sacramento   Columbia, SC

ISBN-13: 978-0-395-97979-2   ISBN-10: 0-395-97979-X

Copyright © 2000 by McDougal, Littell & Company
Box 1667, Evanston, Illinois 60204
All rights reserved. Printed in the United States of America.

14 15 16 17-DWI-08 07 06

CONTENTS

To the Student

Why study vocabulary? Increasing the number of words that you know helps you read, write, and speak better. You'll understand more of what you read with less reliance on the dictionary, and you'll be able to express yourself more accurately. This doesn't mean using twenty-dollar words to amaze others. It just means using the right words to say exactly what you mean.

How to Use This Book

You may notice something unusual about this vocabulary book. Definitions are not given with the word lists. Instead, you are given something more powerful— strategies for determining the meanings of words yourself. You'll find this information in a Special Unit starting on page 1. Then, in the following units, you will master new words using a five step process:

1. First you will infer the word's meaning through context clues.
2. Second you will refine your understanding by studying the word's use in a reading selection.
3. Then your understanding of the words will be reinforced through a variety of exercises.
4. Next you will relate the word to other words in the same family.
5. Finally you will use the word in writing and speaking.

The words in this book are ones you are likely to encounter in your reading. Some you may already know; others may be completely unfamiliar. As you study these words, try to move them into your "active vocabulary," the words you understand well enough to use in your speaking and writing.

A Personal Vocabulary-Building Program

You can apply the vocabulary skills in this book to learning any new words that you encounter. Here are several tips that will help you:

1. Keep a vocabulary notebook. Jot down the new words you encounter. Record the essential information for each word: correct spelling, part of speech, pronunciation, definition.
2. Review the words in your notebook. Take a few minutes each day to study them. Set a realistic goal of learning a certain number of new words per week.
3. Study the words actively. Active study means that you use as many senses as possible in studying the word. Listen to yourself say the word. See it in your mind's eye. Then use the word as soon as possible in speech or in writing. In general, if you use a word twice, it is yours.
4. Invent your own memory devices. Try to associate the word with other similar words you know. Create a mental image that relates to the word and helps you remember its meaning. One student remembered the meaning of the word *pretentious,* "showy, flaunting," by picturing a small boy playing make-believe, *pretending* to be a king.

There is one final reason for studying vocabulary, one that we hope you discover for yourself as you use this book: Words are fascinating! They are as surprising and alive and insightful as the people who use them.

Special Unit Strategies for Unlocking Word Meaning

What happens when you come across an unfamiliar word in your reading? If you have a dictionary at hand, you can look up the word. If you don't have a dictionary, you still have two excellent strategies that can help you make sense of the word: **context clues** and **word parts analysis.** You will be using these strategies in every unit of this book. With practice you can master these strategies and improve your reading skills.

Part A Determining a Word's Meaning from Context

Skilled readers often use context clues to figure out a word's meaning. **Context** refers to the words or sentences before or after a certain word that help explain what the word means. There are several types of context clues you can look for, including **definition and restatement, example, comparison, contrast,** and **cause and effect.**

Definition and Restatement

Sometimes a writer will directly define a word, especially if the word is a technical term that may be unfamiliar to readers. Here is an example:

The new music was *dissonant,* that is, it sounded harsh and incomplete.

More often, a writer will restate the meaning of a word in a less precise form than a dictionary definition.

John sat at the *periphery* of the audience, as far away from the stage as possible.

The meaning of *periphery*—"the outer part; outskirts"—becomes clear from the restatement: "as far away from the stage as possible." Definition and restatement are often signaled by punctuation (note the comma in the preceding examples) and by certain key words and phrases.

Words Signaling Definition and Restatement		
which is	or	also known as
that is	in other words	also called

Example

The context in which a word appears may include one or more **examples** that are clues to its meaning. Look at the following sentence.

Writers use many literary *genres*, such as poetry, the short story, and the novel, to express their ideas.

The phrase *such as,* followed by a list of examples helps explain the meaning of *genre*—"a kind or type, especially of art or literature." The following words and phrases often signal an example:

Words Signaling an Example		
like	for example	other
including	for instance	this
such as	especially	these
		these include

Comparison

Another type of context clue is **comparison.** With this clue the writer compares the word in question with other, more familiar words. By noting the similarities between the things described, you can get an idea of the meaning of the unfamiliar word.

This bike route seems as *arduous* as the one in the Rocky Mountains that's called Agony Trail.

The comparison context clue "as the one in the Rocky Mountains that's called Agony Trail" clearly conveys the meaning of *arduous*—"hard to do." Comparisons are often signaled by one of these key words or phrases.

Words Signaling a Comparison		
like	similar to	similarly
as	resembling	also
in the same way	likewise	identical
		related

Contrast

Context may also help reveal the meaning of a word through **contrast,** as in this example:

Maria was *lethargic* in school, but she was a bundle of energy at cheerleading practice.

In this sentence the word *but* signals a contrast. Therefore, you can assume that *lethargic* means the opposite of *a bundle of energy* (the dictionary defines *lethargic* as "abnormally drowsy or dull"). The following key words and phrases signal a contrast.

Words Signaling a Contrast		
but	on the other hand	instead
although	unlike	different
on the contrary	in contrast to	however

Cause and Effect

Another type of context clue is **cause and effect.** The cause of an action or event may be stated using an unfamiliar word. If, however, the effect is stated in familiar terms, it can help you understand the unfamiliar word. Consider the following example:

Because Marek was a *negligent* babysitter, his younger brother wandered off and fell into the river.

In this sentence the cause—Marek's being negligent—leads to the effect—his brother falling into the river. Therefore, *negligent* must mean "careless or inattentive." Certain key words and phrases may signal cause and effect.

Words Signaling Cause and Effect		
because	consequently	so
since	therefore	as a result

Inference from General Context

Often the clues to the meaning of an unfamiliar word are not in the same sentence. In such cases you will need to look at the sentences that surround the word and **infer,** or draw a conclusion about, the word's meaning. A single piece of information several sentences away from the unfamiliar word may unlock the meaning. Study the following example:

"You can speak *candidly*," the principal said. The student said nothing. The principal tried again, "I can't help you unless I know what really happened."

The clue to the meaning of *candidly* is in the last sentence of the paragraph. The detail "unless I know what really happened" suggests that *candidly* means "honestly and openly."

Sometimes the supporting details in a paragraph must be examined together to help you infer the meaning of an unfamiliar word.

Ellen continued to *vacillate* until it was too late to go to the movies. At first, she was sure she wanted to see the new horror film. Then she chose the comedy. Then she changed her mind again.

A series of descriptive details follows the unfamiliar word *vacillate*. The details help you draw a conclusion about what *vacillate* means—"to waver and be unable to decide."

Determining Meaning from Context Each of the following sentences and paragraphs contains an italicized word you may not know. Look for context clues to help you determine the meaning of the word. Write the definition in the blank.

1. Ellis was *contrite* after breaking the window. He apologized to his mother again and again and promised to be more careful next time. He also offered to pay for the window out of his allowance.

   _____

2. Unlike boring activities, which can *deplete* your energy, activities that you enjoy can actually increase your interest and revive you.

   _____

3. The plot of Mia's story was light and *whimsical*. Humorous and unexpected events followed one another in a way that was very entertaining.

   _____

4. Although that explanation is *plausible*, I can think of one that is even more likely.

   _____

5. "What an *innovative* idea, Jana," said her father. "How did you ever think of something so original?"

   _____

6. I never knew I could be such a *glutton*. I had five ears of corn, two hamburgers, a quart of lemonade, and three pieces of watermelon at the picnic last night.

   _____

7. Because the land was so *arid*, water had to be piped in from miles away to keep the crops from drying up.

   _____

8. The speaker led her listeners carefully from one point to the next. She developed her thoughts logically from beginning to end and never once *digressed*.

    _____

9. That man was considered the city's most *elusive* burglar. It took the police fifteen years to catch him.

    _____

10. Because my baby sister was *premature*, she was not as fully developed as a baby born after nine months. She had to be given food and oxygen through tubes until she was strong enough to eat and breathe on her own.

    _____

11. After the accident, my cousin was *incoherent*, babbling nonsense words that nobody could understand.

    _____

12. Unlike his older sister, who spent every penny as soon as she earned it, Liam was extremely *thrifty*.

    _____

13. My aunt is a musical *prodigy*. She began playing the violin at age two and gave her first concert when she was only four.

    _____

14. Although Jeff was usually quite serious, he sometimes told jokes that sent everyone into fits of *hilarity*.

    _____

15. I had an *erroneous* idea about my lung capacity. I was sure I could swim the length of the pool underwater. When I tried it, though, I had to come up for air halfway across.

    _____

Number correct _____   (total 15)

Understanding Context Clues Choose five of the words below. For each word write a sentence that uses that word. Each of your sentences should contain a different type of context clue—**definition and restatement, example, comparison, contrast,** or **cause and effect.** Then label each sentence according to the type of context clue used.

arrogant   flamboyant   meticulous
condensation   spelunker   sluggish

1. _____

_____

2. _____

_____

3. _____

_____

4. _____

_____

5. _____

_____

Number correct _____ (total 5)

Part B   Determining Meaning Through Word Analysis

Words are made up of various combinations of the following parts: *prefix, suffix, base word,* and *root.* Analysis of these parts is another way to determine an unfamiliar word's meaning. The following terms are used in analyzing word parts.

Prefix   a word part that is added to the beginning of another word or word part

Suffix   a word part that is added to the end of another word or word part

Base word   a complete word to which a prefix and/or a suffix may be added

Root   a word part to which a prefix and/or a suffix must be added. A root cannot stand alone.

For example, the word *undemocratic* is made up of the prefix *un-,* the base word *democrat,* and the suffix *-ic.* If you know the meanings of these parts, you can determine the meaning of the whole word.

un- ("not") + *democrat* ("a person who believes in government by the people") + *-ic* ("relating to")

undemocratic = "relating to something or someone who does not believe in government by the people"

Now look at a word with a root. *Inscription* is made up of the prefix *in-* ("into, on"), the Latin root *script* ("write"), and the suffix *-tion* ("a thing that is"). *Inscription* means "something written on a surface, such as an engraving on a monument."

Prefixes

The following chart contains prefixes that have only one meaning.

Prefixes That Have a Single Meaning

Prefix	Meaning	Example
bene-	good	benefit
circum-	around	circumference
col-, com-, con-, cor-	with, together	collapse, compile construct, correspond
contra-	opposed	contradict
equi-	equal	equidistant
extra-	outside	extraordinary
hemi-	half	hemisphere
inter-	between, among	international
mal-	bad	maltreat, malignant
mid-	halfway	midday
mis-	wrong	misspell
non-	not	nonworking
post-	after in time or space	postpone
pre-	before	predawn
sub-	under, below	subzero

Some prefixes have more than one meaning. Study the common prefixes listed in the following chart.

Prefixes That Have More Than One Meaning

Prefix	Meaning	Example
a-, ab-	up, out	arise
	not	abnormal
	away	absent
anti-	against	antiaircraft
	prevents, cures	antidote
de-	away from, off	derail
	down	decline
	reverse action of	defrost
dis-	lack of	distrust
	not	dishonest
	away	disarm
em-, en-	to get into, on	embark
	to make, cause	enable
	in, into	enclose
il-, im-, in-, ir-	not	illegal
	in, into	investigate
pro-	in favor of	profamily
	forward, ahead	propel
re-	again	rethink
	back	repay
semi-	half	semicircle
	twice in a period	semiannual
	partly	semiconscious
super-	over and above	superhuman
	very large	supertanker
trans-	across	transcontinental
	beyond	transcend
un-	not	unhappy
	reverse of	unfasten

Suffixes

Like a prefix, a suffix has a meaning that can provide a strong clue to the definition of a whole word. Suffixes can also determine the part of speech. Certain suffixes make words nouns; others create adjectives, verbs, or adverbs.

Once you know suffixes and their meanings, you can form new words by attaching suffixes to base words or to roots. For instance, the suffix *-ician* can be added to the base word *politics* to create the word *politician*. Notice that the spelling of a base word may change when a suffix is added. In the preceding example, the *-ics* from *politics* was dropped when *-ician* was added. For information about spelling rules for adding suffixes, see the **Spelling Handbook,** pages 218–243.

Noun suffixes, when added to a base word or root, form nouns. Become familiar with the following common noun suffixes.

Noun Suffixes That Refer to Someone Who Does Something

Suffix	Examples
-ant	commandant, occupant
-eer	auctioneer
-er	manager
-ician	beautician, statistician
-ist	geologist
-or	counselor

Noun Suffixes That Make Abstract Words

Suffix	Examples
-ance, -ancy, -ence	vigilance, vacancy, independence
-ation, -ion, -ition	imagination, inspection, recognition
-cy	accuracy
-dom	freedom, kingdom
-hood	womanhood, brotherhood
-ice	cowardice, prejudice
-ism	realism, federalism
-ity, -ty	sincerity, frailty
-ment	encouragement, commitment
-ness	kindness, fondness
-ship	ownership, worship
-tude	gratitude, solitude

Adjective suffixes, when added to a base word or root, create adjectives—words that are used to modify nouns and pronouns.

Adjective Suffixes

Suffix	Meaning	Example
-able, -ible	able to be	readable, convertible
-al	relating to	musical
-ant	relating to	triumphant
-ar	relating to	polar
-ate	having, full of	passionate
-ful	full of	harmful
-ic	pertaining to, like	heroic
-ish	pertaining to, like	foolish
-ive	pertaining to	descriptive
-less	without	senseless
-like	like	lifelike
-ly	like	scholarly
-most	at the extreme	topmost
-ous	full of	furious

Verb suffixes change base words to verbs. The following chart lists four common verb suffixes.

Verb Suffixes

Suffix	Meaning	Example
-ate	to make	activate
-en	to become	strengthen
-fy	to make	simplify
-ise, -ize	to become	merchandise, computerize

Adverb suffixes change base words to adverbs—words that modify verbs, adjectives, and other adverbs. The following chart lists the most common adverb suffixes.

Adverb Suffixes

Suffix	Meaning	Example
-ily, -ly,	manner	happily, quickly
-ward	toward	skyward
-wise	like	clockwise

Roots and Word Families

A word root cannot stand alone but must be combined with other word parts. A great many roots used in our language come from Greek or Latin. A single root can generate many English words. A **word family** is a group of words with a common root. For example, all of the words in the following word family are derived from the Latin root *gen,* which means "carry."

generate	generous	genesis
genetic	gentle	genus
progenitor	genius	congenial

Learning word roots will help you develop your vocabulary by enabling you to recognize roots in many related words. The following two charts show some common Greek and Latin roots.

Useful Greek Roots

Root	Meaning	Example
anthrop	human	anthropology
aster, astr	star	asterisk
auto	self, alone	autobiography
bibl, biblio	book	bibliography
bi, bio	life	biology
chron	time	chronology
cracy, crat	rule, government	democracy
dem	people	epidemic
gen	birth, race, kind	generation
geo	earth	geography
gram, graph	write, draw, describe	grammar, paragraph
hydr	water	hydogen
log	word, reason, study	dialogue, logic, ecology
meter, metr	measure	barometer
neo	new	neoclassical
nom, nym	name, word, law	nominate, antonym
ortho	straight, correct	orthodontist, orthodox
pan	all, entire	panorama
phil	love	philosopher
phob	fear	claustrophobia
phon	sound	phonograph
psych	mind, soul, spirit	psychology
scope	see	telescope
soph	wise	sophisticated
tele	far, distant	television
theo	god	theology
therm	heat	thermometer

Useful Latin Roots

Root	Meaning	Example
capt, cept	take, have	capture, accept
cede, ceed, cess	go, yield, give way	secede, proceed, recess
cred	believe	credit, creed
dic, dict	speak, say, tell	dictate, dictionary
duc, duct	lead	introduce, conductor
fact, fect	do, make	factory, defect
fer	carry	transfer
ject	throw, hurl	eject, inject
junct	join	junction
miss, mit	send, let go	dismiss, admit
mob, mot, mov	move	mobility, motion, movie
par, para	get ready	prepare, parachute
pon, pos, posit	place, put	opponent, deposit
port	carry	porter, portable
puls	throb, urge	pulsate, compulsory
scrib, script	write	prescribe, scripture
spec, spect, spic	look, see	speculate, spectacle, conspicuous
stat	stand, put in a place	statue, state
tain, ten, tent	hold	contain, tenant, attention
tract	pull, move	tractor, retract
ven, vent	come	convention, event
vers, vert	turn	versatile, invert
vid, vis	see	video, vista
voc, vok	voice, call	vocal, invoke
vol	wish	volunteer, malevolent
volv	roll	revolve, involve

Determining Word Meaning Through Prefixes and Suffixes Draw lines to separate each of the following words into three parts—prefix, base word, and suffix. Determine the meaning of the prefix and the suffix. Then, by adding the meanings of the prefix and the suffix to the base word, determine the meaning of the complete word and write the definition in the blank.

1. antiheroic: _____

2. dishonesty: _____

3. illogical: _____

4. deformity: _____

5. nonpublishable: _____

6. correspondence: _____

7. deactivate: _____

8. circumnavigator: _____

9. hemispheric: _____

10. disrespectful: _____

Number correct _____ (total 10)

Determining Word Meaning Through Prefixes, Suffixes, and Roots Each of the following words consists of a Greek or Latin root and a prefix or suffix. Use your knowledge of roots, prefixes, and suffixes to put together the meanings of the word parts and write a definition for each word. You may check your definitions with a dictionary.

1. chronic: _____

2. compulsory: _____

3. revise: _____

4. program: _____

5. deport: _____

6. disaster: _____

7. transport: _____

8. biography: _____

9. reversible: _____

10. psychic: _____

Number correct _____ (total 10)

Number correct in unit _____ (total 40)

UNIT 1

Part A Target Words and Their Meanings

The twenty words below will be the focus of the first unit. You will find them in the reading selection and in the exercises in this unit. For a guide to their pronunciations, refer to the Pronunciation Key on page 252.

1. alter (ôl′ tər) v.
2. chemist (kem′ ist) n.
3. condition (kən dish′ ən) n., v.
4. conduct (kən dukt′) v. (kän′ dukt′) n.
5. detect (di tekt′) v.
6. development (di vel′ əp mənt) n.
7. establish (ə stab′ lish) v.
8. florist (flôr′ ist, flär′-) n.
9. formation (fôr mā′ shən) n.
10. frequently (frē′ kwənt lē) adv.
11. guarantee (gar′ ən tē′, gär′-) n., v.
12. handicap (han′ dē kap′) n., v.
13. informative (in fôr′ mə tiv) adj.
14. inseparable (in sep′ ər ə b'l) adj.
15. magnificent (mag nif′ ə s'nt) adj.
16. observe (əb zʉrv′, äb-) v.
17. prediction (pri dik′ shən) n.
18. render (ren′ dər) v.
19. safeguard (sāf′ gärd) v., n.
20. seasonal (sē′ z'n əl) adj.

Inferring Meaning from Context

For each sentence write the letter of the word or phrase that is closest to the meaning of the word or words in italics. Use context clues to help you choose the correct answer. (For information about how context helps you understand vocabulary, see pages 1–6.)

__d__ 1. Some scientists warn that if we continue to pollute the world, we could *alter* the earth's climates by raising temperatures significantly.
   a. understand   b. preserve   c. improve   d. change

__d__ 2. Because Jim enjoys working in the science laboratory at school, his teacher has hopes that Jim will become *a chemist* one day.
   a. a janitor   b. a teacher   c. a weather forecaster   d. an expert in chemistry

__b__ 3. We left the room in good *condition*, with the carpet vacuumed and all the furniture dusted and set back in place.
   a. control   b. quality   c. order   d. design

__b__ 4. Detective Hayes *conducted* the investigation of the robbery. He told each member of the team what to do and when to do it.
   a. prevented   b. managed   c. followed   d. aided

14

5. After a careful examination with her stethoscope, Dr. Maeda was able to *detect* a faint murmur in the patient's heart.
   a. remove   b. operate   c. overlook   d. discover

6. The young parents were fascinated by every stage of their baby's *development*, from his first smile to his first wobbly step.
   a. growth   b. education   c. success   d. personality

7. Congressman Romero will *establish* the social service program by organizing volunteers and building neighborhood shelters for the homeless.
   a. close   b. argue for   c. set up   d. overthrow

8. Dad sometimes brings Mom flowers from the *florist* near the train station.
   a. flower seller   b. tile layer   c. restaurant owner   d. engineer

9. Glaciers moving over North America created many of the *formations* of the hills and valleys that we see today.
   a. arrangements   b. future possibilities   c. disappearances
   d. earthquakes

10. Because Renee spends all of her allowance on cassette tapes, she is *frequently* in debt and looking for odd jobs to earn money.
    a. seldom   b. often   c. sometimes   d. never

11. The company *guarantees* in writing that if its audio tape recorder has any defects, the recorder will be repaired or replaced free of charge.
    a. demands   b. admits   c. promises   d. denies

12. Several months after injuring her back in an automobile accident, Becky finally began to accept her *handicap*.
    a. insurance   b. surgery   c. bad luck   d. disability

13. Officer McKenzie's lecture on neighborhood gangs was very *informative*. We learned some things we had not known.
    a. educational   b. casual   c. boring   d. businesslike

14. Mario and Rosa are *inseparable;* they were together all summer and continue to spend time with each other as often as possible.
    a. related   b. close   c. sensible   d. easily angered

15. The big Fourth of July fireworks display was *magnificent*. We'll always remember how beautiful it was.
    a. huge   b. loud   c. splendid   d. ordinary

16. An astronomer *observes* the stars through a telescope, which makes it possible to see incredible distances.
    a. watches   b. connects   c. arranges   d. reveals

___b___ 17. The weather *prediction* was for hot weather—temperatures above one hundred for the next week.

a. invitation   b. forecast   c. contract   d. prayer

___a___ 18. Our teacher *renders* a great service by offering help to students after school.

a. provides   b. endures   c. withholds   d. repeats

___b___ 19. Wearing a life jacket serves as a *safeguard* against drowning.

a. relief   b. protection   c. pad   d. hazard

___a___ 20. The work of migrant farmhands who follow the harvest is *seasonal.* Different crops are ready for harvest at different times of the year.

a. limited to water   b. incredibly difficult   c. never ending
d. dependent on the time of year

Number correct ___18___ (total 20)

Part B Target Words in Reading and Literature

You should now have a general idea of the meaning of each target word. Sharpen your understanding by studying how these words are used in the following selection.

Reading Clouds

Howard Peet

Have you ever noticed the differences in clouds? Some look like fluffy cotton balls, while others look like wide white sheets. The following selection tells you what these differences mean.

If you ranked the topics of conversation in people's lives, weather would probably end up at or near the top. Everyone from philosopher to **florist** feels free to comment on the weather and to try and guess what tomorrow's weather will be. However, the best guessers are people who **observe** the **development** of clouds, for clouds are the makers of weather.   5

In 1803, Luke Howard, an English **chemist,** was the first to **establish** names for different types of clouds. Howard believed that the shapes and forms of clouds were **inseparable** from the weather they caused. By naming the types of clouds, Howard began a scientific means of weather **prediction.**   10

Although there are many combinations of cloud forms, a good observer can **detect** four basic **formations:** cirrus, nimbus, stratus, and cumulus.

16

Clockwise from upper left: Cirrus, Nimbus, Cumulus, and Stratus

The first three types signal that bad weather is either here or on the way.

Cirrus clouds **frequently** soar as high as ten miles. These clouds look 15
like the remains of a pillow fight **conducted** so forcefully that feathers fly
all over the room. Although there is no **guarantee,** cirrus clouds usually
mean rainy or snowy **conditions** within ten to thirty hours.

When it is already raining or snowing, nimbus clouds are probably
responsible. These are the dark rain clouds that often cannot be seen 20
because of the rain or snow falling from them.

Sheetlike clouds that often blanket the ground are called stratus
clouds. They can be a **handicap** to safe driving. Stratus clouds often
appear as fog.

The clouds that people enjoy the most are cumulus clouds. They are 25
beautiful, and their presence usually means fair weather. Floating slowly
along about one mile above ground, these huge heaps of cotton **render
magnificent**-looking scenes.

Identifying these four types of clouds can be **informative** as well as
fun. Professional weather forecasters use information about clouds in a 30
region to make their predictions. Accurate forecasting is very important: it
can **safeguard** people from disastrous storms. However, the forecaster's
job is difficult. For example, **seasonal** differences in weather patterns
must be considered. Also, sudden changes in air pressure and wind
speed can **alter** the weather greatly and unexpectedly. Weather forecast- 35
ing may be a science, but it is not yet an exact one.

Refining Your Understanding

For each of the following items, consider how the target word is used in the passage. Write the letter of the word or phrase that best completes the sentence.

_b_   1. When the author says that Luke Howard was the first scientist "to *establish* names for different types of clouds" (lines 7–8), he means that before 1803   a. no one was interested in clouds   b. there were no official names for different clouds   c. only certain clouds could be created in a laboratory.

_b_   2. An example of a scientific *prediction* (line 11) would not be
a. determining when an eclipse of the sun is coming
b. expecting bad luck after breaking a mirror   c. gauging the future effect of air pollution on a region.

_b_   3. By referring to stratus clouds as a "*handicap* to safe driving" (line 23), the writer implies that the clouds make driving   a. exciting
b. difficult   c. impossible.

_C_   4. When the writer describes cumulus clouds as "huge heaps of cotton [that] *render magnificent*-looking scenes" (lines 27–28), he means that these clouds   a. remind people of their childhoods   b. tear apart the beauty of the sky   c. make beautiful formations in the sky.

_a_   5. By telling us that *seasonal* conditions *alter* our ability to use clouds to predict storms (lines 33–35), the author suggests that   a. clouds will usually give a clear forecast of the weather   b. clouds are not useful weather predictors   c. weather forecasting is difficult.

Number correct ___4___ (total 5)

Part C   Ways to Make New Words Your Own

By now you are familiar with the target words and their meanings. This section presents activities that will help you make the words part of your permanent vocabulary.

Using Language and Thinking Skills

Sentence Completion   Write the word from the list below that best completes the meaning of the sentence.

chemist	development	frequently	magnificent	rendered
conducted	florist	inseparable	observe	seasonal

___chemist___   1. The genius behind the famous cosmetic product is the _?_ in the laboratory.

18

florist 2. Whenever he needs information about house plants, Donald asks the ? on Elm Street.

observe 3. It was enlightening to ? the small children trying to put the puzzle together.

inseparable 4. The friends enjoyed being together so much that they became ? .

conducted 5. The faculty ? an open meeting for parents to discuss methods of improving education at our school.

rendered 6. In order to make his sisters laugh, Luis ? an amusing imitation of an angry dog.

magnificent 7. The red sun setting above the blue water of the Gulf of Mexico was a ? sight.

frequently 8. Because Jennifer has braces on her teeth, she must brush her teeth more ? .

seasonal 9. In addition to being too expensive, the jacket was ? ; it could be worn only during spring.

development 10. The doctors and scientists called a press conference to report a new ? in cancer research.

Number correct __10__ (total 10)

Practicing for Standardized Tests

Synonyms Write the letter of the word that is closest in meaning to the capitalized word.

__C__ 1. DETECT: (A) destroy (B) confuse (C) discover (D) arrest (E) ignore

__A__ 2. ESTABLISH: (A) create (B) change (C) return (D) protect (E) arrive

__A__ 3. FREQUENTLY: (A) often (B) occasionally (C) seldom (D) necessarily (E) honestly

__D__ 4. GUARANTEE: (A) forecast (B) quality (C) advertisement (D) promise (E) repair

__C__ 5. HANDICAP: (A) weaving (B) ability (C) disadvantage (D) error (E) certainty

__E__ 6. INFORMATIVE: (A) imaginative (B) useless (C) entertaining (D) unusual (E) instructive

_C_ 7. MAGNIFICENT: (A) distant (B) expensive (C) glorious (D) smart (E) tiny

_C_ 8. OBSERVE: (A) neglect (B) miss (C) view (D) understand (E) wait

_B_ 9. ALTER: (A) separate (B) change (C) forecast (D) create (E) guard

_D_ 10. SAFEGUARD: (A) hazard (B) fort (C) cruise (D) defense (E) attack

Number correct __10__ (total 10)

Spelling and Wordplay

Word Maze All the words in the list below are hidden in the maze. The words are arranged forward, backward, up, down, and diagonally. Put a circle around each word as you find it and cross the word off the list. Different words may overlap and use the same letter.

```
U N Y L T N E U Q E R F L E O        alter
A S W E S T A B L I S H L L M        chemist
H A N D I C A P T F C B I B H        condition
U F V E R E T L A O A D N E Q        conduct
R E R T O F H I G R N E F V N        detect
E G R E L J Q U A M O V R O         development
N U E C F C A P C A I E R E I       establish
D A D T L R E B O T T L M S T       florist
E R I P A S M R N I I O A B C       formation
R D B N N V K W D O D P T O I       frequently
D K T I Y B F W U N N M I R D       guarantee
S E A S O N A L C E O E V P E       handicap
E L C H E M I S T Y C N E G R       informative
C M A G N I F I C E N T E B P       inseparable
                                    magnificent
                                    observe
                                    prediction
                                    render
                                    safeguard
                                    seasonal
```

20/20

Part D   Related Words

The words below are closely related to the target words. Use your knowledge of the target words and of word parts to determine the meanings of these words. (For information about word parts analysis, see pages 7-13.) Use your dictionary if necessary.

1. alteration (ôl′ tə rā′ shən) n.
2. alternate (ôl′ tər nit, al′-) adj., n. (ôl′ tər nāt′, al′-) v.
3. conductor (kən duk′ tər) n.
4. detection (di tek′ shən) n.
5. detector (di tek′ tər) n.
6. develop (di vel′ əp) v.
7. floral (flôr′ əl) adj.
8. frequency (frē′ kwən sē) n.
9. handicapped (han′ dē kapt′) adj., n.
10. infrequent (in frē′ kwənt) adj.
11. magnification (mag′ nə fi kā′ shən) n.
12. magnificence (mag nif′ ə s'ns) n.
13. magnify (mag′ nə fī′) v.
14. nonchemical (nän′ kem′ i k'l) adj.
15. observation (äb′ zər vā′ shən) n.
16. reestablish (rē′ əs tab′ lish) v.
17. unobserved (un′ əb zʉrvd′) adj.
18. unseasonable (un sē′ z'n ə b'l) adj.

Understanding Related Words

Close Relatives For each sentence below, determine which word in parentheses belongs in each blank.

1. The _____florist_____ delivered the _____floral_____ arrangement just before the party. (floral, florist)

2. We _____frequently_____ have difficulty finding the correct _____frequency_____ of that radio station. (frequency, frequently)

3. Tony _____conducted_____ a tour through the opera house, during which visitors were able to meet the _____conductor_____ of the orchestra. (conducted, conductor)

4. Though Tamika is _____handicapped_____, she does not allow her limitations to _____handicap_____ her daily life. (handicap, handicapped)

5. Though it was cloudy, we tried to _____observe_____ the city from the _____observation_____ deck on the twenty-fifth floor. (observation, observe)

Number correct ___10___ (total 10)

Turn to **The Addition of Prefixes** on page 219 of the **Spelling Handbook**. Read the rule and complete the exercises provided.

Analyzing Word Parts

The Prefix *un-* The prefix *un-* means "not"; for example, the word *unsatisfied* means "not satisfied." *Un-* can also mean the reverse of some situation or condition, as in the word *unfasten*. Match each word on the left with its definition on the right. Write the letter of the definition in the blank on the left.

_d_ 1. undetected   a. not set up, unsettled

_a_ 2. unestablished   b. unusual for a certain time of year

_c_ 3. unobserved   c. not watched

_e_ 4. unaltered   d. not discovered

_b_ 5. unseasonable   e. not changed

Number correct ___5___ (total 5)

The Suffix *-ion* The suffix *-ion*, when added to a verb, means "the act or state of." If the word *predict* means "to foretell the future," the word *prediction* means "the act of foretelling the future." Match each word on the left with its definition on the right. Write the letter of the definition in the blank.

_c_ 1. information   a. the act of observing or watching

_e_ 2. alteration   b. the process of making something look larger

_a_ 3. observation   c. being told of something; knowledge

_b_ 4. magnification   d. the act of discovering

_d_ 5. detection   e. the act of changing something

Number correct ___5___ (total 5)

The Latin Root *magni* The target word *magnificent* comes from the Latin word *magnus*, meaning "great." The two related words *magnificence* and *magnify* also come from this Latin word. Look up the meanings of these two words. Then complete each of the following sentences with one of the words.

magnify 1. A telescope serves to __?__ the stars.

magnificence 2. Visitors to Washington, D.C., are impressed by the __?__ of the Lincoln Memorial.

magnificence 3. The dark blue dress served to __?__ Susan's blue eyes.

magnify 4. Joni's refusal to make friends only served to __?__ her loneliness.

magnificence 5. Stained glass windows in a cathedral add to its __?__ .

Number correct ___4___ (total 5)

Number correct in Unit ___66___ (total 70)

94%

22

Word's Worth: chemist

When the Arabs invaded Europe, they introduced a kind of research they called *al-kimia,* which quickly became known as *alchemy.* The people who practiced alchemy in the Middle Ages invented and used many laboratory procedures that are still being used today in some form. Nevertheless, alchemy was more magic than science. Its chief aims were to turn ordinary metals, such as lead and copper, into silver and gold and to find the secret of eternal youth. Though neither goal was achieved, alchemy is given credit for being the ancestor of chemistry, the science that studies what substances are made of and how they react with one another. Both *chemist* and *chemistry* are forms of the word *alchemy.*

The Last Word

Writing

Many products are sold with a *guarantee*—a declaration that for a certain number of months after the sale, the product will be fixed free of charge to the owner. (This is often referred to as a warranty.) What would be the ideal written guarantee for a CD player or tape deck? For what length of time would the product be guaranteed? What parts and what service would be included? What exclusions, if any, would be mentioned? Where would the product be serviced? Who would be responsible for mailing costs? In no fewer than fifty and no more than one hundred words, write your guarantee.

Speaking

In a short *informative* speech to the class, explain how to do something or make something. Your speech may be as simple as explaining your favorite recipe step-by-step or as complicated as telling how to program a computer to do a specific task. Choose something you are particularly good at doing.

Group Discussion

As described in the reading selection, nineteenth-century chemist Luke Howard *observed* clouds and consequently discovered a means of predicting the weather. Research other observations that have led to discoveries and inventions. Share your examples with the class.

UNIT 2

Part A   Target Words and Their Meanings

1. abnormal (ab nôr′ m′l) adj.
2. accumulate (ə kyo͞om′ yə lāt′) v.
3. cluster (klus′ tər) n., v.
4. curious (kyo͝or′ ē əs) adj.
5. desperate (des′ pər it) adj.
6. effectiveness (ə fek′ tiv nis, i-) n.
7. endear (in dir′) v.
8. mission (mish′ ən) n.
9. mute (myo͞ot′) adj., n., v.
10. mutiny (myo͞ot′ ′n ē) n., v.

11. quest (kwest) n., v.
12. repulsive (ri pul′ siv) adj.
13. suspense (sə spens′) n.
14. technician (tek nish′ ən) n.
15. testimony (tes′ tə mō′ nē) n.
16. transformation (trans′ fər mā′ shən) n.
17. untimely (un tīm′ lē) adj., adv.
18. venture (ven′ chər) n., v.
19. vital (vīt′ ′l) adj.
20. zeal (zēl) n.

Inferring Meaning from Context

For each sentence write the letter of the word or phrase that is closest in meaning to the word or words in italics. Use context clues to help you choose the correct answer. (For information about how context helps you understand vocabulary, see pages 1–6.)

___C___ 1. Eight feet is an *abnormal* height for a man. Only a few men have ever grown that tall.

      a. an impossible   b. a comfortable   c. an unusual   d. a typical

___b___ 2. Over a period of twenty years, Mr. Jefferson *accumulated* a fortune through hard work and wise saving.

      a. spent   b. collected   c. lost   d. altered

___a___ 3. Years ago in California and Nevada, towns often were *clustered* around gold mines. Gold attracted many people to these two states.

      a. grouped   b. disappeared   c. entertained   d. scattered

___d___ 4. Small children are *curious;* they ask many questions about things they see and hear.

      a. fussy   b. clumsy   c. restless   d. eager to learn

___a___ 5. Hanging by one arm from the cliff, Ralph knew he was in *a desperate* situation.

      a. a dangerous   b. a tremendous   c. an uncomfortable
      d. a ridiculous

_____ 6. The *effectiveness* of the cleanup campaign was evident as we drove through the spotless neighborhood.

    a. success b. length c. failure d. difficulty

_____ 7. The courage with which Patrick faced his new handicap *endeared him to* us all. Everyone who knew Patrick liked him.

    a. made him dependent on b. made him different from
    c. made him beloved by d. made him bitter toward

_____ 8. Dr. Jonas Salk's *mission* was to rid the world of polio. In 1955, he succeeded in developing a vaccine that prevented the dreaded disease.

    a. mistake b. special task c. observation d. religion

_____ 9. As Officer Tomito scolded him, Danny was *mute*, unable to speak.

    a. deaf b. amazed c. speechless d. relieved

_____ 10. Because of the terrible conditions aboard the ship, the crew planned a *mutiny*.

    a. party b. cleanup c. rebellion d. robbery

_____ 11. In his *quest for* fame and fortune, Matthew traveled to the big city to try out for the major league team.

    a. search for b. avoidance of c. guarantee of
    d. disappointment with

_____ 12. The refrigerator door was left open for days, and the smell of rotten food was *repulsive*.

    a. harmful b. overflowing c. disgusting d. magnificent

_____ 13. The mystery story kept me in *suspense* until the final chapter, when I found out who the murderer was.

    a. fear b. uncertainty c. laughter d. good spirits

_____ 14. The critics praised the pianist for being a *technician* who performed the music without a flaw.

    a. instructor b. skilled person c. volunteer d. manufacturer

_____ 15. The students and teachers presented their principal with a gold watch as *a testimony* of their respect and affection.

    a. a trace b. an indication c. a denial d. an observation

_____ 16. The *transformation* of a caterpillar into a butterfly is a wonder of nature.

    a. recognition b. changing c. collision d. removal

_____ 17. Eugene's big mistake was his *untimely* interruption during our manager's speech.

    a. thoughtful b. creative c. appropriate d. inappropriate

18. Mr. Lyons's *venture into* the restaurant business proved very successful. He began with one restaurant and expanded to ten.

  a. remark about   b. entry into   c. visit to   d. departure from

19. Concern about the environment is one of the most *vital* issues facing Americans.

  a. important   b. harmless   c. dishonest   d. unnecessary

20. The students had such *zeal for* the project that they enthusiastically devoted their weekend to finishing it.

  a. dislike for   b. mixed feelings about   c. simple regard for
  d. eager interest in

Number correct _____ (total 20)

Part B *Target Words in Reading and Literature*

You should now have a general idea of the meaning of each target word. Sharpen your understanding by studying how these words are used in the following selection.

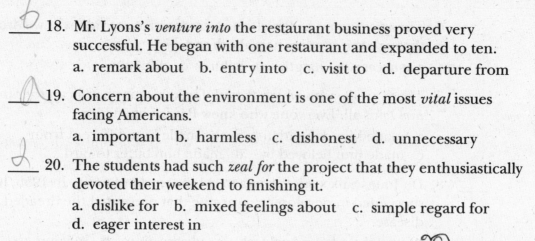

The Final Entry

Howard Peet

What unforeseen problems await future space travelers? In the following science fiction story, a space crew encounters a startling change.

The *Star Shot* burst into outer space. Heading for the Virgo **cluster** of galaxies light years away was a **venture** of faith and courage. The crew approached the **mission** with great **zeal** and confidence. Their spaceship, after all, was a **testimony** to the latest scientific advances. The tremendous speed of the *Star Shot* allowed the crew to go deeper into   5
space than anyone had gone before.

Each crew member, from **technician** to commander, had been carefully chosen. Even the mascot, a monkey named Jocko, was the result of a lengthy **quest**. Jocko was intelligent and **curious**, even for a monkey, and his crazy antics **endeared** him to the crew.   10

The journey went smoothly until the spaceship left the earth's solar system. Then a strange thing began to happen. The farther the *Star Shot* traveled, the more knowledge each crew member's brain **accumulated.** As the crew members' brains accumulated more knowledge, their heads began to grow. Soon their heads were **abnormal** sizes. Worse yet, their heads kept   15
growing. The situation quickly passed from **desperate** to hopeless. Back on earth there was no contact with the *Star Shot;* the ship never returned.

Many years later, the *Star Shot* was found floating aimlessly through the Virgo galaxies. Commander Flynn of the spaceship *Advance* ordered an examining party to board the *Star Shot*. **Suspense** aboard the *Advance* grew as the rescue crew awaited word from the examining party. Had the *Star Shot* fallen victim to a **mutiny** or some strange sickness? 20

The leader of the examining party, Captain Lewis, returned with the leader of the *Star Shot's* logbook gripped tightly in his hand and a look of terror written across his face. Standing **mute,** he pointed to the final entry in the log. It read: 25

November 11, 2101

They are all dead but me. Their huge heads are as large as their bodies. Their staring eyes are so **repulsive** that I must look away as I write these last words. What little **effectiveness** I still have is being poured into this message. I only hope that whoever finds this will be able to read my handwriting. 30

As my **untimely** death draws near, I leave this final message. It is **vital** that future galaxy travelers heed this warning: 35

BEWARE OF THE **TRANSFORMATION**
THAT COMES FROM ACCUMULATING
KNOWLEDGE TOO QUICKLY.

Farewell,
Jocko

Refining Your Understanding

For each of the following items, consider how the target word is used in the passage. Write the letter of the word or phrase that best completes the sentence.

___c___ 1. The word *mission* has several definitions. The definition suggested in line 3 is   a. a small church   b. a military raid
c. an assignment.

___a___ 2. From the word *zeal* (line 3) we gather that the crew members were
a. enthusiastic about their mission   b. forced to make the trip
c. cautious but not fearful.

___b___ 3. If crew members *accumulated* (line 13) more knowledge, they must
have   a. not had any idea what was happening to them
b. quickly realized what danger they were in   c. misinterpreted
the information they received.

___c___ 4. Someone "standing *mute*" (line 26) would be   a. at attention
b. ready to faint   c. silent.

___b___ 5. The *transformation* (line 36) Jocko refers to is   a. the trip into
outer space   b. the abnormal growth of the head
c. his untimely death.

Number correct ___5___ (total 5)

Part C   Ways to Make New Words Your Own

By now you are familiar with the target words and their meanings. This section presents activities that will help you make the words part of your permanent vocabulary.

Using Language and Thinking Skills

True-False Decide whether each statement is true or false. Write **T** for True or **F** for False.

___F___ 1. When a knight went on a *quest*, he stayed home in the castle and
entertained friends.

___F___ 2. A *mutiny* is a celebration held by sailors to honor their captain.

___T___ 3. The human heart is a *vital* organ.

___T___ 4. A house that has been repaired and repainted has undergone a
transformation.

___F___ 5. To be *mute* means to be very talkative.

28

6. To *accumulate* wealth means to lose it gradually over a period of time.

7. A *repulsive* sight is one that appeals to everyone.

8. Telephone poles along a road are a good example of a *cluster.*

9. Eating cake on your birthday is an example of *abnormal* behavior.

10. To *endear* yourself to others means that you do something that causes others to like you.

Number correct _____ (total 10)

Word's Worth: *zeal*

The word *zeal* comes from the Greek word *zelos,* meaning "warmth" or "passion." *Zeal* became a proper noun in the first century A.D., when it was applied to a radical band of Jews who rebelled against their Roman rulers. This group wanted to preserve the national and religious life of the Jewish people at all costs. These Zealots, as they were called, stopped at nothing to gain their ends, including murdering Jews who sought peace with the Romans. The group of Zealots who carried out assassinations were called the *Sicarri,* or "dagger men."

Today, the noun *zeal* means "a devoted enthusiasm for a cause," and *zealous* is the adjective form of the noun. The word *zealot,* however, retains the meaning it had nearly two thousand years ago—"an individual who carries his or her zeal to an extreme."

Finding the Unrelated Word Write the letter of the word that is not related in meaning to the other words in the set.

____ 1. a. mute b. silent c. speechless d. curious

____ 2. a. effectiveness b. competence c. weakness d. usefulness

____ 3. a. defeat b. quest c. adventure d. mission

____ 4. a. abnormal b. different c. irregular d. effective

____ 5. a. gathered b. collected c. annoyed d. accumulated

____ 6. a. necessary b. essential c. untimely d. vital

____ 7. a. suspense b. evidence c. testimony d. proof

_C_ 8. a. devotion b. zeal c. mutiny d. dedication

_b_ 9. a. transformation b. sameness c. alteration d. change

_a_ 10. a. calm b. dangerous c. wild d. desperate

Number correct __10__ (total 10)

Practicing for Standardized Tests

Antonyms Write the letter of the word that is most nearly *opposite* in meaning to the capitalized word.

_E_ 1. CURIOUS: (A) searching (B) clever (C) changeable
(D) gentle (E) uninterested

_C_ 2. EFFECTIVENESS: (A) sinfulness (B) stupidity
(C) uselessness (D) usefulness (E) effort

_E_ 3. UNTIMELY: (A) early (B) fast (C) well-timed (D) famous
(E) exact

_D_ 4. CLUSTER: (A) gather (B) destroy (C) decorate
(D) separate (E) grow

_E_ 5. SUSPENSE: (A) beginning (B) fiction (C) danger
(D) bravery (E) certainty

_C_ 6. DESPERATE: (A) generous (B) usual (C) calm
(D) hopeless (E) wild

_A_ 7. ABNORMAL: (A) natural (B) unnatural (C) incomplete
(D) meaningful (E) skillful

_B_ 8. VENTURE: (A) adventure (B) safety (C) kindness
(D) reward (E) advantage

_B_ 9. ZEAL: (A) eagerness (B) sadness (C) openness
(D) foolishness (E) disinterest

_B_ 10. VITAL: (A) lively (B) unnecessary (C) guaranteed
(D) unknown (E) important

Number correct __8__ (total 10)

Spelling and Wordplay

Crossword Puzzle Read the clues and print the correct answer to each in the proper squares.

ACROSS

1. Producing a desired result
9. A large, nonflying Australian bird
10. To stir or blend ingredients together
11. A female deer
13. Abbr. bushel
15. Abbr. teaching assistant
16. Abbr. southeast
17. To chew and swallow
18. Indefinite article meaning "one"
19. Before noon
20. Objective case of "we"
21. Preposition meaning "in," "on," "near," or "by"
22. A kind of explosive
23. Abbr. Long Island
24. Abbr. Saint
25. Abbr. Latin *id est,* meaning "that is"
26. Contraction of "I would"
28. A short sleep
30. Collected
31. An interjection expressing surprise, doubt, or a question
32. Fourteenth letter of the alphabet
33. Comes after nine
35. Spanish bullfight cheer
36. A rebellion of soldiers or sailors against their officers
37. Abbr. south
38. Phonetic spelling of easy
40. Same as 21 Across
41. 2,000 pounds
42. To drive back an attack
46. Abbr. American Medical Association
48. Not normal

DOWN

1. To make beloved
2. What you stand on
3. Abbr. enlisted man
4. A native of Cuba
5. Contraction of "I am"
6. Necessary to life
7. A test
8. To seek or hunt
12. ___ ___ ___ meal
14. At the wrong time
16. The state of being uncertain
22. Abbr. technician
25. Frozen water
27. A rounded ridge of sand
29. Past tense of "eat"
34. Not speaking
35. Upon
36. Planet noted for its red color
37. Abbr. south
39. Eager interest
41. Same as 33 Across
43. Short for father
44. Abbr. Los Angeles
45. Abbr. stolen base
46. First person singular, present indicative of "to be"
47. Short for mother

Part D   Related Words

The words below are closely related to the target words. Use your knowledge of the target words and of word parts to determine the meaning of these words. (For information about word parts analysis, see pages 7–13). Use your dictionary if necessary.

1. abnormality (ab′ nôr mal′ ə tē) n.
2. accumulation (ə kyōōm′ yə lā′ shən) n.
3. curiosity (kyoor′ ē äs′ ə tē) n.
4. desperation (des′ pə rā′ shən) n.
5. effective (ə fek′ tiv, i-) adj.
6. endearing (in dir′ ŋ) adj.
7. ineffective (in′ i fek′ tiv) adj.
8. suspend (sə spend′) v.
9. suspenseful (sə spens′ fəl) adj.
10. technical (tek′ ni k′l) adj.
11. transfer (trans′ fər) n. (trans fur′, trans′ fər) v.
12. transform (trans fôrm′) v.
13. translate (trans′ lāt, tranz′-) v.
14. transparent (trans per′ ənt, -par′-) adj.
15. transplant (trans′ plant′) n. (trans plant′) v.
16. vitality (vī tal′ ə tē) n.
17. zealot (zel′ ət) n.
18. zealous (zel′ əs) adj.

Understanding Related Words

Finding Examples Write the letter of the situation that best shows the meaning of the boldfaced word.

_____ 1. **effective**

    a. a medicine that did not cure your hay fever

    b. a cleanser that removes stubborn stains from bathroom tile

    c. a drink that leaves you thirsty

_____ 2. **vitality**

    a. baking a fancy cake

    b. sleeping late

    c. running a ten-mile race

_____ 3. **technical**

    a. a school that trains welders

    b. a bright, intense color used in motion pictures

    c. meeting an old friend

_____ 4. **suspenseful**

    a. an exciting movie with a scary ending

    b. a basketball game with a fifty-point margin of victory

    c. a geography lesson

_b_ 5. **curiosity**

    a. an argument between strangers

    b. a little boy taking apart an alarm clock

    c. a music student practicing a lesson

_a_ 6. **desperation**

    a. jumping out of a burning building

    b. a person who gossips

    c. a coach talking to team members

_b_ 7. **accumulation**

    a. winning a race

    b. dishes piled in a sink

    c. refusing to work

_b_ 8. **abnormality**

    a. northern birds flying south for the winter

    b. a four-legged bird

    c. a birdwatcher in a wildlife refuge

_a_ 9. **ineffective**

    a. treating a broken leg with aspirin

    b. paying people well to get them to work better

    c. studying for a spelling test

_c_ 10. **suspend**

    a. setting up a schedule of classes

    b. a teacher meeting with students having trouble

    c. classes called off for several days after a fire in the school

Number correct _9_ (total 10)

Analyzing Word Parts

The Prefix _trans-_ The prefix _trans-_ comes from the Latin word _trans,_ meaning "across." In English, it can mean "on," "to the other side," "over," "across," or "through." Keeping in mind these meanings, match each word below with its correct definition. Write the letter of the appropriate word in the blank.

a. transfer   b. transform   c. translate   d. transparent   e. transplant

_c_ 1. to change the words of one language into those of another (v.)

_e_ 2. something—for example, a human organ or a plant—that is moved from one place to another (n.)

_b_ 3. to change in appearance (v.)

_____ 4. to send from one place to another (v.)

_____ 5. easily seen through (adj.)

Number correct ___5___ (total 5)

Number correct in unit __66__ (total 70)

Turn to **The Final Silent** *e* on page 227 of the **Spelling Handbook.** Read the rule and complete the exercises provided.

The Last Word

Writing

The list of target words on page 24 contains several adjectives: *abnormal, curious, desperate, mute, repulsive, untimely,* and *vital.* Write a short paragraph in which you use one of these adjectives to describe a person, a place, or an incident from your own experience.

Speaking

Prepare a speech on one of the following topics:

- The importance of *curiosity*
- How pets *endear* themselves to people
- A *suspenseful* situation that you or someone you know has experienced

Group Discussion

Medieval French romances were stories about knights on a *quest* or *mission.* Typically, the knight was sent on a quest to conquer an enemy or to retrieve a sacred object. On his return the knight was judged by how well he overcame the obstacles he met, such as dragons and evil knights. In a group create a quest or mission that a knight might undertake. Each member of the group may suggest obstacles for the knight as well as the means for him to overcome these obstacles.

UNIT 3

Part A Target Words and Their Meanings

1. accomplishment (ə käm′ plish mənt) n.
2. advantage (ad vant′ tij) n.
3. constant (kän′ stənt) adj., n.
4. corrective (kə rek′ tiv) adj.
5. credit (kred′ it) n., v.
6. determined (di tur′ mənd) adj.
7. grasp (grasp) n., v.
8. intense (in tens′) adj.
9. involve (in välv′) v.
10. massive (mas′ iv) adj.
11. orthopedic (ôr′ thə pē′ dik) adj.
12. quantity (kwän′ tə tē) n.
13. radiology (rā′ dē āl′ ə jē) n.
14. recall (ri kôl′) v. (ri kôl′, rē′ kôl′) n.
15. sensitivity (sen′ sə tiv′ ə tē) n.
16. sheer (shir) adj.
17. specialist (spesh′ əl ist) n.
18. stamina (stam′ ə nə) n.
19. tranquilize (tran′ kwə līz′, tran′-) v.
20. veterinarian (vet′ ər ə ner′ ē ən,
    vet′ rə ner′-) n.

Inferring Meaning from Context

For each sentence write the letter of the word or phrase that is closest in meaning to the word or words in italics. Use context clues to help you determine the correct answer. (For information about how context helps you understand vocabulary, see pages 1–6.)

_____ 1. Anne is a girl of many *accomplishments;* she has won awards in dancing, singing, and acting.

a. moods b. amusements c. achievements d. embarrassments

_____ 2. An eleven-year-old Oklahoma girl, Metha Brorsen, won the barrel-racing event at the International Rodeo Association competition. She had the *advantage* of a good horse as well as her own exceptional skill.

a. drawback b. lack c. goal d. benefit

_____ 3. After three days of *constant* rain, the river flooded.

a. nonstop b. polluted c. light d. destructive

_____ 4. The captain abruptly changed the ship's course; this *corrective* action prevented a collision with an iceberg.

a. expensive b. foolish c. destructive d. adjusting

_____ 5. Terry, who hit a grand slam home run, deserves most of the *credit* for his team's victory.

a. money b. time off c. honor d. shame

35

_____ 6. The jury spent seven days discussing the case; they were *determined* to reach a fair verdict in the trial.

    a. debating whether b. pretending c. committed d. quick

_____ 7. The drowning man frantically *grasped* the life preserver thrown by the rescue team; the man was pulled to safety.

    a. pushed away b. seized c. noticed d. ripped

_____ 8. Because the pain was so *intense,* the football player knew immediately that he had fractured his leg.

    a. slight b. strong c. dull d. brief

_____ 9. Housekeeping *involves* such tasks as doing laundry, cleaning, cooking, and grocery shopping.

    a. teaches b. encourages c. includes d. postpones

_____ 10. Jupiter is the most *massive* planet in our solar system; it is 318 times bigger than the earth.

    a. immense b. beautiful c. famous d. typical

_____ 11. Jan went to *an orthopedic* doctor to have her broken arm set.

    a. a bones-and-joints b. a children's c. an eye d. a general

_____ 12. Among the potato-growing states, Idaho produces the largest *quantity,* an average of 102,500,000 bags per year.

    a. profit b. industry c. amount d. type

_____ 13. The doctor needed pictures to see whether the bones in his patient's hand were broken; therefore, he sent his patient to the *radiology* department.

    a. science of mechanical devices b. science of X-rays c. science of the brain d. science of infections

_____ 14. My grandfather has an amazing memory. He can *recall* stories that his mother told him when he was a child.

    a. create b. imitate c. memorize d. remember

_____ 15. His *sensitivity to* the problems of others makes Mr. Gomez an excellent counselor.

    a. awareness of b. blindness to c. anger about d. inexperience with

_____ 16. It was *sheer* coincidence that Victoria and Juanita arrived at the same moment and in exactly the same kind of dress.

    a. ordinary b. pure c. sharp d. planned

_____ 17. Doctor Nicholson is an otolaryngologist, *a specialist* in diseases of the ears, nose, and throat.

    a. a student b. an amateur c. a critic d. an expert

_____ 18. A boy of great physical *stamina,* Mark ran ten miles without tiring.

a. size   b. staying power   c. speed   d. weakness

_____ 19. Listening to the soft patter of rain on the roof seemed to *tranquilize* Felicia, and soon she was asleep.

a. relax   b. drug   c. irritate   d. transport

_____ 20. After a lengthy examination, the *veterinarian* determined that the sick cat would not require surgery.

a. doctor of nutrition   b. doctor of animals   c. doctor of veterans   d. doctor of philosophy

Number correct _____ (total 20)

Part B   Target Words in Reading and Literature

You should now have a general idea of the meaning of each target word. Refine your understanding by examining the shades of meaning the words have in the following excerpt.

This Village Blacksmith Is a Woman

Maureen Q. Nichols

From Hollywood westerns, most people have a mental picture of an old-fashioned blacksmith: the village strongman laboring away at his stables on the edge of town. However, modern blacksmithing is quite different from this image, as this reading selection reveals.

When people read the ad "Horseshoeing by Toni Hanna," they think that "Toni" is misspelled. It's no mistake, though; Antoinette Hanna is a blacksmith, the first woman to graduate from Cornell University's Farrier[1] School. Hanna, who was a Girl Scout in Fairfax County, Virginia, for five years, was one of six students chosen to attend the school from over 1,000 applicants.   5

Cornell's program involved four months of **intense** training. Toni, who is five feet tall and weighs 95 pounds, stood on her feet for nine hours a day, hammering. "The forge would blow 2,000 degrees at you, and your face would be black with soot," she **recalled.**   10

It was worth it, though, Toni feels, because she gained a lot of valuable experience. "Since Cornell is a veterinary college, we would go to **radiology** and study the X-rays of diseased horses," Toni explained. "Some of the world's best **veterinarians** were there, and we got the advantage of

---

[1] farrier: British word for a blacksmith who shoes horses

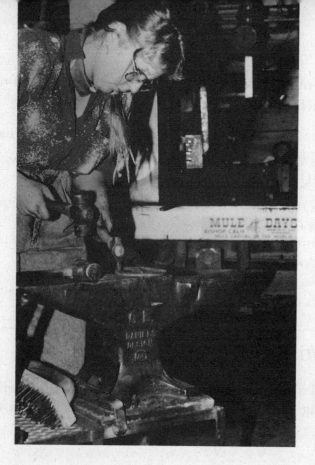

their knowledge. We looked at the horse's foot from a **specialist's** point of view. We were like **orthopedic** surgeons," she laughed.

Horseshoeing has become very scientific. Much of it **involves corrective** shoeing. "In the old days," said Toni, "a blacksmith would put a horse's hoof on a stump, trim it with a chisel, and nail a shoe onto it. Today, a farrier watches a horse travel and observes how his hind foot reaches his front foot. He then measures the angle of the hoof, the slope of the shoulder, and the length of the toe, before shoeing."

After graduation, Toni was eager to start her own business. She needed tools, though, so she advertised in the local paper. A junk dealer called and said he had some old blacksmith tools that he would sell her. Toni rushed over. While there, she saw a 125-pound anvil.[2] Since anvils usually cost about a dollar a pound, Toni was thrilled when the man agreed to sell it for thirty dollars. "I picked up the anvil and marched to the car, which was quite a way down the road," recalled Toni. When she returned and gave the man thirty dollars, he handed it back to her and said, "For any woman who can carry an anvil down that road, it's on the house."

Toni and her **constant** companion, Good Dog, travel all over Oneida County in a pickup truck with a forge[3] in the back. This upstate New York area has many stables, but most of Toni's customers are people who own horses for the **sheer** pleasure of it. "I could make $1,000 a week if I just wanted to shoe at stables," said Toni, "but I prefer quality, not **quantity**."

Toni thinks that, in her line of work, being a woman has both **advantages** and disadvantages. For example, the first horse she ever shod was a huge, unruly Clydesdale. Her male classmates snickered as Toni approached the **massive** animal. "I **grasped** the huge foot that weighed more than I did," she explained. "Suddenly, in one graceful movement,

---

[2] anvil: an iron or steel block on which metal objects are hammered into shape
[3] forge: a place where metal is heated and hammered into shape

the horse lifted me forward and threw me into the side of a truck." Both 55
her pride and the side of the truck were dented, but Toni was **determined**
not to give up. With a toss of her pigtails, she dusted herself off and finished shoeing the horse. Some people feel that a woman handles high-
strung animals better than a man. "That's up to the individual," said Toni.
"You can't just go barging into an animal's stall with your tools. You have 60
to give the animal **credit** for having some **sensitivity**."

Toni recalled a time at Cornell when a fellow was trying to shoe a huge
Tennessee Walker. The horse was fighting and thrashing around. He had
broken his lead[4] several times. Finally the student decided to **tranquilize**
the horse. When he left to get the veterinarian, Toni approached the ani- 65
mal. "The first thing I did was untie him," she said. "Then I began
stroking him and talking softly into his ear. When the men returned," she
laughed, "I had two shoes on him!"

"Horseshoeing takes **stamina**," emphasized Toni, "but the rewards are
great. I go to sleep each night with a sense of personal **accomplish-** 70
ment. I know that I've done some good, honest work."

---

[4] lead: leash

Refining Your Understanding

For each of the following items, consider how the target word is used in the passage. Write the letter of the word or phrase that best completes each sentence.

_____ 1. The best example of *intense* (line 7) training would be   a. a week of hard work followed by a week of vacation   b. two hours of classes every day   c. five hours of classes and five hours of study every day for weeks.

_____ 2. Toni Hanna explains that she prefers quality to *quantity* (line 49). This means that she prefers to   a. do fewer jobs, but do them well   b. change professions   c. work less and enjoy life more.

_____ 3. An example of an animal that is not *massive* (line 53) would be the   a. fox   b. hippopotamus   c. elephant.

_____ 4. When Hanna refers to an animal's *sensitivity* (line 61), she means   a. feelings   b. need for sound nutrition   c. intelligence.

_____ 5. When Hanna describes her "sense of personal *accomplishment*" (line 70–71), she means   a. the feeling that she has done her job well   b. the amount of money she earns   c. the knowledge that her horses will win more races.

Number correct _____ (total 5)

Part C *Ways to Make New Words Your Own*

By now you are familiar with the target words their and meanings. This section presents activities that will help you make the words part of your permanent vocabulary.

Using Language and Thinking Skills

Matching Examples Write the word from the list below that is most clearly related to the situation conveyed in the sentence.

accomplishment	orthopedic	sensitivity
constant	radiology	stamina
corrective	recall	tranquilize
intense		

_____ 1. A long-distance runner must be strong enough to run distances of up to twenty-six miles.

_____ 2. Doctors who specialize in diseases of the bones and joints are particularly helpful to athletes.

_____ 3. Mrs. Winter felt great satisfaction in climbing the mountain on her sixtieth birthday.

_____ 4. An X-ray technician plays an important role in helping doctors diagnose ailments.

_____ 5. You can develop your memory so that you can remember more facts and the details of past incidents.

_____ 6. Becoming more aware of the feelings and attitudes of others is a worthwhile goal.

_____ 7. Eyeglasses help many people to see better.

_____ 8. Sometimes when animals become uncontrollable, veterinarians have to calm them down with medication.

_____ 9. The passing of time never ceases, as evidenced by the continuous ticking of a clock.

_____ 10. The reunion of the two brothers, who had been separated for ten years, was filled with tears and joy.

Number correct _____ (total 10)

Practicing for Standardized Tests

Antonyms Write the letter of the word that is most nearly *opposite* in meaning to the capitalized word.

_____ 1. ACCOMPLISHMENT: (A) mission   (B) failure   (C) goal   (D) viewpoint   (E) achievement

_____ 2. CONSTANT: (A) changing   (B) established   (C) unfortunate   (D) similar   (E) frequent

_____ 3. CORRECTIVE: (A) impossible   (B) destructive   (C) improving   (D) unrewarding   (E) honest

_____ 4. DETERMINED: (A) undecided   (B) guaranteed   (C) content   (D) trustworthy   (E) unsafe

_____ 5. GRASP: (A) settle down   (B) hold   (C) release   (D) venture   (E) suspect

_____ 6. INVOLVE: (A) leave out   (B) realize   (C) dislike   (D) misunderstand   (E) contain

_____ 7. RECALL: (A) remember   (B) forget   (C) forgive   (D) announce   (E) refuse

_____ 8. SENSITIVITY: (A) education   (B) change   (C) feeling   (D) danger   (E) indifference

_____ 9. STAMINA: (A) stupidity   (B) peacefulness   (C) brilliance   (D) weakness   (E) vitality

_____ 10. TRANQUILIZE: (A) feed   (B) comfort   (C) excite   (D) stay   (E) reject

Number correct _____ (total 10)

Word's Worth: stamina

The ancient Romans had a different understanding of the word *stamina* than we do today. The Latin word *stamina* meant "thread." Most Romans believed that the happenings in a person's life were determined by three strange and powerful creatures known as the Fates. Whenever someone was born, one of the Fates spun the thread of life, one determined the length, and one cut the thread when the Fates decided a person should die. Arguing with the Fates was useless.

In the eighteenth century, Jonathan Swift, the author of *Gulliver's Travels*, first used the word *stamina* to refer to the ability to get over an illness. Today when we hear the word, we don't think of threads or Fates but rather of our own ability to withstand fatigue or hardship.

Spelling and Wordplay

Fill-ins Spell the target word correctly in the blanks to the right of its definition.

1. resolved: _ _ t _ _ _ _ _ _ e _

2. endurance: s _ _ _ i _ _

3. achievement: _ _ c _ _ _ _ _ _ _ h _ _ _ _

4. without stopping: _ _ _ _ _ _ n t

5. awareness of feelings: _ _ n s _ _ _ _ _ _ _

6. meant to improve: _ o _ _ e _ _ _ _ _

7. strong; extreme: _ n _ _ n _ _

8. absolute; pure: _ _ e e _

9. science that uses X-rays for medical diagnosis and treatment:

    _ a _ i _ _ _ _ _

10. to seize; to hold: g _ _ _ p

11. to soothe: t _ _ _ q _ _ _ _ _ _

12. expert: s _ _ c _ _ _ _ _ _

13. recognition; regard: _ _ _ d i _

14. to include: _ _ _ _ l _ e

15. related to the study and treatment of bones and joints:

    _ _ t h _ _ _ _ _ _

16. to remember: _ _ _ a l _

17. doctor of animals: v _ t _ _ _ _ _ _ _ _

18. more favorable position: a _ _ _ _ _ _ _ _ _

19. huge; enormous: m _ _ _ _ _ _ _

20. an amount: q _ _ _ _ _ _ _

Number correct _____ (total 20)

Turn to **Words Ending in *-ize* or *-ise*** on page 231 of the **Spelling Handbook**. Read the rule and complete the exercise provided.

Part D Related Words

The words below are closely related to the target words. Use your knowledge of the target words and of word parts to help you determine the meaning of these words. (For information about word parts analysis, see pages 7–13.) Use your dictionary if you are unsure of any definitions.

1. accomplish (ə käm′ plish) v.
2. constantly (kän′ stənt lē) adv.
3. correction (kə rek′ shən) n.
4. creditable (kred′ i tə bəl) adj.
5. determinant (dē tʉr′ mi nənt) adj., n.
6. determination (di tʉr′ mə na′ shən) n.
7. determine (di tʉr′ mən) v.
8. intensify (in ten′ sə fi′) v.
9. intensive (in ten′ siv) adj.
10. involvement (in välv′ mənt) n.
11. orthopedist (ôr′ thə pē′ dist) n.
12. radiologist (rā′ dē äl′ ə jist) n.
13. sensitive (sen′ sə tiv) adj.
14. specialty (spesh′ əl tē) n.
15. tranquil (traŋ′ kwəl, tran′-) adj.
16. tranquillity (traŋ kwil′ ə tē, tran-) n.

Understanding Related Words

Sentence Completion Write the word from the list below that best completes the meaning of the sentence.

accomplish	corrections	intensified	involvement	specialty
constantly	determination	intensive	sensitive	tranquillity

_____ 1. Angie confessed her ? in the scheme to play a trick on her younger brother.

_____ 2. After listening to loud concert music for hours, Lisa enjoyed the ? she found in the silence of her room.

_____ 3. That chef is famous in our city; his ? is French desserts.

_____ 4. This Sunday the Lopez family hopes to ? their goal: to finish a 10K race together.

_____ 5. Richard's friends thought he was being overly ? when he took their joke as an insult.

_____ 6. Following the motorcycle accident, Eustace was treated in the ? care unit of the hospital for six weeks.

_____ 7. Trevor was ? bothering his younger brother; he never left poor Nick alone.

_____ 8. With fierce ? , Elsa was able to accomplish her goal of getting A's in all of her classes.

_____ 9. Ben's English paper needed several spelling ? .

_____ 10. The crowd's anger ? when the umpire made his third terrible call in the inning.

Number correct _____ (total 10)

Analyzing Word Parts

The Suffix -ist The target word *specialist* and the two related words *orthopedist* and *radiologist* all end in the suffix -ist, which means "a person who does, makes, or practices." Using a dictionary when needed, write each of the following -ist words next to its correct definition.

orthopedist   radiologist   psychologist   specialist   sociologist

_____ 1. a person who has skill in a particular kind of work or field of study

_____ 2. a person who diagnoses and treats deformities, diseases, and injuries of the bones and joints

_____ 3. a person who studies X-rays used for the diagnosis and treatment of diseases

_____ 4. a person who studies the behavior of people in groups

_____ 5. a person who studies the human mind and human behavior

Number correct _____ (total 5)

The Suffix -ment The target word *accomplishment* and the related word *involvement* both contain the suffix -ment. This common suffix turns words into abstract nouns that suggest that something is the result of an action or process. For example, *enjoyment* is the result of enjoying. Change each of the following words into nouns by adding the suffix -ment. Write the newly formed word and then write the meaning of the new word, using your dictionary to check your word.

1. disappoint: _____

2. govern: _____

3. encourage: _____

4. employ: _____

5. confine: _____

Number correct _____ (total 5)

Number correct in unit _____ (total 85)

The Last Word

Writing

Think about the word *corrective*. What are some corrective actions taken by people to make the world better? If you could improve or correct one condition in your world, what would it be? What specific corrective actions would you recommend? Write one paragraph on this subject.

Speaking

Tell about a time in which you had *intense* feelings about a goal and great *determination* to achieve it. For example, you might describe your efforts in trying to make a team, obtain a high grade, win a race, or earn a part in a play.

Group Discussion

Two of the target words from this unit, *orthopedic* and *radiology,* refer to particular branches of medical science. See how many different branches of medicine your class can name. Then, working with a partner, find out more about one of the special fields of medicine named. Use a dictionary and an encyclopedia as sources. Share your findings with the rest of the class.

UNIT 4: Review of Units 1–3

Part A Review Word List

Unit 1 Target Words
1. alter
2. chemist
3. condition
4. conduct
5. detect
6. development
7. establish
8. florist
9. formation
10. frequently
11. guarantee
12. handicap
13. informative
14. inseparable
15. magnificent
16. observe
17. prediction
18. render
19. safeguard
20. seasonal

Unit 1 Related Words
1. alteration
2. alternate
3. conductor
4. detection
5. detector
6. develop
7. floral
8. frequency
9. handicapped
10. infrequent
11. magnification
12. magnificence
13. magnify
14. nonchemical
15. observation
16. reestablish
17. unobserved
18. unseasonable

Unit 2 Target Words
1. abnormal
2. accumulate
3. cluster
4. curious
5. desperate
6. effectiveness
7. endear
8. mission
9. mute
10. mutiny
11. quest
12. repulsive
13. suspense
14. technician
15. testimony
16. transformation
17. untimely
18. venture
19. vital
20. zeal

Unit 2 Related Words
1. abnormality
2. accumulation
3. curiosity
4. desperation
5. effective
6. endearing
7. ineffective
8. suspend
9. suspenseful
10. technical
11. transfer
12. transform
13. translate
14. transparent
15. transplant
16. vitality
17. zealot
18. zealous

Unit 3 Target Words
1. accomplishment
2. advantage
3. constant
4. corrective
5. credit
6. determined
7. grasp
8. intense
9. involve
10. massive
11. orthopedic
12. quantity
13. radiology
14. recall
15. sensitivity
16. sheer
17. specialist
18. stamina
19. tranquilize
20. veterinarian

Unit 3 Related Words
1. accomplish
2. constantly
3. correction
4. creditable
5. determinant
6. determination
7. determine
8. intensify
9. intensive
10. involvement
11. orthopedist
12. radiologist
13. sensitive
14. specialty
15. tranquil
16. tranquillity

Inferring Meaning from Context

For each sentence write the letter of the word or phrase that is closest in meaning to the word or words in italics.

_a_ 1. The coach decided to *alter* the game plan in an attempt to stop the team's losing streak.

   a. change   b. recall   c. disrupt   d. foretell

_d_ 2. When Jed ran out of drinking water in the desert, he was in *a desperate* situation.

   a. a predictable   b. an abnormal   c. a seasonal   d. a hopeless

_c_ 3. The manufacturer *guaranteed* that its watch would function flawlessly under water, or the cost of the watch would be cheerfully refunded.

   a. predicted   b. observed   c. pledged   d. realized

_b_ 4. A quality such as talkativeness can be an advantage for a teacher but a *handicap* for a student.

   a. temptation   b. drawback   c. benefit   d. strategy

_a_ 5. The light was so *intense* it hurt our eyes.

   a. strong   b. transparent   c. infrequent   d. effective

_d_ 6. After learning that she had won the lottery, Nadia was totally *mute;* she moved her lips, but no sound came out.

   a. tranquil   b. handicapped   c. nervous   d. silent

_b_ 7. Because Wilma was active in sports and was prone to injury, she felt fortunate that her cousin was *an orthopedic* surgeon.

   a. an eye and ear   b. a bone and joint   c. a nose and throat
   d. a radiological

_d_ 8. The sight of a snake in his back yard was so *repulsive* to Fred that he ran back into the house.

   a. predictable   b. timely   c. contradictory   d. disgusting

_a_ 9. Joann's *sensitivity to* other people's feelings made her a good friend to have.

   a. deep understanding of   b. curiosity about
   c. personal opinion about   d. theory of

_b_ 10. Tracy lifted the refrigerator off the floor through *sheer* willpower.

   a. predictable   b. absolute   c. magnificent   d. mysterious

_d_ 11. The *technician* moved the patient very carefully when taking X-rays to avoid causing injury.

   a. florist   b. developer   c. special teacher   d. skilled specialist _a_ 12. David had to take an oath to tell the truth before he could give his *testimony* in court.

      a. evidence b. accomplishment c. belief d. transformation

_b_ 13. The huge bear had to be *tranquilized* so the dentist could pull its infected tooth.

      a. tricked b. calmed c. involved d. trained

_b_ 14. Because Joe was always bringing home stray animals and nursing them back to health, his family felt sure he would become *a veterinarian.*

      a. a parent b. an animal doctor c. a technician d. a scientist

_d_ 15. The mayoral candidate hoped she would win and not disappoint the supporters who had worked for her campaign with such *zeal.*

      a. curiosity b. carelessness c. profit d. eagerness

Number correct _____ (total 15)

Using Review Words in Context

The story below contains fifteen blanks. For each blank, determine which word from the list best fits the context of the sentence. Write the word in the blank. Each word will be used only once.

accumulate   conditions   curious   guarantees   predict
alter   conduct   establish   mission   quest
chemists   constant   frequently   observe   stamina

Scientists: Nature's Detectives

Scientists have basically one ___mission___—to ___observe___ the natural world and to ___establish___ explanations for what they see. They must be ___curious___ people and must devote themselves to the ___quest___ for knowledge. They also must have the ___stamina___ to work steadily on a problem, even if no solution is in sight. There are no ___guarantees___ in science, and it often takes many people many years to ___predict___ even small pieces in the puzzle. ___Chemists___ for example, ___conduct___ experiments under controlled ___conditions___ in a laboratory. They keep detailed records of their procedures and ___frequently___ redo an experiment. If they think they have found the explanation to a particular problem, they ___accumulate___ what will happen under different circumstances and test their prediction by doing another experiment. For example, they may _alter_ one element, such as temperature, while keeping the other factors in the experiment _constant_. Scientists have all the frustrations—and all the fun—of Sherlock Holmes.

Number correct _____ (total 15)

Part B   Review Word Reinforcement

Using Language and Thinking Skills

Finding the Unrelated Word Write the letter of the word that is not related in meaning to the other words in the set.

__C__ 1. a. alter   b. change   c. detect   d. vary

__b__ 2. a. common   b. abnormal   c. usual   d. typical

__d__ 3. a. remember   b. recollect   c. recall   d. reward

__a__ 4. a. sensitive   b. vital   c. essential   d. required

__d__ 5. a. mission · b. search   c. quest   d. accomplishment

__b__ 6. a. massive   b. sheer   c. huge   d. vast

__C__ 7. a. inseparable   b. attached   c. divorced   d. joined

__a__ 8. a. intense   b. tranquil   c. calm   d. easygoing

__C__ 9. a. venture   b. chance   c. mutiny   d. risk

__d__ 10. a. gather   b. accumulate   c. assemble   d. inform

Number correct _____ (total 10)

Practicing for Standardized Tests

Antonyms Write the letter of the word that is most nearly opposite in meaning to the capitalized word.

__D__ 1. ACCOMPLISHMENT: (A) skill   (B) involvement   (C) observation   (D) failure   (E) development

__A__ 2. ADVANTAGE: (A) drawback   (B) superiority   (C) blessing   (D) convenience   (E) determination

__B__ 3. CORRECTIVE: (A) effective   (B) mistaken   (C) informative   (D) healing   (E) destructive

__B__ 4. DESPERATE: (A) urgent   (B) hopeful   (C) disappointed   (D) mutinous · (E) intense

_A_ 5. DETERMINED: (A) uncertain (B) dependable (C) developed (D) opposed (E) confident

_D_ 6. ENDEAR: (A) charm (B) magnify (C) appreciate (D) disgust (E) attract

_D_ 7. GRASP: (A) suspend (B) understand (C) detect (D) misunderstand (E) develop

_E_ 8. MAGNIFICENT: (A) sheer (B) grand (C) significant (D) sensitive (E) ordinary

_A_ 9. SPECIALIST: (A) generalist (B) chemist (C) technician (D) individual (E) representative

_A_ 10. UNTIMELY: (A) seasonal (B) inconvenient (C) convenient (D) technical (E) interruptive

Number correct _____ (total 10)

Synonyms Write the letter of the word that is *closest* in meaning to the capitalized word.

_E_ 1. DETECT: (A) recall (B) involve (C) transfer (D) hinder (E) notice

_A_ 2. DEVELOPMENT: (A) growth (B) observation (C) solution (D) reversal (E) accumulation

_E_ 3. EFFECTIVE: (A) useful (B) inadequate (C) corrective (D) weak (E) intensive

_E_ 4. INFORMATIVE: (A) ignorant (B) effective (C) unfamiliar (D) guaranteed (E) instructive

_B_ 5. PREDICT: (A) remember (B) foretell (C) remind (D) presume (E) testify

_C_ 6. QUEST: (A) answer (B) conduct (C) search (D) response (E) trust

_A_ 7. REPULSIVE: (A) offensive (B) beloved (C) curious (D) endearing (E) sheer

_B_ 8. SAFEGUARD: (A) retain (B) protect (C) threaten (D) tranquilize (E) handicap

_E_ 9. SUSPENSE: (A) guarantee (B) suspicion (C) insurance (D) prediction (E) uncertainty

_C_ 10. TRANSFORMATION: (A) separation (B) formation (C) alteration (D) information (E) transportation

Number correct _____ (total 10)

Spelling and Wordplay

Word Pyramid Fill in the blanks by following the code at the base of the pyramid.

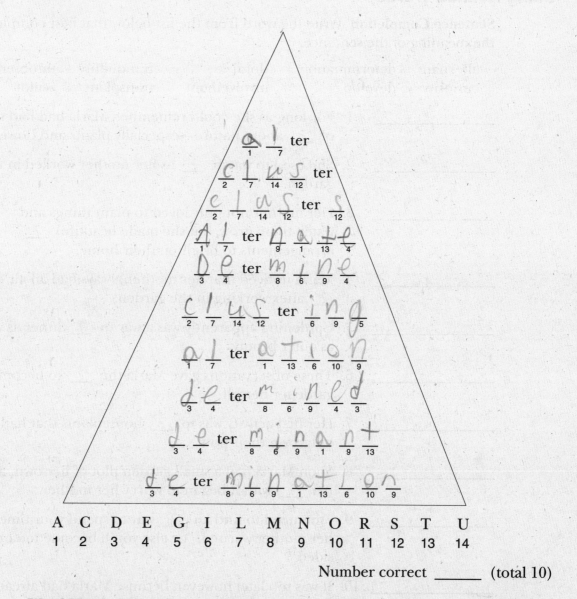

<u>a</u> <u>l</u> ter
 1   7

<u>c</u> <u>l</u> <u>u</u> <u>s</u> ter
 2   7 14 12

<u>c</u> <u>l</u> <u>u</u> <u>s</u> ter <u>s</u>
 2   7 14 12   12

<u>A</u> <u>l</u> ter <u>n</u> <u>a</u> <u>t</u> <u>e</u>
 1   7   9   1 13   4

<u>D</u> <u>e</u> ter <u>m</u> <u>i</u> <u>n</u> <u>e</u>
 3   4   8   6   9   4

<u>c</u> <u>l</u> <u>u</u> <u>s</u> ter <u>i</u> <u>n</u> <u>g</u>
 2   7 14 12   6   9   5

<u>a</u> <u>l</u> ter <u>a</u> <u>t</u> <u>i</u> <u>o</u> <u>n</u>
 1   7   1 13   6 10   9

<u>d</u> <u>e</u> ter <u>m</u> <u>i</u> <u>n</u> <u>e</u> <u>d</u>
 3   4   8   6   9   4   3

<u>d</u> <u>e</u> ter <u>m</u> <u>i</u> <u>n</u> <u>a</u> <u>n</u> <u>t</u>
 3   4   8   6   9   1   9 13

<u>d</u> <u>e</u> ter <u>m</u> <u>i</u> <u>n</u> <u>a</u> <u>t</u> <u>i</u> <u>o</u> <u>n</u>
 3   4   8   6   9   1 13   6 10   9

A	C	D	E	G	I	L	M	N	O	R	S	T	U
1	2	3	4	5	6	7	8	9	10	11	12	13	14

Number correct _____ (total 10)

Word Match Match five words from the pyramid with their correct definition below. Write the words in the blanks.

alternate 1. to do by turns (v.)

predict 2. the act of deciding (n.)

cluster 3. a bunch (n.)

alter 4. to change (v.)

determined 5. decided; settled (adj.)

Number correct _____ (total 5)

51

Part C   Related Word Reinforcement

Using Related Words

Sentence Completion Write the word from the list below that best completes the meaning of the sentence.

| alternate | determination | floral | tranquillity | unobserved |
| curiosity | develop | involvement | transplant | zealot |

curiosity   1. For long as she could remember, Marla had had a lot of ? about nature—especially plants and flowers.

unobserved   2. She used to watch ? as her mother worked in the garden.

floral   3. Her mother not only loved to plant things and watch them grow, but she made beautiful ? arrangements to brighten their home.

tranquillity   4. Marla noticed that her mother always had an air of ? after working in the garden.

develop   5. Gardening apparently was a way to ? inner as well as outer beauty.

determination   6. These observations gave Marla the ? to become a gardener herself.

transplant   7. Her first activity was to ? houseplants that had outgrown their pots.

involvement   8. Soon Marla had a small garden plot of her own, and her ? with it began to worry her mother.

alternate   9. "You need to find an ? way to spend your time," her mother warned, "or else you'll become too one-sided."

zealot   10. It was too late, however, because Marla had already become a ? .

Number correct _____ (total 10)

Reviewing Word Structures

Adding Word Parts Add a word part to each word below to form a new word. Choose from among the word parts listed. Some word parts may be used twice. In some cases the final silent *e* may need to be dropped before a suffix is added.

ab-	-able
en-	-ity
trans-	-ist
	-ion

Words	**New Words**
1. accumulate	*accumylation*
2. credit	*credable*
3. dear	*endear*
4. desperate	*desparation*
5. form	*transform*
6. normal	*abnormal*
7. plant	*transplant*
8. sensitive	*sensitivity*
9. special	*specialty*
10. radiology	*radiologist*

Number correct _____ (total 10)

Number correct in unit _____ (total 95)

Vocab Lab 1

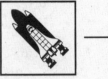

FOCUS ON: **Space Travel**

The following words are related to space travel. Study these words and complete the exercise that follows.

aerospace (er′ ō spās′) n. the earth's atmosphere and the regions of space beyond it. ● As a result of the space program, scientists learned a great deal about traveling in *aerospace.*

artificial satellite (är′ tə fish′ əl sat′ 'l īt′) n. a spacecraft that circles the earth or another heavenly body. ● Unlike the natural moons that orbit planets, *artificial satellites* are produced by humans.

booster (boos′ tər) n. the first stage of a multistage rocket, which provides the power for the launching and early part of the flight. ● The *booster* propelled the spacecraft into orbit.

cosmonaut (käz′ mə nôt) n. a Soviet space pilot. ● Soviet *cosmonauts* and American astronauts conducted scientific experiments together during the Apollo-Soyuz Project.

escape velocity (ə skāp′ və läs′ ə tē) n. the minimum speed a spacecraft must reach to escape the pull of gravity. ● To reach the desired *escape velocity,* a spacecraft must burn a large quantity of fuel.

module (mäj′ ool) n. any section of a spacecraft that can be detached from other sections. ● The lunar *module* separated from the main spacecraft and began its descent to the surface of the moon.

payload (pā′ lōd′) n. cargo aboard the spacecraft. ● On certain spacecraft the *payload* includes a satellite that is eventually released into its own orbit.

probe (prōb) n. a spacecraft designed to explore and to send back information about outer space and other planets. ● Scientists hope one day to create a *probe* that can travel to the nearest star.

reentry (rē en′ trē) n. the return of a space vehicle into the earth's atmosphere. ● The *reentry* is one of the most dangerous parts of space travel.

rendezvous (rän′ dā voo′) n. a maneuver in which two or more spacecraft meet. ● During the *rendezvous* with the space station, astronauts exchanged data.

revolution (rev ə loo′ shən) n. one complete cycle of a heavenly body or an artificial satellite in orbit. ● Early space flights made only a few *revolutions* in their orbit of the earth.

space shuttle (spās′ shut′ 'l) n. a spacecraft used to carry people and equipment between earth and an orbiting space station. ● Because a *space shuttle* can go on more than one mission, using it saves the tremendous cost of building a new vehicle.

space station (spās′ stā′ shən) n. a structure designed to orbit in space and to be used as a laboratory or a launching pad. ● Scientists predict that in the future, some people may permanently live on *space stations.*

trajectory (trə jek′ tə rē) n. the curved flight path of a spaceship shot through space. ● The rocket sped away from Earth on a gradually curving *trajectory.*

zero gravity (zir′ ō, zē′ rō grav′ ə tē) n. the condition in which an object or body appears to be unaffected by gravity; weightlessness. ● The astronaut told funny stories about the effects of *zero gravity*, such as the time his food floated away from him in the space capsule.

Sentence Completion Complete each sentence below by writing the appropriate focus word.

_____ 1. In 1957 *Sputnik I* became the first launch vehicle, or ? to be sent into space.

_____ 2. During ? , a spacecraft plunges through the atmosphere, generating intense heat.

_____ 3. Because of the effects of ? , astronauts must eat with their feet strapped down.

_____ 4. The Viking space ? landed on the surface of Mars and sent back detailed pictures and information.

_____ 5. Until the twentieth century, most people thought travel in ? was impossible.

_____ 6. The *Apollo 11* spacecraft segments separated into the command ? , *Columbia,* which circled the moon, and the *Eagle,* which landed on the moon.

_____ 7. After the spaceship achieved a high enough altitude, the rocket ? detached and parachuted to the earth.

_____ 8. During each ? around earth, a weather satellite takes pictures to monitor cloud movement.

_____ 9. Aerospace scientists can adjust the ? , or curving arch, of a space launch in order to lessen pressure on the astronauts.

_____ 10. *Skylab I* was the first manned ? to be used as an orbiting laboratory.

_____ 11. ? Yuri Gagarin was the first Soviet to orbit the earth.

_____ 12. After leaving the moon, the lunar module had a ? with the command module for the return to earth.

_____ 13. Because the pull of the earth's gravity is so strong, a spacecraft must achieve a(an) ? of 25,000 miles per hour to enter a solar orbit.

_____ 14. Unlike most other spacecraft, the ? can make more than one trip.

_____ 15. On each spaceflight, the ? includes many pounds of equipment for conducting scientific experiments.

Number correct _____ (total 15)

55

FOCUS ON: *Analogies*

Various activities—such as synonym, antonym, and sentence completion exercises—help build vocabulary skills. An analogy exercise is another way to enrich your understanding of words. An **analogy** shows a relationship between words. A typical analogy question might look like this:

> Determine the relationship between the capitalized words. Then decide which other word pair expresses a similar relationship. Write the letter of this word pair.
>
> ____ 1. VIOLIN : INSTRUMENT :: (A) fish : water   (B) bird : eagle
> (C) airplane : hangar   (D) tiger : cat   (E) train : railroad

The analogy can also be stated this way:

"A *violin* is to an *instrument* as a ? is to a(n) ? .

Use the following four steps to find the answer to an analogy.

1. Determine the relationship between the first two words.

2. Make up a sentence using the two words: A *violin* is a type of *instrument*.

3. Decide which of the choices given has a similar type of relationship.

4. Test your choice by substituting the pair of words for the original pair in the sentence you made up.

It becomes obvious that (D) is the best answer to this question when you use the test: "A *tiger* is a type of *cat*."

Below are a few types of relationships used in analogies:

Type of Analogy	Example
part to whole	finger : hand :: spoke : wheel
object to purpose	car : transportation :: lamp : light
action to object	dribble : basketball :: fly : kite
word to synonym	nice : pleasant :: glad : happy
word to antonym	good : bad :: slow : fast
object to its material	shoe : leather :: tire : rubber
product to source	apple : tree :: milk : cow
worker and tool	musician : horn :: carpenter : hammer
time sequence	sunrise : sunset :: winter : spring
word and derived form	act : action :: image : imagination

Analogies Determine the relationship between the capitalized words. Then decide which other word pair expresses a similar relationship. Write the letter of this word pair.

_____ 1. FLORIST : FLOWERS :: (A) paper : wood (B) transplant : heart (C) harvest : crops (D) dentist : teeth (E) grapes : vineyard

_____ 2. TRANQUIL : PEACEFUL :: (A) good : better (B) ugly : attractive (C) gray : black (D) female : feminine (E) weary : tired

_____ 3. ABNORMAL : NORMAL :: (A) angry : furious (B) effective : ineffective (C) medical : dental (D) purple : red (E) bizarre : weird

_____ 4. HOCKEY : SPORT :: (A) doctor : patient (B) mold : bread (C) chemistry : chemist (D) law : justice (E) ballet : dance

_____ 5. MUTE : VOICELESS :: (A) delicate : coarse (B) smart : intelligent (C) vital : lifeless (D) seasonal : daily (E) handicapped : blind

_____ 6. CONDUCTOR : ORCHESTRA :: (A) echo : sound (B) builder : blueprint (C) inventor : patent (D) pianist : violinist (E) coach : team

_____ 7. KNIFE : CUT :: (A) runner : race (B) child : disobey (C) irritation : calm (D) paper : paste (E) hammer : pound

_____ 8. MAGNIFICENT : ORDINARY :: (A) superior : higher (B) recent : current (C) strange : familiar (D) beautiful : conceited (E) polite : quiet

_____ 9. SENSITIVE : SENSITIVITY :: (A) wise : philosopher (B) hopeful : optimist (C) desperate : desperation (D) digestive : food (E) outgoing : personality

_____ 10. EVIDENCE : PROOF :: (A) lecture : professor (B) computer : disk (C) compass : direction (D) thunder : lightning (E) story : tale

Number correct _____ (total 10)

Number correct in Vocab Lab _____ (total 25)

UNIT 5

Part A Target Words and Their Meanings

1. adapt (ə dapt′) n.
2. awkward (ôk′ wərd) adj.
3. characteristic (kar′ ik tə ris′ tik) adj., n.
4. compose (kəm pōz′) v.
5. continuous (kən tin′ yoo wəs) adj.
6. cope (kōp) v.
7. cycle (sī′ k'l) n., v.
8. distribute (dis trib′ yoot) v.
9. efficient (ə fish′ ənt) adj.
10. eventually (i ven′ choo wəl ē, -chə lē) adv.
11. fuse (fyooz) v., n.
12. horizontally (hôr′ ə zän′ tə lē, här′-) adv.
13. maintain (mān tān′) v.
14. merge (murj) v.
15. propel (prə pel′) v.
16. resistant (ri zis′ tənt) adj.
17. rotate (rō′ tāt) v.
18. streamline (strēm′ līn) v.
19. suitable (soot′ ə b'l) adj.
20. vertical (vur′ ti k'l) adj.

Inferring Meaning from Context

For each sentence write the letter of the word or phrase that is closest in meaning to the word or words in italics. Use context clues to help you choose the correct answer. (For information about how context helps you understand vocabulary, see pp. 1–6.)

__b__ 1. The dinosaurs died out because they could not *adapt to* drastic changes in their environment.

a. explain b. adjust to c. reject d. plan

__c__ 2. The newborn colt took a few *awkward* steps, wobbling on its long legs.

a. firm b. small c. clumsy d. graceful

__b__ 3. Mario's *characteristic* honesty made him a trustworthy friend.

a. unpleasant b. basic c. questionable d. occasional

__d__ 4. Two main ingredients, milk and ice cream, *compose* a milkshake.

a. spoil b. are left out of c. cost more than d. make up

____ 5. The *continuous* ticking of a clock reminds people that time is passing.

a. uninterrupted b. annoying c. unpredictable d. irregular

_____ 6. In spite of having to *cope with* blindness and deafness, Helen Keller became an outstanding writer and lecturer.

a. deal with   b. rely on   c. inherit   d. develop

_____ 7. The seasons unfold in a constant *cycle;* winter is followed by spring, spring by summer, summer by fall, and fall by winter.

a. accumulation   b. frequency   c. quest   d. pattern

_____ 8. Once everyone was seated and all books and notes had been put away, the teacher *distributed* the tests to the class.

a. passed out   b. abandoned   c. criticized   d. restored

_____ 9. Because Yuki hated to clean her room and had more interesting ways to spend her time, she tried to discover *an efficient* way to do the chore.

a. a productive   b. an obvious   c. a slow   d. a mechanical

_____ 10. *Eventually,* the rain stopped, and we continued our softball game.

a. Lately   b. Finally   c. Accidentally   d. Remarkably

_____ 11. The welder at the steel mill used a blowtorch to *fuse* the two pieces of metal into one.

a. join   b. cut apart   c. fragment   d. expand

_____ 12. Wearing stripes that run straight up and down tends to make people look slimmer; wearing stripes arranged *horizontally* has the opposite effect.

a. in clusters   b. imaginatively   c. sideways   d. randomly

_____ 13. Try to *maintain* your sense of humor, even when other people are losing theirs.

a. forget about   b. keep   c. abandon   d. share

_____ 14. Because an overturned truck blocked two lanes of the road, three lanes of traffic had to *merge* into one.

a. join   b. disappear   c. transform   d. lengthen

_____ 15. The cannon *propelled* the clown into the air in a graceful arc, but his tiny parachute failed to open and he crashed to the ground.

a. dragged   b. plunged   c. urged   d. thrust

_____ 16. At first Adam was *resistant to* doing his chores, but when he found out that he would not get his allowance until the chores were done, he set about them eagerly.

a. happy   b. opposed to   c. confused by   d. tempted by

_____ 17. The weather vane *rotated* slowly in the wind, pointing first to the north, then to the south, then back again.

a. turned   b. expanded   c. bounced   d. plunged

_____ 18. Over time, engineers have *streamlined* airplanes so that the planes can offer less air resistance and achieve higher speeds.

    a. made underwater   b. made of metal   c. added wings to
    d. shaped for smooth movement

_____ 19. Colleen's outfit is *suitable* for either formal or informal occasions, although she has only worn it to fancy parties so far.

    a. required   b. memorable   c. appropriate   d. guaranteed

_____ 20. If the walls of a building are not *vertical*, the structure will collapse.

    a. straight up and down   b. economical   c. comparable
    d. plastered

Number correct _____ (total 20)

Part B   *Target Words in Reading and Literature*

You should now have a general idea of the meaning of each target word. Sharpen your understanding by studying how these words are used in the following selection.

Shaped Like a Fish, But Not a Fish

Helen Hoke and Valerie Pitt

Many people are surprised to learn that a whale is not a fish. In this reading selection the authors discuss how the whale is similar to and different from other animals.

Although it is a sea creature and it looks somewhat like a huge fish, the whale is actually not a fish at all. Like its land ancestors, it is a mammal.

All mammals have four main **characteristics** in common:

1. They all have lungs and breathe air.

2. They are warmblooded, with body temperatures that remain constant. The whale's temperature is about 96.8°, close to a human's, and it remains the same, whatever the outside temperature.   5

3. All mammals have some hair; although the whale is generally a smooth creature, it does have a few whiskery hairs on its chin or head.

4. Mammals give birth to live young, which they nurse with milk.   10

Nearly all mammals live on land. Humans are mammals. So are tigers and elephants and chimpanzees and cats and dogs. A mammal's characteristics make it highly suited to life on land where there is air to breathe, sunshine and clothes or fur for keeping warm, a great variety of foods, and **suitable** places for giving birth to young.   15

How then does the whale manage to live the life of a mammal in the

60

ocean? The answer is that it has become **adapted,** or fitted, to an ocean life. Take its shape, for instance. Humans cannot move easily through water. For one thing, their legs are too heavy. Normally they must carry their bodies about on land and work against the pull of gravity. In water, humans' strong legs will **eventually** cause them to sink. And besides, the angles of their bodies—their narrow limbs and unwebbed, spreading fingers and toes—are too **awkward** and numerous to **cope** with **resistant** water pressure. For easy traveling in the sea, an animal needs a **streamlined** shape and evenly **distributed** weight.

Whales have been called "**efficient** living submarines." Their huge heads and bodies **merge** into a **continuous** smooth torpedo shape that offers little resistance to water pressure. The head, which may measure a third of the whale's entire body, is supported by neck bones which, in many whales, are **fused** together so that the animal cannot turn its head from side to side. The front limbs have become smooth flippers, which the whale uses for balancing, steering, and braking. They can be **rotated,** which adds to their usefulness when the whale needs to change direction. Some whales have a second balancing-and-steering device, called a dorsal fin, along their backs, near their tails. The tail itself is **horizontally** spread out and ends in two large flukes, or lobes. (A fish's tail is **vertical** and moves from side to side.)

The whale's flukes drive it through the water. **Composed** of tough, flexible tissue, they are powered by strong muscles. As the horizontal tail goes up and down, each fluke moves in turn in opposite **cycles,** twisting through the water with powerful strokes. So strong are the flukes that one lash from them may smash a small boat in two. They **propel** the whale at speeds which, for short bursts, may reach eighteen knots (about twenty-one miles an hour) or more if the whale is frightened. The fin whale can **maintain** a speed of twenty knots for fifteen minutes or more, and the dolphins can go even faster—up to twenty-five knots.

61

Refining Your Understanding

For each of the following items, consider how the target word is used in the passage. Write the letter of the word or phrase that best completes the sentence.

_C_ 1. "*Suitable* places for giving birth to young" (line 15) for animals on land would be   a. spacious and well-lit   b. close to mountains   c. safe from natural enemies.

_C_ 2. Water is more *resistant* (line 23) to movement than air is because water is   a. wetter   b. darker in color   c. heavier.

_b_ 3. Another example of an object that can be *rotated* (line 33) is a a. tree   b. wheel   c. garage door.

_a_ 4. Unlike the fish's tail, which is "*vertical* and moves from side to side" (line 37), the whale's tail is "*horizontally* spread out" (lines 35–36), allowing the tail to move   a. up and down   b. silently c. gracefully.

_b_ 5. Another example of a *cycle* (line 40) would be   a. rocks rolling down a hill   b. the phases of the moon.   c. learning to roller skate.

Number correct _____ (total 5)

Part C   Ways to Make New Words Your Own

By now you are familiar with the target words and their meanings. This section presents activities that will help you make the words part of your permanent vocabulary.

Using Language and Thinking Skills

Verb Match   Match each verb below with its appropriate definition. Write the verb to the left of its definition.

adapt   distribute   maintain   propel   streamline

distribute 1. to divide and hand out

propel 2. to push or make go forward

streamline 3. to shape for smooth movement

maintain 4. to keep up; to hold onto

adapt 5. to change in order to fit a situation or fill a need

Number correct _____ (total 5)

Understanding Multiple Meanings   Each box in this exercise contains a boldfaced word with its definitions. Read the definitions and then the sentences that use the word. Write the letter of the definition that applies to each sentence.

---

compose
  a. to make by putting together different parts or elements (v.)
  b. to create by mental or artistic labor, usually applied to literary or musical work (v.)
  c. to calm; to quiet (v.)

_C_ 1. The class had difficulty *composing* itself after a dog ran through the room.

_a_ 2. The perfect party is *composed* of good friends, good music, and good food.

_b_ 3. The author *composed* her short story in only two weeks of intense work.

_c_ 4. Before competing in the statewide spelling competition, Jeffrey *composed* himself while sitting alone in a dark room.

---

fuse
  a. to mix or join together, often by melting (v.)
  b. an electrical safety device that prevents overloading a circuit (n.)
  c. a strip of combustible material, such as string or cloth, used to set off an explosive charge (n.)

_b_ 5. Using too many appliances at the same time can result in a blown *fuse.*

_c_ 6. The soldier lit the *fuse* on the dynamite, then ran for safety behind a large boulder.

_a_ 7. Certain back problems are treated by *fusing* together sections of the vertebrae in the spine.

---

characteristic
  a. typical of an individual, group, or situation (adj.)
  b. feature or trait that makes something different from others (n.)

_b_ 8. Dedication and the desire to win were *characteristic* of all the football players on the team.

_a_ 9. In his *characteristic,* calm way, Jorge handled the crisis and restored order.

_b_ 10. The single white stripe down its back is one of the skunk's most noticeable *characteristics.*

Number correct _____ (total 10)

Word's Worth: awkward

The word *awkward* has not always meant *clumsy.* In Middle English, *awke* meant "from the left," and *awkward,* "in an *awke* direction." In medieval times, an awkward blow with a sword was merely one delivered from the left side, or backhanded with the right hand. It was not necessarily clumsy or ineffective, and could easily have been fatal. Today, however, *awkward* has a negative association. It means "lacking skill." *Awkward* no longer has any reference to moving to the left.

Practicing for Standardized Tests

Synonyms   Write the letter of the word that is closest in meaning to the capitalized word.

_e_ 1. AWKWARD: (A) massive (B) smooth (C) effective
(D) unsafe (E) clumsy

_e_ 2. CONTINUOUS: (A) frequent (B) interrupted (C) normal
(D) advantageous (E) unbroken

_d_ 3. COPE: (A) alter (B) correct (C) predict (D) handle
(E) transfer

_b_ 4. EFFICIENT: (A) inexpensive (B) effective (C) slow
(D) vital (E) intensive

_d_ 5. EVENTUALLY: (A) slowly (B) urgently (C) fortunately
(D) finally (E) immediately

_a_ 6. HORIZONTALLY: (A) flatly (B) tranquilly (C) unevenly
(D) distantly (E) indirectly

_c_ 7. MERGE: (A) rotate (B) transform (C) fuse (D) invade
(E) emerge

_c_ 8. RESISTANT: (A) fortunate (B) healthful (C) opposed
(D) diseased (E) supportive

___E___ 9. ROTATE: (A) involve (B) drive (C) prefer (D) repair
(E) turn

___b___ 10. VERTICAL: (A) parallel (B) upright (C) normal (D) true
(E) sufficient

Number correct _____ (total 10)

Spelling and Wordplay

Fill-ins   Spell the target word correctly in the blanks.

1. opposed to: r e s i s t a n t
2. without interruption: c o n t i n u o u s
3. clumsy: a w k w a r d
4. straight up and down: v e r t i c a l
5. to join together through heating: f u s e
6. to keep up; to hold onto: m a i n t a i n
7. to combine or blend into one: m e r g e
8. productive; effective: e f f i c i e n t
9. to deal with problems: c o p e
10. repeated pattern: c y c l e
11. finally: e v e n t u a l l y
12. appropriate: s u i t a b l e
13. to shape for smooth movement: s t r e a m l i n e
14. to make by putting together; to create; to calm: c o m p o s e
15. sideways; parallel to the horizon: h o r i z o n t a l l y
16. to adjust to different situations: a d a p t
17. to force into motion: p r o p e l
18. to move around a central point: r o t a t e
19. to divide among many; to hand out: d i s t r i b u t e
20. typical; a noticeable feature: c h a r a c t e r i s t i c

Number correct _____ (total 20)

65

Part D   *Related Words*

The words below are closely related to the target words. Use your knowledge of the target words and of word parts to determine the meanings of these words. (For information about word parts analysis, see pages 7-13.) Use your dictionary if necessary.

1. adaptable (ə dapt′ tə b′l) adj.
2. adaptation (ad′ əp tā′ shən) n.
3. character (kar′ ik tər) n.
4. continuity (kän′ tə nōō′ ə tē, -nyōō′-) n.
5. cyclical (si′ kli k′l, sik′ li k′l) adj.
6. distribution (dis′ trə byōō′ shən) n.
7. efficiency (ə fish′ ən sē, i-) n.
8. event (i vent′) n.
9. eventual (i ven′ chōō wəl) adj.
10. horizontal (hôr′ ə zän′ t′l, här′-) adj.
11. maintenance (mān′ t′n əns) n.
12. propeller (prə pel′ ər) n.
13. recycle (re sī′ k′l) v.
14. resistance (ri zis′ təns) n.
15. rotation (rō tā′ shən) n.
16. suit (sōōt) n., v.

Understanding Related Words

Finding Examples Write the letter of the situation that best shows the meaning of the boldfaced word.

_____ 1. **horizontal**
   a. Milo is doing chin-ups.
   b. A ladder is leaning against the house.
   c. Elsa is turning somersaults.
   d. Hot dogs are cooking on a grill.

_____ 2. **resistance**
   a. Aunt Aiko leaves the door unlocked.
   b. A beaver dam collapses in the flood.
   c. Byron refuses to eat his spinach.
   d. Cecelie decides to buy a magazine subscription from a door-to-door salesperson.

_____ 3. **continuity**
   a. This hamburger is almost raw in the center.
   b. Jerry's father is fired from his job.
   c. A secretary trains her replacement.
   d. There are four or five rotten apples in the bushel.

_____ 4. **adaptation**
   a. Wolves grow thick coats in winter.
   b. Dana forgets his umbrella at home.
   c. Mitzi waters the lawn.
   d. Jesse reads a bestseller.

66

_d_ 5. **rotation**
   a. Kevin does the pole vault.
   b. A truck backs up to the loading dock.
   c. The Statue of Liberty stands near the entrance to New York City's harbor.
   d. A weather vane turns in the wind.

_a_ 6. **efficiency**
   a. A car gets fifty miles per gallon of gas.
   b. A sunbather uses a protective lotion.
   c. Rachel rereads *Gone With the Wind.*
   d. A cactus plant lives for centuries.

_a_ 7. **maintenance**
   a. Alex repairs a flat tire on his bike.
   b. Jean's father washes the car each week and replaces the oil regularly.
   c. Ying buys a new pair of roller blades.
   d. The library upgrades its computer system.

_b_ 8. **recycle**
   a. Niels sells newspapers door to door.
   b. Alicia wears the clothes her sister has outgrown.
   c. Jorge competes in the triathlon.
   d. Katy revises her poem before she hands it in.

_c_ 9. **distribution**
   a. Two magnets are drawn together.
   b. A rose's petals unfold.
   c. Dandelion seeds blow over a field.
   d. Anya rakes leaves.

_b_ 10. **character**
   a. Amy scores 100 on the math quiz.
   b. Marc is the tallest boy in his class.
   c. Sandy locks himself out of the house.
   d. Eduardo reads to children at the local hospital every Saturday.

Number correct _____ (total 10)

Finding the Unrelated Word Write the letter of the word that is not related in meaning to the other words in the set.

_d_ 1. a. match b. suit c. fit d. conflict

_b_ 2. a. adjustable b. rigid c. adaptable d. changeable

_a_ 3. a. happening b. prediction c. occurrence d. event

_b_ 4. a. seasonal b. direct c. cyclical d. repeating

_d_ 5. a. eventual b. future c. coming d. past

Number correct _____ (total 5)

67

Analyzing Word Parts

The Latin Root *sistere*   The target word *resistant* and the related word *resistance* come from the Latin root *sistere,* meaning "to stand." Other words based on this root are listed below.

consistent   desist   persistent   subsistence   transition

Look up these words in your dictionary. Then complete the following sentences using the most appropriate word.

persistant   1. Alex was so _?_ that he continued working on the math problem long after everyone else had given up.

subsistance   2. In _?_ farming, farmers produce only enough goods to provide for their families and have nothing extra to sell.

consistant   3. Ava never won a race, but she was remarkably _?_ , finishing second in each of the five major track meets last season.

desist   4. _?_ , or else!

transition   5. Many children have difficulty making the _?_ from printing to cursive writing.

Number correct _____ (total 5)

Number correct in unit _____ (total 90)

Turn to **The Suffix** *-ion* on page 232 of the **Spelling Handbook.** Read the rule and complete the exercises provided.

The Last Word

Writing

Have you ever wished you could be as friendly (or popular, or confident) as someone else? If you could develop one positive personality *characteristic*, what would it be? How would you develop it? How would you benefit by having it? Discuss these ideas in a well-organized paper.

Speaking

Life is full of difficult situations. Think of a difficulty you faced and were able to *cope* with effectively. Give a short speech to the class in which you describe the situation, the various ways you might have reacted, and how you actually dealt with the problem. You might ask your classmates how they would have coped with that situation and consider if you would act the same way again.

Group Discussion

The whale once lived on land; now it is a sea animal. It has survived because it was able to *adapt* to a new environment. Other animals, such as the dinosaurs, died out because they could not adapt when their environment changed. As a class, discuss what it would be like to live in an environment completely different from your own. This could be somewhere on, in, or above the earth, or an imaginary place. Consider questions such as these in your discussion: What would this environment look like? To what specific differences would you have to adapt? How would your bodies and minds have to change? Do you think some people would be more adaptable than others? Could you, personally, survive?

UNIT 6

Part A Target Words and Their Meanings

1. acknowledge (ək nӑl′ ij, ak-) v.
2. actual (ak′ cho͞o wəl) adj.
3. disclose (dis klōz′) v.
4. douse (dous) v., n.
5. hazardous (haz′ ərd əs) adj.
6. hinder (hin′ dər) v.
7. impure (im pyoor′) adj.
8. intrigue v. (in′ trēg) n., (in trēg′)
9. inviting (in vīt′ iŋ) adj.
10. journalist (jʉr′ n'l ist) n.
11. linger (liŋ′ gər) v.
12. maneuver (mə no͞o′ vər, -nyo͞o′-) v., n.
13. metropolitan (met′ rə pӑl′ ə t'n) adj., n.
14. pursuit (pər so͞ot′, -syo͞ot′) n.
15. reliable (ri lī′ ə b'l) adj.
16. solemn (sӑl′ əm) adj.
17. unaccountable (un′ ə koun′ tə b'l) adj.
18. unaware (un ə wer′) adj.
19. version (vʉr′ zhən, -shən) n.
20. vivid (viv′ id) adj.

Inferring Meaning from Context

For each sentence write the letter of the word or phrase that is closest in meaning to the word or words in italics. Use context clues to help you choose the correct answer. (For information about how context helps you understand vocabulary, see pages 1–6.)

_____ 1. The shoplifter *acknowledged* his guilt and apologized for stealing the tape.

a. admitted b. forgot c. argued d. denied

_____ 2. The *actual* cost of the car rental could be found by adding on the price of insurance and mileage, plus tax.

a. efficient b. reduced c. imaginary d. real

_____ 3. At the press conference the President freely *disclosed* the terms and details of the peace treaty.

a. concealed b. suspended c. resisted d. made known

_____ 4. When the swimming team won, the team members *doused* their coach with lemonade from a huge container.

a. teased b. soaked c. watched d. insulted

_____ 5. The drifting snow made driving *hazardous* and forced many people off the road.

a. suitable b. dangerous c. possible d. vital

_____ 6. Lack of money for costumes and stage sets *hindered* the young theater company and delayed its opening date.

a. encouraged   b. held back   c. developed   d. streamlined

_____ 7. Although the water looked *impure* and unhealthy, tests proved it to be safe.

a. inviting   b. polluted   c. tranquil   d. vital

_____ 8. Mystery stories *intrigue* many readers; these readers eagerly await the next tale by their favorite author.

a. greatly interest   b. bore   c. recall   d. handicap

_____ 9. On a hot summer day a cold, clear lake looks very *inviting*.

a. appealing   b. distant   c. technical   d. threatening

_____ 10. After a verdict was reached, the *journalists* rushed from the courtroom to call their editors and write their stories.

a. technicians   b. judges   c. witnesses   d. news reporters

_____ 11. We *lingered* over dinner, neither of us willing to make the first move toward ending the meal.

a. hurried   b. met   c. skipped   d. took extra time

_____ 12. After receiving field reports, the general decided on the army's next *maneuver:* it would attack by night from the rear.

a. resting place   b. movement   c. testimony   d. mutiny

_____ 13. The weather forecast was only for the *metropolitan* area, not the outlying farm communities.

a. rural   b. distant   c. urban   d. inhabited

_____ 14. *In pursuit of* world conquest, Alexander the Great led his armies across Asia.

a. Avoiding   b. Resisting   c. Suspending   d. Seeking

_____ 15. That encyclopedia is a *reliable* source of information; each fact has been carefully checked.

a. favorite   b. personal   c. dependable   d. neglected

_____ 16. The nation was in *a solemn* mood for some time after President John F. Kennedy was assassinated in 1963.

a. a serious   b. a suspenseful   c. a tranquil   d. an untimely

_____ 17. James was considered to be *unaccountable for* the loss of the necklace because it had disappeared before his employment began.

a. a suspect for   b. guilty of   c. not responsible for
d. unhappy about

_____ 18. The deer calmly munched the grass, *unaware* of the mountain lion's presence.

   a. suspicious   b. not knowing   c. glad   d. conscious

_____ 19. Hugo and Eduardo had different *versions of* the accident. Hugo claimed the driver was at fault; Eduardo said the driver was innocent.

   a. reactions to   b. fears about   c. dreams of
   d. descriptions of

_____ 20. The interior decorator recommended *vivid* colors to brighten the drab room.

   a. bright   b. soft   c. pale   d. plain

Number correct _____ (total 20)

Part B Target Words in Reading and Literature

You should now have a general idea of the meaning of each target word. Sharpen your understanding by studying how these words are used in the following selection.

The Press and Free Speech

Howard Peet

The following reading selection explains why reporting a news story is often difficult and sometimes dangerous.

Inviting as it may sound, the job of a **journalist** is not an easy one. In any one day on the job, a reporter may be **doused** with rain or threatened with a lawsuit. Whatever happens, the most important task is to give an honest account of **actual** events. When two reporters write different **versions** of the same story, one version might be more colorful than the other. However, accuracy is what counts most. In giving the news it is better to be **reliable** than **vivid.** A good reporter will try for both.   5

Reporters, like the rest of us, live in an **impure** world, so the **pursuit** of the news sometimes involves mystery and **intrigue.** Especially in **metropolitan** areas, people with inside information about crime may be   10
afraid to talk about it. They may feel threatened by the people who committed the crime. They may not want to be seen **lingering** at the scene of a crime, talking to reporters. Sometimes a person with inside information can only be **maneuvered** into giving information by being promised complete privacy. The reporter must promise not to reveal the person's name.   15

Freedom of the press is guaranteed by the First Amendment to the U.S. Constitution. Journalists—and most courts—have interpreted freedom of the press as meaning that journalists need not reveal their sources for a story. The public is often **unaware** of the **hazardous** situation journalists could face if this were not true. Journalists are caught between wanting to **acknowledge** their sources and needing to protect them. Judges and attorneys sometimes claim that members of the media **hinder** justice by failing to **disclose** the insider's name. The journalist, however, may insist that the only way the insider will give information is if he or she remains nameless. In extreme circumstances, the informant's life may be in danger if his or her name is made public.

Knowing this, journalists may face a **solemn** decision. They know that they cannot be **unaccountable** for their actions. They may decide to go to jail rather than reveal the names of informants who trusted them. Over the years a number of journalists have, in fact, been jailed for this reason. However, all of the journalists who have refused to reveal the names of their informants have eventually been released.

73

Refining Your Understanding

For each of the following items, consider how the target word is used in the passage. Write the letter of the word or phrase that best completes each sentence.

_____ 1. A *vivid* account of the news (line 7) is likely to be
a. dramatic   b. boring   c.   hard to follow.

_____ 2. The fact that obtaining news sometimes involves *intrigue* (line 9) suggests that obtaining news may be
a. enjoyable   b. easy   c. complicated.

_____ 3. To "*hinder* justice" (line 23) is the opposite of
a. promoting justice   b. preventing justice   c. forgetting justice.

_____ 4. A "*solemn* decision" (line 27) is one that
a. is not very important   b. should not be taken lightly
c. changes frequently.

_____ 5. A reporter who *acknowledges* (line 21) a source is
a. giving credit to a person   b. asking what is known about a person   c. hiding a person's identity.

Number correct _____   (total 5)

Part C   Ways to Make New Words Your Own

By now you are familiar with the target words and their meanings. This section presents activities that will help you make the words part of your permanent vocabulary.

Using Language and Thinking Skills

Finding the Unrelated Word Choose the word that does not mean the same as the other words in the set.

_____ 1. a. soak   b. douse   c. grasp   d. drench

_____ 2. a. impure   b. clean   c. dirty   d. polluted

_____ 3. a. scheme   b. intrigue   c. plot   d. stamina

_____ 4. a. solid   b. faithful   c. reliable   d. magnificent

_____ 5. a. acknowledge   b. admit   c. predict   d. confess

_____ 6. a. proceed   b. linger   c. pause   d. delay

_____ 7. a. disclose   b. show   c. reveal   d. hide

_____ 8. a. hunt   b. chase   c. cluster   d. pursuit

_____ 9. a. blameable   b. unaccountable   c. guilty   d. responsible

_____ 10. a. report   b. version   c. writer   d. description

Number correct _____ (total 10)

Practicing for Standardized Tests

Antonyms Write the letter of the word that is most nearly *opposite* in meaning to the capitalized word in each set.

_____ 1. ACKNOWLEDGE: (A) know   (B) deny   (C) recognize
(D) agree   (E) misunderstand

_____ 2. ACTUAL: (A) dishonest   (B) imaginary   (C) realistic
(D) unusual   (E) truthful

_____ 3. DISCLOSE: (A) hide   (B) emphasize   (C) display
(D) decide   (E) plan

_____ 4. HAZARDOUS: (A) brave   (B) dangerous   (C) safe
(D) cowardly   (E) wise

_____ 5. HINDER: (A) obstruct   (B) establish   (C) assist   (D) follow
(E) create

_____ 6. LINGER: (A) decide   (B) merge   (C) spread   (D) hurry
(E) pause

_____ 7. METROPOLITAN: (A) crowded   (B) awkward   (C) rural
(D) urban   (E) rhythmical

_____ 8. RELIABLE: (A) undependable   (B) true   (C) determined
(D) strange   (E) continuous

_____ 9. SOLEMN: (A) heavy   (B) false   (C) repulsive   (D) technical
(E) humorous

_____ 10. VIVID: (A) memorable   (B) polite   (C) natural   (D) dull
(E) colorful

Number correct _____ (total 10)

Spelling and Wordplay

Crossword Puzzle Read the clues and print the correct answer to each in the proper squares. There are several target words in the puzzle.

ACROSS

1. Not responsible
11. Dependable
12. Noah built it
13. Abbr. fullback
15. Unfeeling
16. To ask to come somewhere
19. Much __ __ __ about nothing
20. Observed
21. Wood twists or bends; it _____
25. Abbr. railroad
26. Short for Albert
28. Abbr. lower case
29. To free oneself of
31. Abbr. Long Island
32. Of a city area
35. Abbr. Dutch
36. Either __ __
37. Long story of heroic deeds
38. The earth revolves around it
40. That man
41. An elevated railway
42. More than one female deer
44. Average or normal
45. Twice five
46. Unhappy

DOWN

1. Not knowing
2. To admit to be true
3. To stuff
4. Abbr. Old English
5. Abbr. ultimate
6. Abbr. nickel
7. One who prepares hides
8. First two letters of the alphabet
9. Abbr. Blue
10. Past participle of "to leave"
14. To exist
16. Form of "to be"
17. One account of what happened
18. Not out
22. Real
23. To supply
24. To drink slowly
26. Abbr. American Library Association
27. To delay leaving
30. To drench; to put out
33. Abbr. translation
34. Covered with ashes; ash-colored
39. You and me
40. Past tense of "have"
43. Above and in contact with
44. Short for "father"

76

Word's Worth: *hazard*

In the twelfth century, *hazard* was the name of a game of chance played with dice. It is said to have been invented by bored knights in the Crusades as they sat around waiting for people in a castle to surrender. The word *hazard* can be traced back to the Arabic word for dice, *al-zahr*. This passed into Spanish as *azar*, meaning "a losing throw" of the dice. Over time, that idea extended to any kind of chance, accident, or misfortune. *Azar* became *hasard* in French and *hazard* in English. So a word that in the beginning simply referred to a roll of the dice gradually came to mean anything that is dangerous or uncertain—whether in a game or in life itself.

Part D **Related Words**

The words below are closely related to the target words. Use your knowledge of the target words and of word parts to determine the meaning of these words. (For information about word parts analysis, see pages 7–13.) Use your dictionary if necessary.

1. accountable (ə kount′ ə b'l) adj.
2. acknowledgment (ək näl′ ij mənt, ak-) n.
3. actuality (ak′ choo wal′ ə tē) n.
4. aware (ə wer′) adj.
5. awareness (ə wer′ nis, -nes) n.
6. disclosure (dis klō′ zhər) n.
7. hazard (haz′ ərd) n., v.
8. hindrance (hin′ drəns) n.
9. impurity (im pyoor′ ē tē) n.
10. intriguing (in trē′ giŋ) adj.
11. invitation (in′ və tā′ shən) n.
12. journalism (jur′ n'l iz'm) n.
13. pursue (pər soo′, -syoo′) v.
14. reliability (ri lī′ ə bil′ ə tē) n.
15. reliance (ri lī′ əns) n.
16. rely (ri lī′) v.
17. solemnity (sə lem′ nə tē)
18. vividness (viv′ id nəs) n.

Understanding Related Words

Finding Examples Write the letter of the situation that best demonstrates the meaning of the boldfaced word.

_____ 1. **hazard**

  a. Maria left her roller skates at the bottom of the stairs.
  b. The highway department installed traffic signals at the busy intersection.
  c. No matter how late he goes to bed, Kyle always gets up early.

_____ 2. **hindrance**

  a. The company sponsors an annual race.
  b. Lack of experience can make it difficult to get a job.
  c. Your work has shown steady improvement.

_____ 3. **reliance**

  a. In the attic we found trunks filled with scrapbooks.
  b. The Armstrongs know they can count on their friends to help with the move.
  c. Susan often trusts the wrong people.

_____ 4. **impurity**

  a. The bakery's specialty is four-grain bread.
  b. The jeweler examined the diamond for flaws.
  c. A witness testifies without fear of punishment.

_____ 5. **awareness**

  a. Northern China has a cold, dry climate.
  b. Lydia looks forward to her camping trip.
  c. When a car pulls into the driveway, the dog begins barking.

_____ 6. **invitation**

  a. The police officer directed motorists around the accident.
  b. Tina asked ten friends to attend her birthday party.
  c. The bill arrived in today's mail.

_____ 7. **reliability**

  a. The most brilliant student does not always earn the highest grades.
  b. Keiko has never failed to turn in his assignments on time.
  c. The Chinese invented gunpowder.

_____ 8. **disclosure**

  a. The veterans will march at the head of the parade.
  b. Chief Tanaka explained what the department knew about the case.
  c. The city erected a high fence around the swimming pool.

_____ 9. **solemnity**
  a. A square dance followed the wedding.
  b. The funeral procession moved slowly down the street.
  c. The hail destroyed the corn crop.

_____ 10. **intriguing**
  a. Germany invaded Poland during World War II.
  b. Steel is a mixture of iron and other metals.
  c. Jan finds anything related to computers fascinating.

Number correct _____ (total 10)

Turn to **The Prefix in-** on page 223 of the **Spelling Handbook.** Read the rule and complete the exercise provided.

True-False Decide whether each statement is true (**T**) or false (**F**).

_____ 1. A sleeping person is usually _aware_ of his or her surroundings.

_____ 2. People usually _pursue_ hobbies they dislike.

_____ 3. An _acknowledgment_ of guilt is made by a person who is innocent.

_____ 4. A degree in _journalism_ prepares a person to be a professional salesperson.

_____ 5. An _actuality_ is a real event.

_____ 6. Adding a chemical _impurity_ improves the quality of drinking water.

_____ 7. The _vividness_ of Claire's description helped the audience picture the scene.

_____ 8. You can _rely_ on an honest plumber.

_____ 9. To extend an _invitation_ to someone is to demand that he or she attend.

_____ 10. Newborn babies are _accountable_ for their actions.

Number correct _____ (total 10)

Analyzing Word Parts

The Prefixes *im-* and *un-* The prefixes *im-* and *un-* generally mean "not." In this unit, the target words *impure, unaccountable,* and *unaware* are examples of words that use these prefixes. (Other prefixes that often mean *not* are *in-, il-, ir-,* and *non-.*)

Add either *im-* or *un-* to the words below. Write the newly formed word and then write the meaning of the new word, using a dictionary to check your work.

1. reliable   New word: _____

Definition: _____

_____

2. inviting   New word: _____

Definition: _____

_____

3. mature   New word: _____

Definition: _____

_____

4. suitable   New word: _____

Definition: _____

_____

5. movable   New word: _____

Definition: _____

_____

Number correct _____ (total 5)

Number correct in unit _____ (total 70)

The Last Word

Writing

Choose one item from each of the three columns below. Using your imagination, write a story based on these three items.

Characters
- an eager *journalist*
- a *reliable* friend
- a person *unaware* of danger
- a person *accountable* for his or her actions
- a *solemn* judge

Incidents
- *lingering* without reason
- *maneuvering* around obstacles
- *acknowledging* the truth
- *disclosing* the secret
- *intrigued* by the mystery

Conditions
- in an *inviting* way
- with a *vivid* imagination
- in hot *pursuit* of the criminal
- in a *metropolitan* area
- in a *hazardous* situation

Speaking

A *vivid* description can bring an object to life. Think of a favorite possession and prepare a speech in which you describe this object without actually naming it. Choose specific adjectives and adverbs that will give the class a vivid picture of the object. Your word choice should not only describe the object but also show why it is important to you. Have other members of the class guess what you are describing.

Group Discussion

Divide into small groups and select a book, a movie, or a television special that all members of the group have read or seen. Each person should write down his or her *version* of the story. Then members of the group should take turns reading their accounts aloud. Compare your versions. In what ways are the versions similar or different? Discuss why people have different explanations of the same story. In what situations could problems result from different interpretations of the same event? Try to decide which version is the most accurate, according to the majority of students in your group.

UNIT 7

Part A *Target Words and Their Meanings*

1. apply (ə plī′) v.
2. ceaselessly (sēs′ lis lē) adv.
3. fanciful (fan′ si fəl) adj.
4. fantasy (fan′ tə sē, -zē) n.
5. frenzied (fren′ zēd) adj.
6. govern (guv′ ərn) v.
7. idle (ī′ d'l) adj., v.
8. laboratory (lab′ rə tôr′ ē, -ər ə tôr′ ē) n.
9. logic (läj′ ik) n.
10. lurk (lurk) v.
11. mythical (mith′ i k'l) adj.
12. peculiarly (pi kyo̅o̅l′ yər lē) adv.
13. poise (poiz) n., v.
14. regain (ri gān′) v.
15. reveal (ri vēl′) v.
16. situation (sich′ o̅o̅ wā′ shən) n.
17. suspend (sə spend′) v.
18. trait (trāt) n.
19. transition (tran zish′ ən, -sish) n.
20. vaguely (vāg′ lē) adv.

Inferring Meaning from Context

For each sentence write the letter of the word or phrase that is closest in meaning to the word or words in italics. Use context clues to help you choose the correct answer. (For information about how context helps you understand vocabulary, see pages 1–6.)

_____ 1. Michael bought a medium brown stain for the bookshelves he built, but because he didn't *apply* it properly, the shelves turned out black.
a. safeguard b. return c. use d. maneuver

_____ 2. The students are working *ceaselessly* to clean up the school grounds. Shifts of five students work during their study periods and before and after school from 7:30 a.m. to 7:30 p.m.
a. predictably b. indirectly c. increasingly d. continuously

_____ 3. One reason that *fanciful* tales like the stories of Paul Bunyan and Pecos Bill are entertaining is that they aren't bound by the laws of reality.
a. fancy b. unfamiliar c. imaginary d. frightening

_____ 4. My favorite *fantasy* is to imagine that I become a major league baseball star.
a. dream b. prediction c. quest d. accomplishment

_____ 5. Uncle Oscar was in *a frenzied* state when, ten minutes before his plane was scheduled to depart, he realized that he had lost his wallet and airline ticket.

a. a zealous   b. a forgetful   c. a handicapped   d. an excited

_____ 6. The tides are *governed* primarily by the gravitational pull of the moon and the sun.

a. transformed   b. controlled   c. used   d. hindered

_____ 7. During the workers' strike, all the machines in the factory were *idle*.

a. not in use   b. broken   c. desperate   d. resistant

_____ 8. Working in her *laboratory,* the cancer researcher discovered a substance that stopped the growth of cancer cells.

a. residence   b. hospital   c. place for experiments   d. darkroom

_____ 9. Although Zhou Yu's parents agreed that his decision to continue his education in the United States was based on sound *logic,* they knew they would miss him terribly and did not want him to go.

a. reasoning   b. prejudice   c. feelings   d. imagination

_____ 10. When the car thieves heard the police siren, they ran into the alley and *lurked* in the shadows until the patrol car had passed.

a. participated   b. maneuvered   c. plotted   d. lay hidden

_____ 11. The stories of the Trojan War presented in Homer's *Iliad* contain both *mythical* and historical elements.

a. complicated   b. warlike   c. adventurous   d. imaginary

_____ 12. Brian was *peculiarly* dressed for warm weather with a knit hat, wool coat, and leather gloves.

a. seasonally   b. oddly   c. fashionably   d. sensitively

_____ 13. Ira showed remarkable *poise* when the fire broke out, keeping everyone calm and making sure they left the building quickly.

a. level-headedness   b. courage   c. zeal   d. force

_____ 14. Muhammad Ali first won the heavyweight boxing championship in 1964. He lost his title to Joe Frazier in 1971 but *regained* it by defeating George Foreman in 1974.

a. safeguarded   b. earned   c. magnified   d. recovered

_____ 15. Susan's smile *revealed* a mouth full of braces.

a. hid   b. resembled   c. established   d. showed

_____ 16. What an embarrassing *situation:* Nora misspelled the title of the book in her book report.

a. position   b. condition   c. transformation   d. accomplishment

_____ 17. Leo was *suspended from* school for two weeks as punishment for cheating on a math test. He would have to make up the days missed during summer school.

a. abandoned   b. prevented from attending   c. locked in
d. ignored in

_____ 18. Common sense and kindness are desirable personality *traits*.

a. benefits   b. appearances   c. talents   d. characteristics

_____ 19. The teenage years are the *transition* from childhood to adulthood.

a. mutiny   b. passage   c. return   d. translation

_____ 20. The stunned victim could only *vaguely* describe his attacker. In fact, he remembered only that the person was a tall, thin man.

a. unclearly   b. angrily   c. fearfully   d. awkwardly

Number correct _____ (total 20)

Part B *Target Words in Reading and Literature*

You should now have a general idea of the meaning of each target word. Sharpen your understanding by studying how these words are used in the following selection.

Sleep and Dreams

Alvin Silverstein and Virginia Silverstein

All people—and even some animals—dream. Yet, the purpose of dreaming is as mysterious as dreams themselves. In this selection Alvin and Virginia Silverstein explore some aspects of dreams and dreaming.

What did you dream last night? Can you remember? Some people can recall portions of their nighttime **fantasy** in vivid detail. Others claim they never dream at all. Yet, studies in sleep **laboratories** have **revealed** that people normally dream as many as four or five or even six separate times each night.

What are your dreams like? Bits and pieces of your waking experiences are woven into them: people you know or used to know; houses, cars, clothes; trips you have taken; everyday **situations** in the classroom, the sports field, or at work; things you have read about; strange animals, foreign places. Most of these are things you might think about in the moments before you go to sleep or in a spell of daytime woolgathering.[1] However, there are differences between a dream and a train of **idle** thoughts. In a dream the usual **logic** that your brain follows often does

5

10

---
[1] woolgathering: daydreaming

84

not seem to **apply;** the laws that normally **govern** events in the world are **suspended.** In a dream you may at one moment be sitting comfortably in your living room, and then, without any real **transition,** you are somewhere else—scuba diving in the Caribbean, trekking across the snow-swept Russian steppes,[2] or riding downtown on the bus.

Have you ever dreamed that something—a tiger, perhaps, or a **fanciful mythical** beast or some **vaguely** defined horror—was pursuing you? On you fled through the mysterious dreamland until there was no longer anywhere to run and the beast was almost upon you. You tried to scream, but no sound came out. In a second it would be upon you, but you were paralyzed. Then you awoke, shaken and drenched in a sweat, unable to move for a moment, unsure exactly where you were. In a few moments your muscles **regained** their tone, and you stirred restlessly, **poised** for a time in wakefulness, a little afraid to go back to sleep lest the vivid dream monster might still be **lurking** in wait.

Dreams have been reported since the beginnings of recorded history, and indeed, studies of animals suggest that the first ape-like ancestors of humans undoubtedly dreamed, too. Yet it is perhaps a **peculiarly** human **trait** to search **ceaselessly** for the meaning of dreams. It seems logical that all this **frenzied** mental activity must have some meaning.

15

20

25

30

---

[2] steppes: the great, treeless plains of southeastern Europe and Asia

Refining Your Understanding

For each of the following items, consider how the target word is used in the passage. Write the letter of the word or phrase that best completes the sentence.

_____ 1. The person most likely to be having a *fantasy* (line 2) would be
a. a surgeon performing an operation   b. a teenager in love
c. a policeman at the scene of a crime.

_____ 2. A person might tend to have *idle* thoughts (line 12) while
a. taking a shower   b. solving a math problem   c. watching the
World Series.

_____ 3. A world in which normal laws are *suspended* (line 15) might include
a. people doing chin-ups   b. an author writing mystery stories
c. time running backwards.

_____ 4. The authors claim that trying to find the meaning of dreams is "a
peculiarly human trait" (line 31). By this they mean that   a. being
interested in dreams is strange   b. it is mostly strange people who
are interested in dreams   c. people are apparently the only beings
who are interested in dreams.

_____ 5. The authors describe dreams as "*frenzied* mental activity" (line 33)
because of the fact that dreams   a. are often filled with turmoil
b. occur many times a night in all people and in some animals
c. are usually frightening.

Number correct _____ (total 5)

Part C Ways to Make New Words Your Own

By now you are familiar with the target words and their meanings. This section presents activities that will help you make the words part of your permanent vocabulary.

Using Language and Thinking Skills

True-False Decide whether each statement is true (**T**) or false (**F**).

_____ 1. The unicorn is a *mythical* beast.

_____ 2. Everyday *logic* is useful in the study of dreams.

_____ 3. Most history books are about *fanciful* characters.

_____ 4. Answering questions *vaguely* is the best way to get a good test grade.

_____ 5. For most people, becoming a millionaire is an *idle* dream.

_____ 6. Time moves *ceaselessly* onward.

_____ 7. Being held hostage is an unusual *situation*.

_____ 8. Before making their first jumps, skydivers may stand *poised* in the door of the airplane for several minutes.

_____ 9. Obedience is an undesirable *trait* in a pet.

_____ 10. Mice and guinea pigs are common *laboratory* animals.

Number correct _____ (total 10)

Sentence Completion Write the word from the list below that best completes the meaning of the sentence.

apply   govern   poise   reveal   trait
fantasy   lurk   regain   suspend   transition

_____ 1. Honesty is an important character ? and one we should all try to develop.

_____ 2. Who knows what scary creatures ? in the shadows of the dark forest?

_____ 3. Alex used a roller to ? the paint, making his job go much faster.

_____ 4. My favorite daydream is a(an) ? in which I win the lottery.

_____ 5. In order to ? his health after suffering a heart attack, Father had to rest and eat low-fat food.

_____ 6. Few people have the knowledge of domestic and international affairs and the leadership qualities necessary to ? a country well.

_____ 7. The mayor cautioned that she would ? the carnival if the crowd became unruly.

_____ 8. Jamie had a difficult time making the ? when his family moved from southern California to northern Minnesota.

_____ 9. With great ? and grace, the actress walked to the stage to accept her award.

_____ 10. I'll tell you a secret, but only if you promise not to ? it to anyone.

Number correct _____ (total 10)

Finding the Unrelated Word Write the letter of the word that is not related in meaning to the other words in the set.

_____ 1. a. clearly b. hazily c. indistinctly d. vaguely

_____ 2. a. frightful b. fanciful c. dreadful d. terrible

_____ 3. a. position b. place c. accomplishment d. situation

_____ 4. a. calm b. tranquil c. frenzied d. serene

_____ 5. a. definitely b. strangely c. oddly d. peculiarly

_____ 6. a. genuine b. real c. mythical d. actual

_____ 7. a. sense b. reason c. logic d. confusion

_____ 8. a. occupied b. idle c. busy d. employed

_____ 9. a. ceaselessly b. constantly c. steadfastly d. seldom

_____ 10. a. club b. organization c. laboratory d. society

Number correct _____ (total 10)

Practicing for Standardized Tests

Synonyms Write the letter of the word that is closest in meaning to the capitalized word.

_____ 1. FANCIFUL: (A) beautiful (B) dreamy (C) decorated
(D) real (E) confusing

_____ 2. APPLY: (A) conduct (B) alter (C) accumulate (D) rotate
(E) relate

_____ 3. GOVERN: (A) determine (B) obey (C) campaign
(D) tranquilize (E) rule

_____ 4. REGAIN: (A) retreat (B) recall (C) resist (D) discover
(E) recover

_____ 5. MYTHICAL: (A) unreal (B) magnificent (C) ancient
(D) factual (E) unusual

_____ 6. REVEAL: (A) propel (B) lie (C) venture (D) disclose
(E) return

_____ 7. LURK: (A) linger (B) intensity (C) sneak (D) reveal
(E) lunge

_____ 8. TRAIT: (A) guarantee (B) mission (C) feature (D) version
(E) advantage

_____ 9. TRANSITION: (A) change (B) transportation
(C) accumulation (D) permission (E) difficulty

____ 10. VAGUELY: (A) irresponsibly   (B) abnormally   (C) uncertainly
(D) slowly   (E) unfortunately

Number correct _____ (total 10)

Word's Worth: peculiar

If someone suddenly dropped onto all fours and began mooing like a cow, you'd probably think he or she was a little *peculiar.* Although most observers probably would agree with you, the person might argue that he or she was just demonstrating a knowledge of the origin of that word.

In ancient Rome, before there were coins, cattle took the place of money. The more cattle a person owned, the wealthier that person was. The Latin word for cattle was *pecus.* The Latin word *peculiaris* came from *pecus* and meant "belonging to one's private property." *Peculiaris* became *peculiar* in English and originally referred to property that belonged exclusively to one person. Later the word was used to refer to a person's characteristics that were distinct from those of other persons. It was a short step from this meaning to its common meaning today —"odd or strange."

Spelling and Wordplay

Word Maze Find and circle each target word in this maze.

D	Y	L	A	C	I	H	T	Y	M	I	D	L	E
Y	L	R	A	I	L	U	C	E	P	F	A	U	S
L	S	D	P	B	V	Y	S	A	T	N	A	F	O
E	S	S	P	Q	O	N	I	A	G	E	R	I	E
U	E	X	L	U	N	R	E	V	O	G	R	C	C
G	L	M	Y	D	A	L	A	E	V	E	R	N	D
A	E	T	R	A	N	S	I	T	I	O	N	A	N
V	S	R	B	L	U	R	K	U	O	H	Z	F	E
S	A	A	Q	D	E	I	Z	N	E	R	F	B	P
W	E	I	M	E	S	I	O	P	S	L	Y	J	S
A	C	T	C	I	G	O	L	Z	U	M	A	E	U
T	M	C	L	C	N	O	I	T	A	U	T	I	S

apply
ceaselessly
fanciful
fantasy
frenzied
govern
idle
laboratory
logic
lurk
mythical
peculiarly
poise
regain
reveal
situation
suspend
trait
transition
vaguely

89

Part D Related Words

The words below are closely related to the target words. Use your knowledge of the target words and of word parts to determine the meaning of these words.

1. application (ap′ lə kā′ shən) n.
2. deceased (di sēst′) adj.
3. fancy (fan′ sē) n., adj., v.
4. frenzy (fren′ zē) n., v.
5. governess (guv′ ər nəs) n.
6. government (guv′ ər mənt, -ərn mənt) n.
7. laborious (lə bôr′ ē əs) adj.
8. logistics (lō jis′ tiks) n.
9. myth (mith) n.
10. mythology (mi thäl′ ə jē) n.
11. peculiar (pi kyōōl′ yər) adj., n.
12. peculiarity (pi kyōō′ lē ar′ ə tē, -kyōol yar′-) n.
13. situate (sich′ ōō wāt′) v.
14. suspension (sə spen′ shən) n.
15. transit (tran′ sit, -zit) n.
16. transmission (trans′ mish′ ən) n.
17. vague (vāg) adj.

Understanding Related Words

Matching Ideas Write the word from the list below that is most clearly related to the situation described in each sentence.

| application | laborious | mythology | situate | transit |
| governess | logistics | peculiarity | suspension | transmission |

_____ 1. Maya discovered that she could get to school faster by rollerblading than by taking the bus.

_____ 2. Lisa put skin lotion on her chapped hands.

_____ 3. Joey had one strange habit—he never took off his hat.

_____ 4. The landscapers planted the elm tree next to the house to shade the front lawn and the porch.

_____ 5. It took Sasha all weekend to paint the wooden fence.

_____ 6. The freshman English class read the stories of the Greek gods and goddesses.

_____ 7. Nick caught chicken pox from his younger brother.

_____ 8. After high school, Janice spent a year with a Brazilian family teaching English to the two children.

_____ 9. When Jon returned from his camping trip, he hung the sleeping bags on the clothesline to air.

_____ 10. The general met with his staff to plan the battle details.

Number correct _____ (total 10)

Analyzing Word Parts

The Suffixes -al and -ical These two suffixes have the meaning "characterized by" or "related to." They are added to nouns to form adjectives. For example, the word *mythical* includes the suffix *-ical*.

Form adjectives from each of the following nouns by adding *-al* or *-ical*. If necessary, use your dictionary. Then complete the sentences using the most appropriate adjective.

government   logistics   mythology   situation   transition

_____   1. Many people were willing to donate old clothes and furniture for the school rummage sale. There was a __?__ problem, however, in getting all the items to the school and finding a place to store them.

_____   2. Because Alan's stuttering was __?__, he tried to avoid circumstances that triggered it.

_____   3. Grassroots citizens' groups often are more effective than __?__ programs in solving social problems.

_____   4. Many popular heroes are based on __?__ characters.

_____   5. The community was in a __?__ period as it changed from being a small rural town to a fast-growing suburb.

Number correct _____ (total 5)

Number correct in unit _____ (total 80)

Turn to **Words Ending in *y*** on page 225 of the **Spelling Handbook**. Read the rule and complete the exercises provided.

The Last Word

Writing

Something is lurking in the shadows. Write a story, poem, or news report about this thing. You may or may not choose to reveal its identity to your readers.

Speaking

Work together in groups of four or five to create a modern myth. The myth should explain a natural phenomenon, such as earthquakes, and may include gods and goddesses or other imaginary characters. Select one person from your group to present the myth to the class.

Group Discussion

As a class, discuss how people acquire the traits that make up their personalities. Think about whether we inherit characteristics from our parents or develop them based on our individual experiences in life. Perhaps you think that both ways apply. Be sure to support your point of view with specific examples.

UNIT 8: Review of Units 5–7

Part A Review Word List

Unit 5 Target Words

1. adapt
2. awkward
3. characteristic
4. compose
5. continuous
6. cope
7. cycle
8. distribute
9. efficient
10. eventually
11. fuse
12. horizontally
13. maintain
14. merge
15. propel
16. resistant
17. rotate
18. streamline
19. suitable
20. vertical

Unit 5 Related Words

1. adaptable
2. adaptation
3. character
4. continuity
5. cyclical
6. distribution
7. efficiency
8. event
9. eventual
10. horizontal
11. maintenance
12. propeller
13. recycle
14. resistance
15. rotation
16. suit

Unit 6 Target Words

1. acknowledge
2. actual
3. disclose
4. douse
5. hazardous
6. hinder
7. impure
8. intrigue
9. inviting
10. journalist
11. linger
12. maneuver
13. metropolitan
14. pursuit
15. reliable
16. solemn
17. unaccountable
18. unaware
19. version
20. vivid

Unit 6 Related Words

1. accountable
2. acknowledgment
3. actuality
4. aware
5. awareness
6. disclosure
7. hazard
8. hindrance
9. impurity
10. intriguing
11. invitation
12. journalism
13. pursue
14. reliability
15. reliance
16. rely
17. solemnity
18. vividness

Unit 7 Target Words

1. apply
2. ceaselessly
3. fanciful
4. fantasy
5. frenzied
6. govern
7. idle
8. laboratory
9. logic
10. lurk
11. mythical
12. peculiarly
13. poise
14. regain
15. reveal
16. situation
17. suspend
18. trait
19. transition
20. vaguely

Unit 7 Related Words

1. application
2. deceased
3. fancy
4. frenzy
5. governess
6. government
7. laborious
8. logistics
9. myth
10. mythology
11. peculiar
12. peculiarity
13. situate
14. suspension
15. transit
16. transmission
17. vague

Inferring Meaning from Context

For each sentence write the letter of the word or phrase that is closest in meaning to the word or words in italics.

_____ 1. After the last votes had been tallied, Mario sadly *acknowledged* his defeat in the student council election.
a. denied   b. forgot   c. admitted   d. guaranteed

_____ 2. The *actual* location of the buried treasure may never be known.
a. real   b. imaginary   c. efficient   d. untimely

_____ 3. When we moved from Florida to Minnesota, we had to *adapt to* the cold winter climate.
a. understand   b. forget   c. adjust to   d. regain

_____ 4. Though the weather forecast was for sunny skies, it rained *ceaselessly* all weekend.
a. horizontally   b. vaguely   c. peculiarly   d. continually

_____ 5. The Sunday edition of the newspaper is *composed of* ten sections.
a. made up of   b. fused into   c. maintained by
d. acknowledged by

_____ 6. *A continuous* line of cars blocked the intersection.
a. A loud   b. A mythical   c. An uninterrupted   d. An idle

_____ 7. Counseling has not eliminated Alex's problems, but it has taught him how to *cope* more successfully.
a. manage   b. escape   c. complain   d. rotate

_____ 8. *An efficient* worker may finish a task in half the time an inefficient worker takes.
a. A productive   b. A fanciful   c. An unaware   d. An awkward

_____ 9. No one has bad luck all the time; *eventually* the tide turns.
a. sadly   b. vaguely   c. ultimately   d. idly

_____ 10. Jenny was in *a frenzied* state after she discovered that she had left her diary in the cafeteria.
a. a fanciful   b. a sad   c. a tranquil   d. a frantic

_____ 11. The early New England colonies were often *governed* by men with strong religious beliefs.
a. hindered   b. ruled   c. safeguarded   d. maintained

_____ 12. The carefully prepared food on the buffet table looked very *inviting*.
a. vivid   b. streamlined   c. untimely   d. tempting

_____ 13. Due to declining enrollments, the two schools *merged* into one.

      a. separated b. joined c. rotated d. developed

_____ 14. The Declaration of Independence states that all people have the right to life, liberty, and the *pursuit* of happiness.

      a. seeking b. application c. guarantee d. establishment

_____ 15. The former world-champion ice skater tried to *regain* her title.

      a. disclose b. win back c. apply for d. suspend

_____ 16. Many people are *resistant to* change—they want things to stay the same.

      a. curious about b. aware of c. opposed to d. sensitive to

_____ 17. Many states *suspend* the driver's licenses of drunken drivers.

      a. disclose b. discontinue c. adapt d. observe

_____ 18. Determination is one of the most important *traits* needed for success.

      a. qualities b. tests c. specialties d. developments

_____ 19. Sandford *vaguely* resembles my cousin Bob.

      a. curiously b. in a vivid way c. remotely d. definitely

_____ 20. Haim's *version* of the accident differed from mine only in unimportant details.

      a. acknowledgment b. pursuit c. translation d. description

Number correct _____ (total 20)

Using Review Words in Context

Using context clues, determine which word from the list below best fits in each blank. Write the word in the blank. Each word will be used only once.

adapt	eventually	hazardous	maintains	reveal
apply	fanciful	logic	maneuver	situations
efficient	governs	lurk	reliable	vaguely

Triskaidekaphobia

Is Friday the thirteenth _____ to your health? Does bad luck _____ around every corner on that day? _____ may say that fearing Friday the thirteenth is silly, but this _____ notion _____ the lives of some people.

The roots of *triskaidekaphobia*—fear of the number thirteen—reach down into the sixth century B.C. Pythagoras, a famed mathematician of that time, believed that the number twelve represented completeness. Thirteen got a bad reputation simply because it is the number that comes after twelve and supposedly breaks the whole. _____, the number thirteen became associated with bad luck.

Many otherwise dependable and _____ people think that thirteen is an unlucky number. Even though they may be only _____ aware of their fear, their actions _____ their true feelings. Continually trying to _____ daily activities to avoid something as common as a number, however, can make life difficult. Persons with triskaidekaphobia will never plan a party or _____ for a job on the thirteenth of the month; they avoid the thirteenth floor of any building; they _____ their way out of all kinds of _____ in order to avoid contact with the dreaded number thirteen.

Triskaidekaphobia can even interfere with _____ work production. One expert _____ that employee absenteeism, cancellation of plane and train reservations, and reduced business activity on the thirteenth of each month costs American businesses about $1 billion a year.

Number correct _____ (total 15)

Part B   Review Word Reinforcement

Using Language and Thinking Skills

Matching Examples Write the word from the list below that is most clearly related to the situation described in each sentence.

disclose	fantasy	journalist	solemn	transition
douse	fuse	propel	streamline	vertical

_____ 1. The pot cooked dry and then began to melt into the top of the stove.

_____ 2. After college Maria hopes to get a job as a reporter.

_____ 3. Changing schools in midyear was difficult for Anna.

_____ 4. The booster on a rocket lifts it off the launching pad.

_____ 5. A true friend is one who does not reveal a secret.

_____ 6. The janitor plunged the burning rags into a nearby bucket of water.

_____ 7. Instead of doing his math homework, Eugene began daydreaming of being a famous basketball star.

_____ 8. The height of the telephone pole was thirty feet.

_____ 9. Jill could tell by the serious look on her mother's face that something was wrong.

_____ 10. The superintendent asked the teachers to eliminate all unnecessary expenses from the school's budget.

Number correct _____ (total 10)

Practicing for Standardized Tests

Analogies Determine the relationship between the capitalized pair of words. Then decide which other word pair expresses a similar relationship. Write the letter of this word pair in the blank.

____ 1. CYCLE : EVENTS ::   (A) calendar : months   (B) Labor Day : holiday   (C) history : nonfiction   (D) war : treaty   (E) author : editor

____ 2. HAZARDOUS : POTHOLE ::   (A) freezing : frost   (B) electrical : wiring   (C) dangerous : risk   (D) beautiful : rainbow (E) digestive : food

____ 3. JOURNALIST : WORDS ::   (A) artist : creativity   (B) teacher : school   (C) farmer : harvest   (D) chemist : chemistry (E) carpenter : wood

____ 4. LABORATORY : SCIENTIST ::   (A) experiment : test (B) banker : loan   (C) doctor : medicine   (D) garage : mechanic   (E) city : mayor

____ 5. LOGIC : LOGICAL ::   (A) ice : slippery   (B) sense : sensible (C) east : eastern   (D) circle : triangular   (E) secret : hidden

____ 6. METROPOLITAN : CITY ::   (A) suburban : street   (B) rural : country   (C) friendly : neighborhood   (D) noisy : playground (E) expensive : resort

____ 7. POISE : DANCER ::   (A) clay : potter   (B) sensitivity : counselor (C) balance : scale   (D) music : composer   (E) self-control : calmness

____ 8. ROTATE : PROPELLER ::   (A) gather : harvest   (B) command : pilot   (C) drive : car   (D) dissolve : pill   (E) turn : wheel

____ 9. TRAIT : BOLDNESS ::   (A) builder : blueprint   (B) optimistic : hopeful   (C) glacier : ice   (D) storm : tornado   (E) hope : despair

_____ 10. VERTICAL : HORIZONTAL ::   (A) up : slant   (B) parallel : mathematical   (C) flat : sloping   (D) below : beside   (E) left : right

Number correct _____ (total 10)

Synonyms Write the letter of the word that is closest in meaning to the capitalized word.

_____ 1. CHARACTERISTIC: (A) typical   (B) suitable   (C) vital   (D) unusual   (E) continuous

_____ 2. FANCIFUL: (A) intriguing   (B) logical   (C) imaginative   (D) realistic   (E) abnormal

_____ 3. HINDER: (A) support   (B) help   (C) alter   (D) guarantee   (E) delay

_____ 4. LINGER: (A) restrict   (B) stay   (C) recall   (D) leave   (E) detect

_____ 5. LURK: (A) cope   (B) trap   (C) venture   (D) sneak   (E) strut

_____ 6. MAINTAIN: (A) suspend   (B) neglect   (C) adapt   (D) regain   (E) preserve

_____ 7. PECULIARLY: (A) violently   (B) peacefully   (C) uniquely   (D) commonly   (E) horizontally

_____ 8. POISE: (A) self-confidence   (B) condition   (C) zeal   (D) frenzy   (E) courtesy

_____ 9. RELIABLE: (A) sheer   (B) eventual   (C) dependable   (D) massive   (E) disloyal

_____ 10. SOLEMN: (A) actual   (B) serious   (C) casual   (D) seasonal   (E) unbroken

Number correct _____ (total 10)

Antonyms Write the letter of the word that is most nearly _opposite_ in meaning to the capitalized word.

_____ 1. AWKWARD: (A) graceful   (B) safe   (C) clumsy   (D) abnormal   (E) peculiar

_____ 2. DISTRIBUTE: (A) credit   (B) give out   (C) assign   (D) collect   (E) maintain

_____ 3. IDLE: (A) foolish   (B) busy   (C) relaxed   (D) lazy   (E) godless

____ 4. IMPURE: (A) common (B) wise (C) polluted
(D) immortal (E) clean

____ 5. MYTHICAL: (A) fanciful (B) timely (C) actual
(D) Grecian (E) magnificent

____ 6. REVEAL: (A) expose (B) suspend (C) hide (D) betray
(E) propel

____ 7. SUITABLE: (A) frenzied (B) proper (C) adequate
(D) unlikely (E) inappropriate

____ 8. UNACCOUNTABLE: (A) peculiar (B) intriguing
(C) extreme (D) usual (E) official

____ 9. UNAWARE: (A) conscious (B) asleep (C) idle
(D) ignorant (E) uninformed

____ 10. VIVID: (A) lively (B) impure (C) dull (D) happy
(E) intense

Number correct _____ (total 10)

Spelling and Wordplay

Latin Roots Crossword Puzzle Many English words have been adapted from Latin words. Fill in the puzzle's blanks with the target words that have grown out of the Latin words listed below.

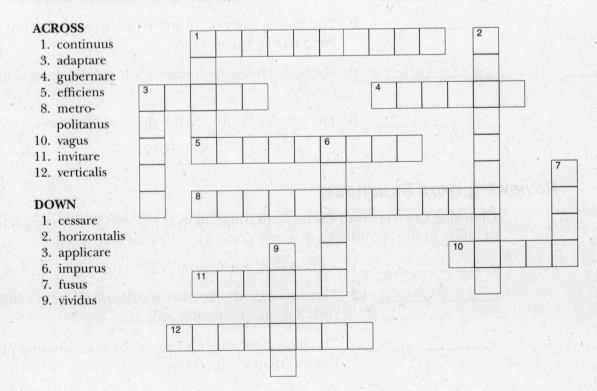

ACROSS
1. continuus
3. adaptare
4. gubernare
5. efficiens
8. metro-
    politanus
10. vagus
11. invitare
12. verticalis

DOWN
1. cessare
2. horizontalis
3. applicare
6. impurus
7. fusus
9. vividus

Part C   Related Word Reinforcement

Using Related Words

Matching Examples Write the word from the list below that is most clearly related to the situation described in each sentence.

adaptable	government	impurity	pursue	rotation
cyclical	horizontal	logical	rely	vague

_____ 1. In a democracy the officials are accountable to the people who elect them.

_____ 2. Many department stores do more than seventy percent of their business between Thanksgiving and New Year's.

_____ 3. Lynne is as comfortable at a formal party with acquaintances as she is at a cookout with friends.

_____ 4. We all need people on whom we can depend.

_____ 5. The moon goes around the earth once every twenty-four hours.

_____ 6. The cowboys rode off to capture the runaway horse.

_____ 7. Mrs. Rio's recollection of the incident was hazy.

_____ 8. The player had not only been knocked down but was lying flat on the ground.

_____ 9. Sherlock Holmes is known for his ability to reason clearly.

_____ 10. The jeweler examined the diamond for flaws.

Number correct _____ (total 10)

Reviewing Word Structures

Choosing Correct Word Parts Read the sentences below. Choose the prefix or suffix in the parenthesis that best completes the italicized word.

_____ 1. A good (-ist; -ism) *journal* can write quickly and well.

_____ 2. The new cars are (re-; stream-) *lined*; they cut wind resistance for better gas mileage.

_____ 3. The final clue (dis-; en-) *closed* the secret hiding place was less than a mile away.

_____ 4. Both paper and aluminum are good items to (bi-; re-) *cycle*.

_____ 5. The (in-; -ful) *fancy* costumes were made with chicken wire and old sheets.

Now add the suffix or prefix you did not use in the above sentences to each word. Write the new word in the blank and define it. Use your dictionary if necessary.

6. journal   New word: _____

Definition: _____

_____

7. lined   New word: _____

Definition: _____

_____

8. closed   New word: _____

Definition: _____

_____

9. cycle   New word: _____

Definition: _____

_____

10. fancy   New word: _____

Definition: _____

_____

Number correct _____ (total 10)

Number correct in unit _____ (total 95)

Vocab Lab 2

FOCUS ON: *Computers*

This is the computer age. To check your knowledge of the vocabulary related to computers, study these words and complete the exercise that follows.

bit (bit) n. [b(inary) (dig)it] the basic unit of information in a computing system • Even a small computer can store thousands of *bits* of information.

cursor (kʉr′ sər) n. a symbol on a computer's video screen indicating where the next character will appear. The cursor may be moved from place to place by the operator to mark where insertions or corrections will be made. • Lynn moved the *cursor* to the beginning of the misspelled word.

data base (dāt′ ə, dat′ ə bās) n. a collection of information stored in a computer. • A large government organization, such as the Internal Revenue Service, needs an extensive *data base*.

disk (disk) or **diskette** (di sket′) n. a thin round plate made of plastic or metal (floppy or hard) on which data for a computer can be stored. • Eleanor made a copy of the *disk* containing the first draft of her story.

DOS (däs) n. [an acronym for D(isk) O(perating) S(ystem)] a microcomputer operating system that is stored on a disk. • Our microcomputer's *DOS* is on a floppy disk.

hard copy (härd käp′ ē) n. a computer's output that is printed on paper. • After making all the corrections on his essay, Alan printed out a *hard copy*.

hardware (härd′ wer′) n. the physical parts that make up a computer. • The designers of the computer for the space shuttle used minimal *hardware* in order to keep the weight down.

input (in′ pʊt) n., v. information fed into a computer through the use of such devices as electronic keyboards and punch cards; to enter information into a computer. • The *input* to the class data base included the names and addresses of all the new students.

memory (mem′ ər ē, -rē) n. the part of the computer that stores information. • A computer sometimes contains a short-term *memory* for information being used in the near future and a long-term *memory* for information that will not be recalled for a longer time.

menu (men′ yo͞o) n. a list of user options displayed on a computer's video screen. • Item number three on my computer's *menu* is the print command.

network (net′ wʉrk′) n. a system made up of two or more computers connected by communication lines. • A computer *network* enables people living vast distances apart to exchange information.

output (oʊt′ pʊt) n., v. information fed out of a computer; to produce output. • The *output* of the program was an alphabetized mailing list.

program (prō′ gram, -grəm) n., v. a set of instructions that a computer must follow in order to carry out a task; to feed a set of instructions into a computer. • The new self-teaching *program* helps students learn to use the computer.

software (sôft′ wer′, säft′-) n. computer programs. ● The latest computer *software* includes programs that allow artists to create visual images on the screen.

terminal (tʉr′ mə n'l) n. a device through which a person can receive information from and give information to a computer. ● Types of computer *terminals* include automatic typewriters, high-speed printers, and visual-display screens.

Matching Definitions Match each definition in the list with the appropriate focus word. Write the letter of the focus word in the blank.

_____ 1. unit of information

_____ 2. information received from a computer

_____ 3. the part of a computer that stores information

_____ 4. information given to a computer

_____ 5. large quantity of information organized and stored in a computer

_____ 6. a computer screen, for example

_____ 7. a computer program

_____ 8. two or more computers connected to one another

_____ 9. instructions to the computer

_____ 10. what a computer is made of

_____ 11. a disk operating system

_____ 12. a position-indicator symbol appearing on a video display

_____ 13. a list of the options a computer user has

_____ 14. a computer's printed output

_____ 15. a device for storing computer memory outside the computer

a. bit

b. cursor

c. data base

d. disk

e. DOS

f. hard copy

g. hardware

h. input

i. memory

j. menu

k. network

l. output

m. program

n. software

o. terminal

Number correct _____ (total 15)

FOCUS ON: *Multiple Meanings*

Many words in our language have several, or multiple, meanings.

Familiar words with multiple meanings may cause more confusion than words that are completely unfamiliar. When we see a familiar word, we may assume we know its meaning, when in fact it may have several meanings.

To be a careful reader, you must learn the various meanings of a word as well as the situation in which each meaning applies. For example, look at the following dictionary entry for the word *civil:*

> **civil** (siv′ ′l) **adj.** [OFr.< L. *civilis < civis,* see CITY]
> **1.** of a citizen or citizens *[civil* rights] **2.** of a community of citizens, their government, or their interrelations **3.** civilized **4.** polite or courteous, esp. in a merely formal way **5.** not military or religious *[civil* marriage] **6.** *Law* relating to private rights and legal actions involving these

Which of the definitions of *civil* would apply to the situation described in this sentence?

General Lee greeted General Grant in a *civil* way at Appomattox.

From your knowledge of American history, you know that Appomattox was where General Lee surrendered to General Grant, ending the Civil War. The meaning of *civil* in this sentence, however, is not the same as its meaning in *Civil War* (definition 2—"of a community of citizens, their government, or their interrelations"). The word is used here to describe General Lee's personal manner, which would best be covered by definition 3—"civilized"— or definition 4— "polite or courteous."

This book contains several exercises dealing with the multiple meanings of words. In doing these exercises, make sure you understand the various definitions of the word before proceeding.

Definitions Listed below are five words that have multiple meanings. Each word is followed by two sentences using that word. Write your own definition of the word as it is used in each sentence. Then compare your definitions with those in the dictionary.

   stake
 1. Kurt and Earl drove a *stake* into the ground to mark the boundary of their property.

104

2. Wendy had a considerable *stake* in the outcome of the race because she wanted to make the high school track team and knew the coach would be watching.

_____

fraction

3. The mathematics teacher insisted that we express all *fractions* as decimals on the test.

_____

4. By midwinter California had received only a *fraction* of its normal rainfall, and many people feared that there would be a drought.

_____

cement

5. Our *cement* driveway cracked under the weight of the truck.

_____

6. The student exchange was designed to *cement* relationships between the two countries.

_____

common

7. Joan and Juan became good friends after discovering they had many *common* interests.

_____

8. Beavers are *common* in many parts of Arkansas.

_____

still

9. Just before the tornado struck, the sky became an eerie green and the air became ominously *still*.

_____

10. When the bell rang, Marc was *still* completing the test.

_____

Number correct _____ (total 10)

Number correct in Vocab Lab _____ (total 25)

Special Unit Taking Standardized Vocabulary Tests

At various times during your years in school, you have taken standardized tests. These tests are given to large groups of students around the country. Teachers use the test scores to compare your knowledge and skills with those of other students who have completed the same number of years of school.

During the next few years you will be taking many other standardized tests. Because most of these tests contain vocabulary questions, it is to your advantage to spend time becoming familiar with the major types of vocabulary test questions. These types of questions include **synonyms, antonyms,** and **sentence completion**.

This special unit offers specific strategies for taking standardized tests, as well as additional practice.

Part A Synonyms

As you know, **synonyms** are words that have the same meaning. Standardized test questions covering synonyms are answered by selecting the word that is closest in meaning to the given word. A typical synonym question looks like this:

> LEAD: (A) handle (B) cooperate (C) direct (D) own
> (E) follow

To answer a synonym question, use the following guidelines:

1. Try to determine the meaning of the given word before you look at the answer choices. Pay attention to any prefix, suffix, or root that may help reveal the meaning.
2. Look carefully at the answer choices. Remember to look only for words with *similar* meanings. Do not be thrown off by *antonyms*—words that are opposite in meaning. In the example above, choice (E), *follow,* is an antonym for the given word, *lead.*
3. Keep in mind that many words have more than one meaning. For example, *lead* means both "to guide" and "to be ahead of." If none of the answer choices seems to fit your sense of the given word's meaning, think about other meanings.
4. If you cannot readily identify the correct answer, try to eliminate any obviously incorrect answers.
5. Remember that you are looking for the *best* answer, the word that is *closest* in meaning to the given word. In the example above, *own* and *handle* have meanings related to control. However, choice (C), *direct,* is closest in meaning to *lead.*

Exercise Write the letter of the word that is closest in meaning to the capitalized word.

_____ 1. ATTEMPT: (A) complete (B) try (C) watch (D) protect (E) begin

_____ 2. FINALLY: (A) greatly (B) briefly (C) simply (D) ultimately (E) happily

_____ 3. ASTONISH: (A) worry (B) attract (C) calm (D) annoy (E) surprise

_____ 4. DESPERATE: (A) unwise (B) joyous (C) determined (D) hopeless (E) grateful

_____ 5. INVESTIGATE: (A) ignore (B) explore (C) criticize (D) delay (E) demand

_____ 6. GRATITUDE: (A) sincerity (B) grief (C) difficulty (D) thankfulness (E) pleasantness

_____ 7. OCCASIONALLY: (A) always (B) sometimes (C) lately (D) promptly (E) commonly

_____ 8. DEMAND: (A) tell (B) allow (C) require (D) prevent (E) anger

_____ 9. YEARN: (A) hate (B) shout (C) tie (D) desire (E) discuss

_____ 10. AWKWARD: (A) clumsy (B) slow (C) graceful (D) quiet (E) fast

Number correct _____ (total 10)

Part B Antonyms

As you know, **antonyms** are words that are opposite in meaning. Standardized test questions covering antonyms are answered by selecting the word that is most nearly _opposite_ in meaning to a given word. A typical question looks like this:

ANXIOUS: (A) calm (B) bored (C) alone (D) angry (E) worried

To complete an antonym question, use the following guidelines:

1. Try to determine the meaning of the given word before you look at the answer choices. Pay attention to any prefix, suffix, or root that may help reveal the meaning.

2. Look carefully at the answer choices. Remember that you must find a word that is opposite in meaning. Do not be thrown off by *synonyms*— words that are similar in meaning. In the example above, choice (E), *worried*, is a synonym for the given word, *anxious*.

3. Keep in mind that many words have more than one meaning. For example, *anxious* means both "worried" and "eager." If none of the answer choices seems to fit your sense of the opposite meaning, think about other meanings for the given word.

4. If you cannot readily identify the correct answer, try to eliminate any obviously incorrect answers.

5. Remember that you are looking for the *best* answer, the word that is *most nearly opposite* in meaning. In the example above, *bored* has a meaning related to a lack of anxiety. However, choice (A), *calm*, is the most nearly opposite in meaning to *anxious*.

Exercise Write the letter of the word that is most nearly *opposite* in meaning to the capitalized word.

_____ 1. ELIMINATE: (A) remove (B) include (C) grow (D) guess (E) evade

_____ 2. CLUTTERED: (A) large (B) messy (C) empty (D) orderly (E) beautiful

_____ 3. USELESS: (A) ineffective (B) exhausted (C) rare (D) active (E) worthwhile

_____ 4. INCREASE: (A) diminish (B) multiply (C) delay (D) raise (E) preserve

_____ 5. CONQUER: (A) fight (B) overthrow (C) surrender (D) guide (E) agree

_____ 6. FREEDOM: (A) power (B) right (C) message (D) slavery (E) government

_____ 7. ADVANTAGE: (A) victory (B) benefit (C) contest (D) kindness (E) obstacle

_____ 8. CARELESS: (A) sloppy (B) cautious (C) reckless (D) capable (E) forgetful

_____ 9. VIOLENT: (A) calm (B) allergic (C) stormy (D) easy (E) fierce

_____ 10. UNEXPECTED: (A) surprising (B) shocking (C) anticipated (D) pleasant (E) innocent

Number correct _____ (total 10)

Part C Sentence Completion

Sentence completion questions test your ability to use words and to recognize relationships among parts of a sentence. A sentence completion question gives you a sentence in which one or two words are missing. You must then choose the word or set of words that best completes the sentence. A typical sentence completion question looks like this:

A _?_ of the class needed extra instruction on the homework assignment, but only a _?_ of the students stayed after school for help.
(A) student ... few   (B) part ... portion   (C) majority ... few
(D) teacher ... minority   (E) leader ... group

To answer sentence completion questions, use the following guidelines:

1. Read the entire sentence carefully, noting key words. Pay particular attention to words such as *but* and *however,* which indicate contrast. Note any words that might indicate similarity, such as *and, the same as,* and *another.* Also look for words that might indicate cause and effect, such as *because, as a result,* and *therefore.* In the example question, the word *but* suggests that the correct word pair may contain words that are opposite in meaning.

2. Try each of the choices in the sentence. Eliminate those choices that make no sense or those that contradict some other part of the statement. In a sentence with two blanks, the right answer must correctly fill *both* blanks. A wrong answer choice often includes one correct and one incorrect word.

3. After choosing an answer, reread the entire sentence to make sure that it makes sense. Be sure that you have not ignored an answer that would create a more logical sentence than your choice.

Exercise Write the letter of the word or words that best completes the sentence.

_____ 1. The club members _?_ their approval by shouting "aye."
(A) denied   (B) postponed   (C) showed   (D) whispered
(E) prepared

_____ 2. The jeweler assured Mr. Goode that the stone was a _?_ diamond and not an imitation.
(A) pretty   (B) large   (C) fake   (D) genuine   (E) beautiful

_____ 3. Julie was _?_ with her birthday present; it was exactly what she had wanted.
(A) delighted   (B) disappointed   (C) bored   (D) uneasy
(E) disturbed

_____ 4. A ? reward was given to the two ? boys who turned in the money they found.

(A) stingy … athletic   (B) sincere … helpful
(C) generous … honest   (D) modest … dishonest
(E) large … helpless

_____ 5. Terry was quite ? after ? all the way to his friend's house, only to learn that his friend had already left.

(A) happy … running   (B) ambitious … walking
(C) angry … talking   (D) satisfied … jogging
(E) disappointed … going

_____ 6. When Ms. Wendorf's business became ? , she lost her life savings.

(A) popular   (B) profitable   (C) bankrupt   (D) public
(E) efficient

_____ 7. Although Ralph's ? were good, his actions only ? more trouble.

(A) methods … promised   (B) intentions … caused
(C) solutions … prevented   (D) motives … stopped
(E) grades … created

_____ 8. The department store planned to ? the sale of ? clothes because no one bought them.

(A) continue … unfashionable   (B) discontinue … expensive
(C) announce … colorful   (D) cancel … popular
(E) correct … missing

_____ 9. Louise is very ? to have such loving grandparents.

(A) fortunate   (B) unlucky   (C) disappointed   (D) frustrated
(E) wise

_____ 10. Even though the robber crept ? out of his secret hiding place, the police eventually ? him.

(A) loudly … followed   (B) carefully … lost
(C) quickly … addressed   (D) bravely … left
(E) silently … caught

Number correct _____ (total 10)

Number correct in unit _____ (total 30)

Part D *General Strategies*

No matter what type of question you are answering, certain strategies can be applied to any part of a standardized test. Keep the following guidelines in mind. They can help you increase your chance of success. Remember, too, that a good mental attitude, plenty of rest the night before a test, and the ability to relax will further improve your test performance.

Basic Strategies for Taking Standardized Tests

1. **Read and listen to directions carefully.** This may seem obvious, but many students do poorly on tests because they misunderstand the directions or fail to read each item completely. For each question, read all of the choices before choosing an answer.

2. **Budget your time carefully.** Most standardized tests are timed, so it is important that you not spend too much time on any single item.

3. **Complete the test items you know first.** Skip items that you do not know the answer for, but mark them so that you can return to them later. After you have answered the items that you know, go back and tackle the more difficult items.

4. **Mark the answer sheet carefully and correctly.** Most standardized tests make use of computerized answer sheets. You are required to fill in a circle corresponding to the correct answer in the test booklet, as follows:

When using such computerized answer sheets, follow these guidelines:

a. Always completely fill in the circle for the correct answer.

b. Periodically check your numbering on the answer sheet, especially if you skip an item. Make sure your answer matches the number of the test item.

c. Never make notes or stray marks on the answer sheet. These could be misread as wrong answers by the scoring machine. Instead, write on the test booklet itself or on scratch paper, whichever is indicated in the directions.

5. **Make guesses only if you can eliminate some of the answer choices.** Random guessing is unlikely to improve your score. In fact, on some standardized tests, points are subtracted for incorrect answers. In such cases it is a better idea to leave an item blank rather than to guess wildly. However, if you can eliminate one or more of the choices, then your chance of guessing the correct answer is increased.

UNIT 9

Part A Target Words and Their Meanings

1. account (ə kount´) n., v.
2. adverse (ad vʉrs´, əd-) adj.
3. circulate (sʉr´ kyə lāt´) v.
4. confederate (kən fed´ ər it) n., adj. (-ə rāt´) v.
5. execute (ek´ sə kyo͞ot´) v.
6. expedition (ek´ spə dish´ ən) n.
7. fate (fāt) n.
8. ferocious (fə rō´ shəs) adj.
9. gigantic (jī gan´ tik) adj.
10. incredible (in kred´ ə b'l) adj.
11. inherit (in her´ it) v.
12. intention (in ten´ shən) n.
13. invade (in vād´) v.
14. noble (nō´ b'l) n., adj.
15. objective (əb jek´ tiv, äb-) n., adj.
16. prevail (pri vāl´) v.
17. quality (kwäl´ ə tē) n.
18. scanty (skan´ tē) adj.
19. substantial (səb stan´ shəl) adj.
20. vigorous (vig´ ər əs) adj.

Inferring Meaning from Context

For each sentence write the letter of the word or phrase that is closest in meaning to the word or words in italics. Use context clues to help you choose the correct answer. (For information about how context helps you understand vocabulary, see pages 1–6.)

_____ 1. When she got home, Sarah gave her parents a complete *account* of her heroics in the soccer game. She described each of her goals.

a. performance   b. movie   c. report   d. score

_____ 2. Most of the citizens had *adverse* reactions to the news that a factory would be built less than a mile from their homes. They were concerned about noise and pollution.

a. favorable   b. unfavorable   c. positive   d. unusual

_____ 3. By telling everyone they saw in their classes that school would be dismissed early, Jason and his friends *circulated* a rumor.

a. wanted   b. believed   c. heard   d. spread

_____ 4. Dan knew he could not pull off the complicated practical joke by himself. He would need *a confederate* to assist in the preparations.

a. an enemy   b. a machine   c. a helper   d. a traitor

_____ 5. Perhaps the most shocking act of the English Civil War was the beheading of King Charles I. Parliament had the king *executed*.

a. jailed   b. praised   c. put to death   d. rewarded

_____ 6. With plenty of supplies for the long months ahead, the determined group began its *expedition* into unknown territory.

a. exploration   b. vacation trip   c. exit   d. transformation

_____ 7. The *fate* of Charles Lindbergh's solo flight across the Atlantic Ocean was unknown until he arrived safely in France.

a. crash   b. name   c. advantage   d. outcome

_____ 8. The wild dog looked *ferocious* with its fur standing up and its fangs showing.

a. friendly   b. fierce   c. silly   d. peculiar

_____ 9. From a distance Mount Rainier looked very big. But it wasn't until we arrived at its base that we realized how *gigantic* it really was.

a. small   b. old   c. dangerous   d. huge

_____ 10. Lupita thought that Harry's tale of jumping out of an airplane, landing in a haystack, and not getting hurt was *incredible*. Such a thing could not be possible!

a. believable   b. unbelievable   c. true   d. courageous

_____ 11. We *inherited* the grandfather clock in our living room from Aunt Betty when she died.

a. acquired   b. bought   c. borrowed   d. wound

_____ 12. Carol said it was not her *intention* to get rich; she only wanted to earn enough money to live comfortably.

a. condition   b. accomplishment   c. plan   d. result

_____ 13. In 1990, armed Iraqi soldiers crossed their country's southeastern border and *invaded* Kuwait, attacking the small, neighboring country.

a. recalled   b. retreated from   c. enjoyed   d. forcefully entered

_____ 14. The king gathered a few *nobles* and some other important people to advise him.

a. low-ranking persons   b. servants   c. high-ranking persons
d. priests

_____ 15. Because knowledge was important to her, Linda's *objective* was to learn, not just to pass tests.

a. logic   b. goal   c. success   d. failure

_____ 16. The coach said that good, basic ball handling would help us defeat each opposing team and eventually *prevail* in the state basketball tournament.

a. triumph   b. stay even   c. lose   d. remain

_____ 17. Christina has many wonderful characteristics, but I believe her best *quality* is her friendly attitude toward others.

a. hope b. decision c. trait d. potential

_____ 18. The bears feasted on our supplies and left us with only a *scanty* amount of food.

a. large b. extra c. small d. unusual

_____ 19. That flimsy tent will not protect us all winter. We need a *substantial* shelter.

a. solid b. weak c. quick d. beautiful

_____ 20. My grandfather walks several miles each day, and he even lifts weights! At seventy years of age, he is still *vigorous*.

a. tired b. strong c. mythical d. suitable

Number correct _____ (total 20)

Part B *Target Words in Reading and Literature*

You should now have a general idea of the meaning of each target word. Sharpen your understanding by studying how these words are used in the following selection.

John Smith and the Virginia Settlement

Clifford Lindsey Alderman

Three ships left England in 1606 headed for the New World. This selection tells about the voyage, the settlement that became Jamestown, Virginia, and an unusual leader, John Smith.

The great city of London was getting ready to celebrate Christmas when three ships, the *Susan Constant, Godspeed,* and *Discovery,* sailed down the Thames in December of 1606. The vessels were bound for the New World. The largest, the *Susan Constant,* was of only 100 tons burden, while the smallest, the *Discovery,* was a tiny 20-tonner.   5

Aboard the ships were more than 140 persons. Some, listed as "gentlemen," had no **intention** of doing any work when they reached the distant land of Virginia. They were thinking mainly of the gold they were sure could be picked up with no trouble.

Many of these gentlemen were the younger sons of English **nobles.**   10
Under English law a nobleman's oldest son **inherited** his property. The others had to find ways of supporting themselves.

The Trial of John Smith,
C.Y. TURNER.
Smith is shown standing
with his arms crossed
on the left.

The rest of the colonists were of humbler birth. Some had signed for the voyage to escape the terrible conditions under which the poor lived in England. Others had come along because the trip offered excitement and adventure. There was not a woman or child among them.

John Smith, who would later write an **account** of the voyage and the settlement of Virginia, was not listed as a "gentleman." However, he was no ordinary person, either. A short, sturdy man of twenty-seven, he looked as if he had a ramrod[1] down the back of his doublet[2]. Like the men of **quality,** he wore knee breeches[3], boots with flared tops reaching halfway to his knees, shoes with bows, and a broad-brimmed hat. A beard and a long, thin, **ferocious** mustache that curled at the tips decorated his face.

Money for the venture had been provided by the London Company, which hoped to earn a handsome profit. First and foremost, the settlers were to find gold. They were also to seek a passage to the South Sea (the Pacific Ocean), which would be shorter than the long one around Africa. Such a passage would provide a speedier and safer route to the spices, silks, and tea of the East Indies. A third **objective** was to find the colonists sent to America by Sir Walter Raleigh in 1587. Raleigh's colonists had landed at Roanoke Island. However, four years later, when ships returned there, the colony had vanished and nothing was known of its **fate.**

The voyagers' Christmas was not merry. They spent it in the English Channel, beset by **adverse** winds. Six weeks passed before the wind shifted at last.

John Smith's air of self-confidence, his **vigorous** personality, and his common sense won him respect. Many of the colonists, however, could

---

1 ramrod: a rod used to push a charge down the muzzle of a gun
2 doublet: a short jacket, commonly worn in Smith's lifetime
3 breeches: knee-length trousers

not stand his know-it-all ways. For a time he was surrounded by an open-mouthed audience when he told **incredible** tales of his adventures. However, some of his listeners who had had no such thrilling experiences became jealous.

As a very young man, Smith had made his way to Hungary to fight the Turks who had **invaded** that country. According to the stories he told, he had slain the **gigantic** Turbashaw, their leader, in combat and cut off his head. He had fought in bloody battles, and religious pilgrims had thrown him overboard from a ship as an unbeliever. He had been captured and sold into slavery in Turkey.

At least so said John Smith, and who was to deny the truth of it? His enemies **circulated** a story that he planned to seize control of the colony in Virginia with the aid of some **confederates.** Worse yet, they claimed he intended to murder the leaders of the **expedition** and make himself king.

He was arrested for mutiny and clapped into irons. When the fleet arrived in the West Indies, a gallows was constructed to hang him. Luckily, not only for him but for the rest of the colonists, cooler heads **prevailed** and he was not **executed.**

Early in May 1607, the vessels entered Chesapeake Bay. At the mouth of a river which the colonists called the James, after King James I of England, they established a settlement. It was named Jamestown. The land was marshy, and therefore unhealthy, and the water was impure. But the site did have a good anchorage where the ships could tie up to trees. It could also be defended against Indian attacks.

The London Company had appointed seven settlers as a council to govern the Colony. One of the seven was John Smith. Although he was no longer confined, Smith was still charged with mutiny. So the others forbade him to sit on the council.

The colonists pitched tents they had brought with them. For a time they were too busy looking for gold to put up more **substantial** houses. Nor did they think of how they were to exist once their **scanty** supply of food ran out. During the summer the heat and humidity of the Virginia coast exhausted them. Great numbers fell ill from dysentery and malaria. Before the summer was over, half of them were dead.

They found no gold nor any trace of the lost Roanoke colonists. And at last they had to face the approach of winter and the problem of food.

Without John Smith they would have been lost. They had expected to trade hatchets, beads, copper and other goods with nearby Indians for food. But the natives refused to give up the precious corn and beans they had raised to get them through the winter. Smith, however, made voyages to other Indian villages on the bay and its tributary rivers. By shrewd bargaining he obtained enough food for the colony to survive until spring.

Refining Your Understanding

For each of the following items, consider how the target word is used in the passage. Write the letter of the word or phrase that best completes each sentence.

_____ 1. Some men on the ships "had no *intention* of doing any work" (line 7) in North America. We might conclude that these men were
a. on vacation b. in poor health c. planning on an easy life.

_____ 2. "Under English law a nobleman's oldest son *inherited* his property." (line 11) Therefore, the oldest son of a nobleman would most likely
a. stay in England b. move to North America c. send his family to North America.

_____ 3. The phrase "men of *quality*," as it is used in line 21, means
a. religious people b. people of high social position
c. common people.

_____ 4. The winds were *adverse* (line 36) because they a. made the passengers comfortable b. stopped blowing c. blew in the wrong direction.

_____ 5. John Smith was not hanged because "cooler heads *prevailed*" (lines 57–58). This probably means that a. some people remained reasonable and stopped the execution b. the reasonable people killed the "hotheads" c. the gallows were not finished in time.

Number correct _____ (total 5)

Part C Ways To Make New Words Your Own

By now you are familiar with the target words and their meanings. This section presents activities that will help you make the words part of your permanent vocabulary.

Using Language and Thinking Skills

Finding Examples Write the letter of the situation that best shows the meaning of the boldfaced word.

_____ 1. **inherit**
a. When her grandmother died, Lisa received ownership of her grandmother's car.
b. When Joe's sister was sick, she let him use her car.
c. After the accident, Dad bought a new car.

_____ 2. **expedition**
a. A group of students changes classes.
b. Researchers set out to find and explore an uninhabited island.
c. A family plays a game of basketball before dinner.

_____ 3. **scanty**

    a. After the earthquake, the Forest family could find only two unbroken jars of food in their shattered apartment.

    b. The visitors from the Soviet Union were amazed to find all the shelves stocked with food in the American supermarket.

    c. The hikers had plenty of food and water to last them until they reached their destination.

_____ 4. **incredible**

    a. Sachi told her friend a story about finding a lost dog.

    b. Mr. Washington told his students a story about traveling to Nebraska.

    c. Matt told his mother a story about aliens from Saturn making him late for school.

_____ 5. **circulate**

    a. Wanda kept Kate's secret to herself.

    b. Theo told everyone on his block about the quarrel, and soon the whole neighborhood knew the story.

    c. The police officer instructed Jesse and Lee to keep their bicycles on the sidewalk.

Number correct _____ (total 5)

Understanding Multiple Meanings Each box in this exercise contains a boldfaced word with its definitions. Read the definitions and then the sentences that use the word. Write the letter of the definition that applies to each sentence.

---

account

    a. a record or list of money taken in and paid out (n.)

    b. a credit arrangement with a business firm (n.)

    c. a record, report, or description of an event (n.)

    d. to explain or offer reasons for something (v.)

_____ 1. Bill entertained us with his _account_ of the time he got lost in the woods.

_____ 2. When they moved to Topeka, the Wilsons opened a charge _account_ with the largest department store in town.

_____ 3. After he is sworn in, the defendant will _account_ for his actions on the night of the crime.

_____ 4. Our _account_ showed that we spent more money on the party than we had planned.

> **objective**
> a. not influenced by personal feelings or thoughts (adj.)
> b. something one is trying to achieve, reach, or capture (n.)

____ 5. Jan found it hard to be *objective* when she described her horse.

____ 6. The *objective* of the U. S. space program in the late 1960's was to put people on the moon.

____ 7. The author tried to give an *objective* evaluation of her latest book.

> **execute**
> a. to carry out or complete (v.)
> b. to put to death, particularly as punishment for a crime (v.)
> c. to perform, such as to play a piece of music (v.)

____ 8. In the Old West, hanging was the method used to *execute* murderers.

____ 9. My violin teacher said that I would have to practice hard to be able to *execute* the piece properly.

____ 10. The firefighters *executed* their captain's orders precisely.

Number correct _____ (total 10)

Practicing for Standardized Tests

Synonyms Write the letter of the word that is closest in meaning to the capitalized word.

____ 1. VIGOROUS: (A) weak (B) energetic (C) loose (D) mute (E) feeble

____ 2. EXECUTE: (A) locate (B) die (C) examine (D) forgive (E) kill

____ 3. EXPEDITION: (A) journey (B) assassination (C) involvement (D) obstacle (E) circulation

____ 4. FATE: (A) intention (B) destiny (C) time (D) hope (E) festival

____ 5. INTENTION: (A) objective (B) venture (C) examination (D) accident (E) handicap

____ 6. OBJECTIVE: (A) argument (B) goal (C) observation (D) account (E) stamina

_____ 7. PREVAIL: (A) detect   (B) lose   (C) win   (D) prevent   (E) resist

_____ 8. QUALITY: (A) amount   (B) objective   (C) formation
(D) suspense   (E) characteristic

_____ 9. SUBSTANTIAL: (A) firm   (B) attractive   (C) special
(D) underground   (E) shaky

_____ 10. ACCOUNT: (A) mission   (B) silence   (C) banker
(D) report   (E) safeguard

Number correct _____ (total 10)

Antonyms Write the letter of the word that is most nearly *opposite* in meaning to the capitalized word.

_____ 1. CONFEDERATE: (A) enemy   (B) partner   (C) technician
(D) governor   (E) character

_____ 2. FEROCIOUS: (A) deceased   (B) inhuman   (C) cruel
(D) strange   (E) meek

_____ 3. GIGANTIC: (A) enormous   (B) hazardous   (C) magnificent
(D) tiny   (E) vertical

_____ 4. INCREDIBLE: (A) brief   (B) grand   (C) believable
(D) doubtful   (E) substantial

_____ 5. SCANTY: (A) vague   (B) serious   (C) skimpy   (D) plentiful
(E) silly

Number correct _____ (total 5)

Word's Worth: gigantic

The word *gigantic* comes from *gigas*, the Greek word for *giant*. In Greek mythology the Giants were an ancient race of monstrous creatures. They were manlike in shape, but they were huge. This savage race began and ended with violence. The Giants were born from the blood of Uranus, the god of the sky, who had been wounded by his own son, Cronus. The Giants' purpose in life was to find sinners and punish them. Eventually the god Zeus and the hero Hercules battled the Giants and hurled them down to the Underworld. According to legend, the anger of the Giants is still felt today in the form of volcanic eruptions and earthquakes.

Spelling and Wordplay

Spell the Correct Word Use the clues to answer with the correct target word. Then write the word in the blank.

_____ 1. This word rhymes with *shanty*.

_____ 2. Change one letter in *qualify*.

_____ 3. This word contains a word used to describe poetry.

_____ 4. This word contains a word that is the opposite of *yes*.

_____ 5. This word has a number in it.

_____ 6. This word contains a word that means *tardy*.

_____ 7. Add *in* and *it* to *her*.

_____ 8. Begin this word with the shortened word for an underwater boat.

_____ 9. This word rhymes with *delayed*.

_____ 10. Look for the object in this word.

Number correct _____ (total 10)

Part D   Related Words

The words below are closely related to the target words. Use your knowledge of the target words and of word parts to determine the meanings of these words. (For information about word parts analysis, see pages 7–13.) Use your dictionary if necessary.

1. accountable (ə kount′ ə b'l) adj.
2. accounting (ə koun′ tiŋ) n.
3. adversity (ad vʉr′ sə tē, əd-) n.
4. circulation (sʉr′ kyə lā′ shən) n.
5. confederacy (kən fed′ ər ə sē) n.
6. credible (kred′ ə b'l) adj.
7. execution (ek′ sə kyo͞o′ shən) n.
8. expeditious (ek′ spə dish′ əs) adj.
9. fatal (fāt′ 'l) adj.
10. fateful (fāt′ fəl) adj.
11. inheritance (in her′ it əns) n.
12. intend (in tend′) v.
13. intent (in tent′) n.
14. invasion (in vā′ zhən) n.
15. nobility (nō bil′ ə tē) n.
16. objection (əb jek′ shən) n.
17. prevalent (prev′ ə lənt) adj.
18. vigor (vig′ ər) n.

Turn to **The Prefix ad-** on page 221 of the **Spelling Handbook.** Read the rule and complete the exercise provided.

Understanding Related Words

Sentence Completion Write the word from the list below that best completes the meaning of the sentence.

accountable   fatal   intend   nobility   prevalent
adversity   inheritance   invasion   objection   vigor

_____ 1. At the reading of the will, Tim learned that his _?_ from his grandfather would include a gold pocket watch.

_____ 2. Because no one at the meeting offered an _?_, the plan was approved.

_____ 3. The plane crash proved _?_ to everyone on board. Not a single person survived.

_____ 4. Corina did not _?_ to tell her friends about the incident. She was just too embarrassed.

_____ 5. Babysitting is a responsible job. A babysitter is _?_ for the children's safety.

_____ 6. The army tanks rolled in, and then came the marching soldiers; we knew the _?_ had begun.

_____ 7. People with titles such as earl or duke make up the _?_ of England.

_____ 8. Lately, we have had our share of _?_. After the fire destroyed our house, Mom lost her job.

_____ 9. Although Leroy was sick for some time, he is now feeling better and is beginning to regain his _?_.

_____ 10. Cactuses and other desert plants are _?_ in Arizona.

Number correct _____ (total 10)

Analyzing Word Parts

The Latin Root *cred* The Latin root *cred* means "believe." In this unit, the target word *incredible* and its antonym, the related word *credible,* contain the *cred* root and come from the Latin verb *credere,* meaning "to trust." Other words that derive from *credere* are *credit, creditor, credentials,* and *creed.* Using this knowledge, write the word from the list below that best completes the meaning of the sentence. You may use a dictionary if necessary.

creed   credentials   credible   credit   creditor

_____ 1. If we do not pay that bill, we will soon receive another angry call from the _?_.

122

2. I don't find Tony's story far-fetched. In fact, I think it is quite ___?___.

3. What is the ___?___ of the Greek Orthodox Church?

4. Considering that Anna organized the entire farewell party, she should get most of the ___?___ for its success.

5. The woman who will speak to us about juvenile delinquency has college degrees in law and psychology. She certainly has impressive ___?___.

Number correct _____ (total 5)

Number correct in unit _____ (total 80)

The Last Word

Writing

Use your imagination to write a story about a *ferocious* animal. Include many descriptive details to help readers picture this animal.

Speaking

Choose a famous *expedition* from the list below. Use an encyclopedia to find out what happened during the expedition. Then prepare a short talk in which you give an *account* of the expedition. Include enough specific details in your talk to make your account vivid and interesting.

1. Lewis and Clark's overland expedition to the Pacific Ocean in 1804–1806
2. Sir Edmund Hillary and Tenzing Norgay's expedition to the top of Mt. Everest in 1953
3. The *Apollo XI* expedition to the moon in 1969

Group Discussion

What personal *quality* makes someone a good leader? The following are some possible answers to this question:

1. A good leader remains calm in the face of *adversity*.
2. A good leader is *objective*.
3. A good leader has *noble* goals.
4. A good leader is *vigorous*.

Discuss what each of these statements means. Give examples to demonstrate each statement. Then discuss what other qualities could be added to the list.

UNIT 10

Part A   Target Words and Their Meanings

1. accommodate (ə kăm′ ə dāt′) v.
2. available (ə vā′ lə b'l) adj.
3. besiege (bi sēj′) v.
4. congregate (kăŋ′ grə gāt′, kăn-) v.
5. demolish (di mäl′ ish) v.
6. discount (dis′ kount, dis kount′) v. (dis′ kount) n.
7. domestic (də mes′ tik) adj., n.
8. hesitation (hez′ ə tā′ shən) n.
9. humiliate (hyōō mil′ ē āt′, hyoo-) v.
10. incident (in′ si dənt) n.
11. induce (in dōōs′, -dyōōs′) v.
12. meager (mē′ gər) adj.
13. miraculous (mi rak′ yōō ləs) adj.
14. morale (mə ral′, mô-) n.
15. obvious (äb′ vē əs) adj.
16. option (ăp′ shən) n.
17. permeate (pur′ mē āt′) v.
18. petrify (pet′ rə fī′) v.
19. placid (plas′ id) adj.
20. smolder (smōl′ dər) v.

Inferring Meaning from Context

For each sentence write the letter of the word or phrase that is closest in meaning to the word or words in italics. Use context clues to help you choose the correct answer. (For information about how context helps you understand vocabulary, see pages 1–6.)

_____ 1. The booths can *accommodate* four diners comfortably. Larger parties must sit at one of the long tables.

a. hold   b. choose   c. guide   d. exclude

_____ 2. Under attack by a swarm of hornets, Anne raced for the only *available* shelter—a hedge—and jumped in.

a. usable   b. beautiful   c. legal   d. comfortable

_____ 3. The king was trapped inside the castle, *besieged* by enemy forces.

a. adopted   b. deserted   c. surrounded   d. neglected

_____ 4. Arriving by car and bus, people began to *congregate* at the airport to welcome the winning team.

a. laugh   b. depart   c. disperse   d. gather

_____ 5. The accident *demolished* the car. Not one part of it could be salvaged.

a. scratched   b. dented   c. repaired   d. destroyed

_____ 6. Kyoko *discounted* Marcy's story of having amazing adventures while on vacation. Kyoko knew Marcy had a wild imagination.

    a. forgot   b. did not believe   c. added to   d. did not understand

_____ 7. Bob disliked *domestic* chores, especially washing dishes.

    a. home   b. neighborhood   c. community   d. school

_____ 8. Officer Mariano saw the blazing house. With no *hesitation,* he rushed to rescue the trapped child.

    a. concern   b. hurrying   c. running   d. delay

_____ 9. The cruel boy tried to *humiliate* Becky by calling her names.

    a. correct   b. flatter   c. degrade   d. help

_____ 10. During the flood, Sandra, Julie, and Anne spent a night huddled on a rooftop. After that *incident,* the three became friends.

    a. joke   b. event   c. job   d. patrol

_____ 11. The salesperson tried to *induce* me to buy both pairs of slacks by offering the second pair at half price.

    a. persuade   b. instruct   c. bribe   d. trick

_____ 12. Jonathan didn't want to begin his long hike on a *meager* breakfast of toast. He wanted eggs, juice, bacon, and cereal.

    a. generous   b. little   c. huge   d. necessary

_____ 13. It seemed *miraculous* that the storm let up just long enough for us to paddle our boat back to shore.

    a. wondrous   b. cruel   c. untimely   d. normal

_____ 14. After losing ten games in a row, the team had such low *morale* that several players talked of quitting.

    a. awareness   b. talent   c. ability   d. confidence

_____ 15. The skid marks made it *obvious* that the driver had applied the brakes but could not stop the car in time.

    a. possible   b. clear   c. lucky   d. unfortunate

_____ 16. Don has the *option* of playing in the school band or singing in the chorus. He must pick one by Tuesday.

    a. choice   b. courage   c. joy   d. work

_____ 17. The odor from the skunk began to *permeate* the neighborhood.

    a. please   b. amuse   c. freshen   d. spread throughout

_____ 18. When Mike heard footsteps behind him, he stopped in his tracks, *petrified* that someone was following him home.

    a. frozen with fear   b. curious   c. calm   d. overwhelmed with anger

_____ 19. Not a breath of wind disturbed the *placid* surface of the lake.
   a. rough   b. choppy   c. calm   d. violent

_____ 20. Careless campers left the ashes of their campfire *smoldering*.
   a. completely out   b. cold   c. smoking   d. blazing

Number correct _____ (total 20)

Part B *Target Words in Reading and Literature*

You should now have a general idea of the meaning of each target word. Sharpen your understanding by studying how these words are used in the following selection.

The Great Stone Bridge Legend

Marion E. Gridley

Several native American legends concern the natural world. The following legend recalls an extraordinary event that involved a great stone bridge.

As the sun rose that morning, an air of suspense **permeated** the small Indian camp. The camp was pitched at the edge of a deep gorge—so deep one could barely see the **placid** water at the bottom. Some braves **congregated** beside a **smoldering** campfire. They murmured and fixed their eyes on the dying embers. Women nervously performed their 5 **domestic** tasks, preparing **meager** meals. Several sad, old men sat silent, their **morale** very low.

The Indians had been taken by surprise and **besieged** by enemy forces. They had fought bravely but were **humiliated** by defeat. Their homes were **demolished.** Those who survived fled the enemy. 10 **Induced** by their leaders to press on, they had made a wrong turn. Their hazardous journey ended at the rim of a canyon. Before them was a great hole in the earth. Behind them was the enemy. No wonder they were **petrified** with fear. Where could they go?

Just when no **option** seemed **available**, several young braves dashed 15 into camp. Excitedly, they reported seeing a **miraculous** stone bridge that crossed the canyon just a short distance from camp. Most of the tribe **discounted** this story. But a few warriors hurried to the spot to see for themselves. Seeing was believing! A stone bridge, large enough to **accommodate** several people and horses, stretched across the canyon. 20 Without **hesitation,** the people gathered their children and belongings and hurried across the bridge.

Enemy braves watched but did not follow. It was **obvious** that the Great Spirit sided with 25 the defeated. Safe on the other side of the canyon, the wanderers thanked the Great Spirit for saving them.

For hundreds of miles around, 30 Indians recounted this **incident**. From near and far many came to see the magnificent bridge. You too can see and even cross it—in southwestern Virginia. 35

Refining Your Understanding

For each of the following items, consider how the target word is used in the passage. Write the letter of the word or phrase that best completes the sentence.

_____ 1. *Permeated* (line 1) is synonymous with   a. disappeared from
b. filled   c. strengthened.

_____ 2. Other examples of *domestic* (line 6) tasks might include
a. hunting   b. sewing clothes   c. scouting enemy warriors.

_____ 3. The stone bridge was considered *miraculous* (line 16) because
a. many braves had crossed the bridge in the past   b. the Indians
did not expect to find it there   c. it was solid enough to support
the horses.

_____ 4. At first, most members of the tribe *discounted* (line 18) the story of
the stone bridge because they   a. had already seen the bridge
b. knew that the speakers were liars   c. thought that they could
not be saved.

_____ 5. The people crossed the stone bridge "without *hesitation*" (line 21)
because they were   a. afraid of their enemies   b. adventurous
c. careless.

Number correct _____ (total 5)

Part C   Ways to Make New Words Your Own

By now you are familiar with the target words and their meanings. This section presents activities that will help you make the words part of your permanent vocabulary.

Using Language and Thinking Skills

Understanding Multiple Meanings   Each box in this exercise contains a boldfaced word with its definitions. Read the definitions and then the sentences that use the word. Write the letter of the definition that applies to each sentence.

> **discount**
> a. a reduction from the usual price (n.)
> b. to sell for less than the regular price (v.)
> c. to disbelieve a story entirely or in part (v.)

_____ 1. All merchandise at the camping store was sold at a twenty-percent *discount*.

_____ 2. People often *discount* stories about huge fish that barely got away.

_____ 3. Carlos *discounted* Len's stories about his adventures with pirates in the South Seas.

_____ 4. Mr. Charnes, who owns Old Towne Bakery, *discounts* the day-old bread.

> **domestic**
> a. of the home or family (adj.)
> b. of one's own country or of the country referred to (adj.)
> c. a servant in the home (n.)

_____ 5. *Domestic* goods sometimes are less expensive than foreign goods.

_____ 6. Today, many men and women share *domestic* chores such as cooking, cleaning, and washing dishes.

_____ 7. Dale, who had extensive experience as a *domestic,* started a house-cleaning service.

> **accommodate**
> a. to make fit; adjust; adapt (v.)
> b. to do a favor for (v.)
> c. to have room for (v.)

____ 8. The pupil of the eye *accommodates* itself to the intensity of light.

____ 9. The hotel *accommodated* hundreds of tourists.

____ 10. Yoko tried to *accommodate* her friend by lending him her class notes.

Number correct _____ (total 10)

Finding the Unrelated Word Write the letter of the word that is not related in meaning to the other words in the set.

____ 1. a. compliment b. humiliate c. shame d. embarrass

____ 2. a. amazing b. astonishing c. ordinary d. miraculous

____ 3. a. permeate b. spread c. penetrate d. contain

____ 4. a. rule b. choice c. option d. alternative

____ 5. a. persuade b. prevent c. influence d. induce

____ 6. a. avoid b. surround c. besiege d. encircle

____ 7. a. collect b. congregate c. assemble d. disperse

____ 8. a. excited b. peaceful c. placid d. calm

____ 9. a. wreck b. create c. demolish d. destroy

____ 10. a. incident b. event c. idea d. occurrence

Number correct _____ (total 10)

Word's Worth: petrify

Have you ever been so afraid that you couldn't even move? Most people have. When you are *petrified,* it's as though you have turned to stone. *Petrify,* meaning "to paralyze, as with fear," comes from the Greek word *petra,* meaning "stone," and the Latin verb *ficare,* meaning "to make." Interestingly, the name *Peter* also comes from the Greek word for stone. In addition, you may have heard of, or even visited, *petrified* forests in eastern Arizona, where trees have changed from living tissue into solid rock.

Word Map Create a word map for *placid*. Include two synonyms and two antonyms of *placid*. Also use the word *placid* in a sentence of your own.

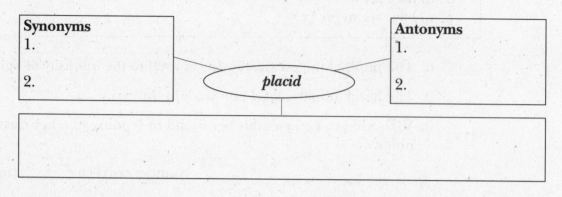

Synonyms		Antonyms
1.		1.
2.	*placid*	2.

Number correct _____ (total 5)

Practicing for Standardized Tests

Antonyms Write the letter of the word that is most nearly *opposite* in meaning to the capitalized word.

____ 1. OBVIOUS: (A) striking   (B) open   (C) clear   (D) slow   (E) hidden

____ 2. DEMOLISH: (A) cease   (B) build   (C) smash   (D) detect   (E) wreck

____ 3. CONGREGATE: (A) scatter   (B) compose   (C) collect   (D) govern   (E) swing

____ 4. PLACID: (A) repulsive   (B) quiet   (C) hazardous   (D) turbulent   (E) calm

____ 5. MEAGER: (A) scanty   (B) efficient   (C) plentiful   (D) mute   (E) little

____ 6. INDUCE: (A) discourage   (B) urge   (C) predict   (D) propel   (E) question

____ 7. DOMESTIC: (A) reasonable   (B) awkward   (C) homelike   (D) difficult   (E) public

____ 8. MIRACULOUS: (A) wondrous   (B) peaceful   (C) common   (D) ferocious   (E) unearthly

____ 9. DISCOUNT: (A) trick   (B) believe   (C) ignore   (D) attract   (E) doubt

____ 10. PETRIFY: (A) calm   (B) terrify   (C) baffle   (D) horrify   (E) search

Number correct _____ (total 10)

Spelling and Wordplay

Word Maze Find and circle each target word in this maze.

```
Y  C  P  B  M  E  C  U  D  N  I  S  A
F  I  M  E  O  I  N  H  C  O  N  C  E
I  T  E  S  R  O  V  Q  W  I  C  O  N
R  S  A  I  A  M  F  H  R  T  I  N  T
T  E  G  E  L  Z  E  E  X  P  D  G  N
E  M  E  G  E  U  D  A  Y  O  E  R  U
P  O  R  E  Q  L  T  P  T  M  N  E  O
L  D  E  M  O  L  I  S  H  E  T  G  C
A  H  U  M  I  L  I  A  T  E  K  A  S
C  D  S  O  B  V  I  O  U  S  G  T  I
I  A  C  C  O  M  M  O  D  A  T  E  D
D  S  M  I  R  A  C  U  L  O  U  S  A
A  E  S  E  L  B  A  L  I  A  V  A  P
X  H  E  S  I  T  A  T  I  O  N  V  Q
```

accommodate
available
besiege
congregate
demolish
discount
domestic
hesitation
humiliate
incident
induce
meager
miraculous
morale
obvious
option
permeate
petrify
placid
smolder

Part D Related Words

The words below are closely related to the target words. Use your knowledge of the target words and of word parts to determine the meanings of these words. (For information about word parts analysis, see pages 7–13.) Use your dictionary if necessary.

1. accommodation (ə käm′ ə dā′ shən) n.
2. avail (ə vāl′) v., n.
3. congregation (käŋ′ grə gā′ shən) n.
4. demolition (dem′ ə lish′ ən, de′ mə-) n.
5. hesitate (hez′ ə tāt′) v.
6. humiliation (hyo͞o mil′ ē ā′ shən, hyo͝o-) n.
7. humility (hyo͞o mil′ ə tē) n.
8. incidence (in′ si dəns) n.
9. incidental (in′ si den′ t′l) adj.
10. inducement (in do͞os′ mənt, -dyo͞os′-) n.
11. induct (in dukt′) v.
12. induction (in duk′ shən) n.
13. miracle (mir′ ə k′l) n.
14. moral (môr′ əl, mär′-) adj., n.
15. optional (äp′ shən ′l) adj.
16. permeation (pur′ mē ā′ shən) n.
17. siege (sēj) n., v.

Understanding Related Words

Sentence Completion Complete each sentence with a related word from the list on page 131. A word may be used only once.

_____ 1. As an ? , the teacher awarded extra credit points for additional book reports.

_____ 2. His dream as a baseball player was to be ? into the Hall of Fame.

_____ 3. For a week he dieted to no ? , he did not shed a single pound.

_____ 4. The newlyweds loved their hotel ? , a bridal suite overlooking the lake.

_____ 5. Despite additional police patrols, the ? of crime increased.

_____ 6. Though she was the leading scorer in the state, the basketball player answered reporters' questions with ? .

_____ 7. The minister's sermon stirred the hearts of the ? .

_____ 8. It seemed almost a ? when the team that had the worst record in the league last year finished first this year.

_____ 9. Many citizens protested the proposed ? of the oldest stadium in the city.

_____ 10. Besides paying for food, lodging, and airfare, we had to cover several ? expenses during our vacation.

Number correct _____ (total 10)

Finding Examples Write the word from the list below that is most clearly related to the situation conveyed in the sentence.

congregation	hesitate	induction	moral	permeation
demolition	humiliation	miracle	optional	siege

_____ 1. During the ceremony five members of the organization were installed as officers for the coming year.

_____ 2. The odor from the burnt toast soon spread from the kitchen through the entire house.

_____ 3. The church members waited for Sunday morning services to begin.

_____ 4. Aesop's fable of the fox and the crow teaches an important lesson—do not trust flatterers.

inducement

_____ 5. Yoko may choose silver or gold buckles for her new dress.

_____ 6. Because the old building was in poor condition, the owner chose to have it torn down. When the workers finished, not one brick of the original structure remained.

_____ 7. During World War II, the German army surrounded the Russian city of Leningrad. For more than three years the city was under attack, and food and supplies were scarce.

_____ 8. Ed, one of the best students in the class, was distracted. When the teacher called on him, Ed had no idea what the class was studying! His face turned bright red.

_____ 9. The witness paused before answering the lawyer's question.

_____ 10. Although the accident destroyed both automobiles, neither the drivers nor the passengers were even scratched.

Number correct _____ (total 10)

Analyzing Word Parts

The Latin Root _greg_ The target word _congregate_ and the related word _congregation_ contain the Latin root _greg_. This root comes from the Latin word _gregare_, which means "to gather into a flock." Other English words that contain this root include _congregationalism, gregarious, segregate,_ and _segregation._ Match each of the following words on the left with its definition on the right. Write the letter of the definition. Use your dictionary to check your work.

_____ 1. the bringing of different racial groups into equal association

_____ 2. a group of distinct things considered as a whole

_____ 3. the policy of having different races live apart

_____ 4. liking the company of others

_____ 5. remarkably bad

a. egregious
b. aggregate
c. gregarious
d. integration
e. segregation

Number correct _____ (total 5)

The Latin Root *duc* The target word *induce* and the related words *inducement, induct,* and *induction* contain the Latin root *duc.* This root comes from the Latin word *ducere,* which means "to lead." Other English words formed from this root include *conducive* and *reduce.* Use your dictionary to examine the meanings of these words. Then write the word from this list that completes the meaning in the following sentences.

conducive   conductor   deduce   induction   reduce

_____ 1. If we __?__ our speed, we'll use less gas.

_____ 2. The __?__ inspired the orchestra to perform magnificently.

_____ 3. Soothing music is sometimes __?__ to sleep.

_____ 4. Based on her understanding of people, the lawyer was led to __?__ that her client was innocent.

_____ 5. After visiting several classrooms, she made an __?__ about the quality of education at the school.

Number correct _____ (total 5)

Number correct in unit _____ (total 90)

Turn to **Words with *ie* and *ei*** on page 233 of the **Spelling Handbook.** Read the rule and complete the exercises provided.

The Last Word

Writing

Describe an *incident* in which you learned something important about yourself or someone you care about.

Speaking

Imagine that you are the captain of a team that has lost the first two games of a twelve-game schedule. What would you say to your teammates to bolster their *morale*? Prepare a speech to give to your classmates.

Group Discussion

As a class, discuss what it means to be a *moral* person. Think of different situations that require you to choose between right and wrong. Why is it sometimes difficult to make the right choice?

UNIT 11

Part A Target Words and Their Meanings

1. appoint (ə point′) v.
2. bitterly (bit′ ər lē) adv.
3. campaign (kam pān′) n., v.
4. correspond (kôr′ ə spänd′, kär′-) v.
5. decency (dē′ s'n sē) n.
6. dispose (dis pōz′) v.
7. engagement (in gāj′ mənt) n.
8. institution (in′ stə too′ shən, -tyoo′-) n.
9. mortal (môr′ t'l) adj., n.
10. oust (oust) v.
11. parallel (par′ ə lel′, -ləl) adj., n., v.
12. percussion (pər kush′ ən) n.
13. practical (prak′ ti k'l) adj.
14. repercussion (rē′ pər kush′ ən, rep′ ər-) n.
15. resign (ri zīn′) v.
16. snipe (snīp) v., n.
17. suite (swēt) n.
18. sympathy (sim′ pə thē) n
19. token (tō′ k'n) adj., n.
20. wage (wāj) v., n.

Inferring Meaning from Context

For each sentence write the letter of the word or phrase that is closest in meaning to the word or words in italics. Use context clues to help you choose the correct answer. (For information about how context helps you understand vocabulary, see pages 1–6.)

_____ 1. The President of the United States *appoints* the members of the Cabinet.

a. names b. rejects c. suspends d. scorns

_____ 2. The captured soldier stared *bitterly* at his cruel enemies.

a. sadly b. happily c. with love d. with hatred

_____ 3. The general's *campaign* to reach the capital city included several battles intended to weaken the enemy.

a. series of planned military actions b. negotiations c. treaty
d. retreat

_____ 4. Although my mother has not seen her best friend from high school since graduation, they still *correspond*.

a. quarrel b. attend school c. exchange letters d. visit

_____ 5. "It is a matter of *decency*," Mike explained. "Mrs. Cruz is sick, and it's only right to do whatever I can to help her."

a. proper behavior b. earning extra money c. getting even
d. dishonesty

135

_____ 6. Nancy's neighbor used to blast his stereo in the middle of the night. Nancy *disposed of* this problem by having her landlady tell him to turn it down.

a. ignored   b. accepted   c. created   d. settled

_____ 7. The first *engagement* of the Revolutionary War took place in Massachusetts when the minutemen fired at the redcoats.

a. political meeting   b. election   c. game   d. battle

_____ 8. Summer vacation is *an institution* of long standing. For generations, kids have expected to be out of school each summer, but there's talk of changing this practice.

a. a problem   b. a necessity   c. a custom   d. a belief

_____ 9. The two men were *mortal* enemies for years, but suddenly, to everyone's surprise, they became friends.

a. harmless   b. hateful   c. trustworthy   d. pleasant

_____ 10. During the revolution in Camillo's native country, the old government was *ousted* and replaced by a new one.

a. praised   b. hired   c. forced out   d. formed

_____ 11. The shelves were *parallel,* one exactly twelve inches above the other.

a. sloping   b. the same distance apart   c. sideways   d. backwards

_____ 12. As the players entered the gymnasium, the *percussion* of drums and cymbals stirred the crowd.

a. crash   b. screech   c. moan   d. whisper

_____ 13. Andrew's mother thinks that he should learn *practical* skills, such as cooking and home repairs.

a. outdoor   b. academic   c. useless   d. useful

_____ 14. The elimination of bus service had several *repercussions,* including the creation of huge traffic jams.

a. advantages   b. results   c. benefits   d. predictions

_____ 15. Though he hated to leave his job, Mr. Santiago *resigned* to accept a managerial position with another company.

a. returned   b. accepted   c. quit   d. stayed

_____ 16. During war, soldiers sometimes hide and *snipe* at the enemy. Their deadly fire catches the enemy by surprise.

a. shoot from hiding   b. charge   c. look   d. yell insults

_____ 17. For her sixteenth birthday, Donna's older sister got a new bedroom *suite* that included a beautiful bed, dresser, and night stand.

a. bookcase   b. set of matched furniture   c. decoration
d. set of matched luggage

_____ 18. In *sympathy* with the homeless, we joined their march on city hall.
a. a feeling of disagreement   b. a feeling of agreement
c. a lack of interest   d. anger

_____ 19. Convinced that the party had made a mistake, the governor gave only *token* support to its candidate for senator.
a. sincere   b. costly   c. noble   d. pretended

_____ 20. The shortest war ever *waged* lasted thirty-eight minutes. It was fought between Great Britain and Zanzibar.
a. planned   b. threatened   c. carried on   d. prevented

Number correct _____ (total 20)

Part B   Target Words in Reading and Literature

You should now have a general idea of the meaning of each target word. Sharpen your understanding by studying how these words are used in the following selection.

Grandma and the Sea Gull

Louise Dickinson Rich

Have you ever known two neighbors who just couldn't get along? In this selection a teenager recalls the feud between her grandmother and the next-door neighbor.

My grandmother had an enemy named Mrs. Wilcox. Grandma and Mrs. Wilcox moved, as brides, into next-door houses on the sleepy, elm-roofed Main Street of the tiny town in which they were to live out their lives. I do not know what started the war—that was long before my day—and I do not think that by the time I came along, over thirty years later, they remembered themselves what started it. Nevertheless, it was still being **bitterly waged**.

Make no mistake. This was no polite sparring[1] match. This was War Between Ladies, which is total war. Nothing in town escaped **repercussion**. The 300-year-old church, which had lived through the Revolution, the Civil War, and the Spanish-American War, almost went down when Grandma and Mrs. Wilcox fought the Battle of the Ladies' Aid. Grandma won that **engagement** but it was a hollow victory. Mrs. Wilcox, since she could not be president, **resigned** in a huff, and what is the fun of running a thing if you cannot force your **mortal** enemy to eat crow?[2] Mrs. Wilcox

5

10

15

---
[1] sparring: boxing, as in practice matches
[2] to eat crow: to be humiliated

won the Battle of the Public Library, getting her niece, Gertrude, **appointed** librarian instead of Aunt Phyllis. The day Gertrude took over was the day Grandma stopped reading library books—"filthy germ things" they had become overnight—and started buying her own. The Battle of the High School was a draw. The principal got a better job and left before Mrs. Wilcox succeeded in having him **ousted** or Grandma in having him given life tenure[3] of office.

In addition to these major engagements, there was constant sallying and **sniping** back of the main line of fire. When as children we visited my grandmother, part of the fun was making faces at Mrs. Wilcox's impossible grandchildren—nearly as impossible as we were, I now see. . . .

We chased the Wilcox hens, too, and put **percussion** caps, saved from July 4, on the rails of the trolley line right in front of the Wilcox house, in the pleasant hope that when the trolley went by, the explosion—actually a negligible[4] affair—would scare Mrs. Wilcox into fits. One banner day we put a snake in the Wilcox rain barrel. My grandmother made **token** protests but we sensed tacit[5] **sympathy**, so different from what lay back of my mother's noes, and went merrily on with our career of brattishness. If any child of mine—but that's another story.

Do not think for a minute that this was a one-sided **campaign**. Mrs. Wilcox had grandchildren too, remember; more and tougher and smarter grandchildren than my grandmother had. Grandma did not get off scot-free. She had skunks introduced into her cellar. On Halloween all loose forgotten objects, such as garden furniture, miraculously flew to the ridgepole[6] of the barn, whence they had to be lowered by strong men hired at exorbitant[7] day rates. Never a windy washday went by but what the clothesline mysteriously broke, so that the sheets wallopsed around in the dirt and had to be done over. . . . I do not know how Grandma could have borne[8] her troubles so long if it had not been for the household page of her daily Boston newspaper.

This household page was a wonderful **institution**. Besides the usual cooking hints and cleaning advice, it had a department composed of letters from readers to each other. The idea was that if you had a problem —or even only some steam to blow off—you wrote a letter to the paper, signing some fancy name like Arbutus. That was Grandma's pen name. Then some of the other ladies who had had the same problem wrote

---

[3] tenure: the holding of a position, especially in teaching, on a permanent basis
[4] negligible: unimportant
[5] tacit: quiet
[6] ridgepole: the horizontal beam at the ridge of a roof
[7] exorbitant: expensive
[8] borne: past participle of bear, meaning to put up with

back and told you what they had done about it, signing themselves One Who Knows or Xanthippe or whatever. Very often, the problem **disposed** of, you kept on for years writing to each other through the column of the paper, telling each other about your children and your canning and your new dining room **suite**. This is what happened to Grandma. She and a woman called Sea Gull **corresponded** for a quarter of a century and Grandma told Sea Gull things that she never breathed to another soul. . . . Sea Gull was Grandma's true, bosom friend. 55

When I was about sixteen, Mrs. Wilcox died. In a small town, no matter how much you have hated your next-door neighbor, it is only common **decency** to run over and see what **practical** service you can do the bereaved.[9] Grandma, neat in a percale[10] apron to show that she meant what she said about being put to work, crossed the two lawns to the Wilcox house, where the Wilcox daughters set her to cleaning the already immaculate[11] front parlor for the funeral. And there on the parlor table in the place of honor was a huge scrapbook; and in the scrapbook, pasted neatly in **parallel** columns, were her letters to Sea Gull over the years and Sea Gull's letters to her. Grandma's worst enemy had been her best friend. 60 65 70

---

9 bereaved: those mourning one who has recently died
10 percale: tightly woven cotton cloth
11 immaculate: completely clean

Refining Your Understanding

For each of the following items, consider how the target word is used in the passage. Write the letter of the word or phrase that best completes the sentence.

_____ 1. An example of someone being *ousted* (line 21) would be   a. a teacher being hired   b. a soldier going to war   c. a governor being removed from office.

_____ 2. "*Token* protests" (line 32) show that Grandma   a. did not really oppose her grandchildren's dropping a snake in the neighbor's rain barrel   b. was very much against her grandchildren's dropping a snake in the neighbor's rain barrel   c. did not understand what her grandchildren planned to do.

_____ 3. Which of the following people would most likely take part in a *campaign* (line 35)?   a. a carpenter   b. a soldier   c. a grocer.

_____ 4. To *dispose* of a problem (line 53) means to   a. ignore it   b. put it off   c. deal with it.

_____ 5. A *practical* (line 62) service that Grandma might do for the bereaved would be   a. reviewing Mrs. Wilcox's scrapbook   b. preparing dinner for those attending the funeral   c. writing a poem about her relationship with Sea Gull.

Number correct _____ (total 5)

Part C   Ways to Make New Words Your Own

By now you are familiar with the target words and their meanings. This section presents activities that will help you make the words part of your permanent vocabulary.

Using Language and Thinking Skills

Finding Examples Write the letter of the situation that best shows the meaning of the boldfaced word.

_____ 1. **campaign**
   a. General Sherman's "March to the Sea" was a series of battles that helped bring the Civil War to a close.
   b. Louis spent a weekend in a tent in the forest.
   c. Samuel Clemens's experience as a steamboat captain gave him the background for writing *Life on the Mississippi*.

_____ 2. **engagement**
   a. Two sisters have a birthday party.
   b. Two doctors discuss a patient's condition.
   c. Two armies meet in a small battle.

_____ 3. **appoint**

    a. The club president names Harry the leader of a committee.

    b. A judge gives a criminal a long sentence.

    c. A hiker selects the supplies she needs.

_____ 4. **mortal**

    a. Two newlyweds have their first fight.

    b. Two friends say goodbye at an airport.

    c. Two enemies vow never to make peace.

_____ 5. **suite**

    a. A lawyer chose a matching jacket and skirt.

    b. A woman arrived with a set of matching luggage.

    c. A salesperson showed us a set of living room furniture.

_____ 6. **bitterly**

    a. The defeated wrestler stared at the winner with deep resentment.

    b. The winning cook gave the judges a grateful smile.

    c. The losing coach shook hands with the winning coach and congratulated her on the victory.

_____ 7. **decency**

    a. Jeff walked to school along a different route to avoid meeting Calvin.

    b. Mallorie admitted to her neighbor that she had broken the window.

    c. Tom lied to his parents about his conduct at school.

_____ 8. **parallel**

    a. Workers were laying rails for the new train.

    b. An animal trainer was teaching a new lion.

    c. A map maker traced the path of a stream to its source in the mountains.

_____ 9. **practical**

    a. Michelle likes to daydream about having dates with movie stars.

    b. Stan spends weekends at his uncle's garage learning to repair car engines.

    c. Pat wants to quit school and travel throughout the state.

_____ 10. **resign**

    a. Mr. Amsted began working for a large corporation.

    b. Gregory forgot his math book and returned home to get it.

    c. Mrs. Stinson gave up her job at the library.

Number correct _____ (total 10)

Practicing for Standardized Tests

Synonyms Write the letter of the word that is closest in meaning to the capitalized word.

_____ 1. APPOINT: (A) sharpen (B) select (C) recall (D) notify
(E) reject

_____ 2. BITTERLY: (A) unusually (B) disagreeably (C) satisfactorily
(D) agreeably (E) awkwardly

_____ 3. DECENCY: (A) rightness (B) pride (C) rudeness
(D) curiosity (E) selfishness

_____ 4. DISPOSE OF: (A) receive (B) besiege (C) handle
(D) prepare (E) stall

_____ 5. MORTAL: (A) kind (B) inhuman (C) calm (D) cheerful
(E) severe

_____ 6. OUST: (A) elect (B) remove (C) douse (D) propel
(E) admit

_____ 7. PRACTICAL: (A) favorite (B) difficult (C) artistic
(D) workable (E) costly

_____ 8. REPERCUSSION: (A) effect (B) trial (C) cause
(D) instrument (E) plan

_____ 9. RESIGN: (A) agree (B) leave (C) apply (D) regain
(E) meet

_____ 10. SYMPATHY: (A) orchestra (B) dislike (C) doubt
(D) fear (E) agreement

Number correct _____ (total 10)

Word's Worth: percussion

The _percussion_ section of the band or orchestra includes instruments like drums, cymbals, and chimes. What do these instruments have in common that makes them different from other instruments? You strike them. The Latin root of _percussion_ is _percutere_, meaning "to strike." A _repercussion_ is a far-reaching reaction to some event, an echo or a "striking again." A word related to _percussion_ is _concussion_, an injury caused by a blow to the head.

Spelling and Wordplay

Crossword Puzzle Read the clues and print the correct answers in the proper squares. There are several target words in this puzzle.

ACROSS

1. To force out
2. Next to
5. To shoot from a hidden position
7. Right conduct
9. An organ of sight
10. Someone who jumps into a swimming pool
11. Severe, extreme
12. An automobile
14. Type of airplane
18. A signal for help
19. Shared feeling
21. A hole
22. Ripped
23. A custom of long standing
25. Name for first or last tone on musical scale
27. Coin worth five cents
29. A series of battles

DOWN

1. Unusual
2. To purchase
3. Something inserted in a lock
4. A battle
5. Set of matching furniture
6. A sound caused by striking something
8. To write a letter to someone
13. To quit
15. Something to play with
16. To carry on
17. Drawing with water colors or oils
20. Stop!
22. Pretended
24. A solvent used for cleaning
26. Abbreviation for District of Columbia
28. Prefix meaning "not"

Turn to **The Letter _g_** on page 237 of the **Spelling Handbook**. Read the rule and complete the exercises provided.

Part D   Related Words

The words below are closely related to the target words. Use your knowledge of the target words and of word parts to determine the meanings of these words. (For information about word parts analysis, see pages 7–13.) Use your dictionary if necessary.

1. appointee (ə poin′ tē′) n.
2. appointment (ə point′ mənt) n.
3. bittersweet (bit′ ər swēt′) adj., n.
4. correspondence (kôr′ ə spän′ dens, kär′-) n.
5. correspondent (kôr′ ə spän′ dent, kär′-) adj., n.
6. decent (dē′ s'nt) adj.
7. disposition (dis′ pə zish′ ən) n.
8. engage (in gāj′) v.
9. immortal (i môr′ t'l) adj., n.
10. institute (in′ stə tōot′, -tyōot′) v., n.
11. percussive (pər kus′ iv) adj.
12. practicality (prak′ ti kal′ ə tē) n.
13. resignation (rez′ ig nā′ shən) n.
14. sniper (snī′ pər) n.
15. sympathetic (sim′ pə thet′ ik) adj.
16. sympathize (sim′ pə thīz′) v.
17. wager (wā′ jər) n., v.

Understanding Related Words

True-False   Decide whether each statement is true or false. Write **T** for True or **F** for False.

_____ 1. If you submit your *resignation*, you expect to continue in the same job.

_____ 2. A superstar might not be able to *sympathize* with a mediocre player's frustrations.

_____ 3. Anyone who reaches the age of seventy can be considered *immortal*.

_____ 4. If your brother and his girlfriend are *engaged*, they have decided to get married.

_____ 5. A *decent* person is generally rude and thoughtless.

_____ 6. An *appointee* has been selected for a job or position.

_____ 7. A newspaper *correspondent* usually is not interested in world events.

_____ 8. Someone with a pleasant *disposition* is probably well liked.

_____ 9. Nothing sad or troubling ever happens in a *bittersweet* friendship.

_____ 10. A person who never takes risks probably would not *wager* on sporting events.

Number correct _____ (total 10)

Analyzing Word Parts

The Suffix *-ion* You can sometimes turn verbs into nouns by adding the suffix *-ion*. The target word *institution,* for example, was formed by adding the suffix *-ion,* meaning "the act, condition, or result of," to the noun *institute.* Add *-ion* to each of the following verbs. Then define each noun.

regulate   1. _____   _____

_____

correct   2. _____   _____

_____

translate   3. _____   _____

_____

hesitate   4. _____   _____

_____

educate   5. _____   _____

_____

Number correct _____ (total 5)

The Suffix *-ment* The target word *engagement* is formed by adding the suffix *-ment* to the verb *engage.* This suffix can have several meanings. It may mean "a result," "a means or way," "the act or process," or "the state, fact, or degree." Examples include *improvement, discouragement, measurement, inducement,* and *government.* Complete each of the following sentences using one of these words.

_____   1. The carpenter needed to make a(n) _?_ before sawing the new door.

_____   2. Mr. Ray was looking for some _?_ in Megan's grades before allowing her to watch television.

_____   3. Hector couldn't hide his _?_ after losing his fourth tennis match in a row.

_____   4. The _?_ might raise taxes to pay for rising costs in education.

_____   5. Helen had a(n) _?_ to do her chores without being reminded: her mother had promised her a new bike as a reward for handling her responsibilities.

Number correct _____ (total 5)

Number correct in unit _____ (total 65)

145

The Last Word

Writing

Imagine that you and a pen pal *correspond* frequently. Write a letter of advice to your pen pal about one of the following situations:
- how to deal with bullies at school
- how to achieve higher grades
- how to handle annoying brothers or sisters

Speaking

Prepare a speech in which you give the class some *practical* advice regarding a topic of your choice. Your advice may involve any subject that you know well.

Group Discussion

The two characters in the reading selection were *mortal* enemies yet best friends. Discuss the following questions as a group: What might have happened to make the two women dislike each other so much? How might Grandma have felt after realizing who Sea Gull was? What lessons might be learned from this story?

UNIT 12: Review of Units 9–11

Part A Review Word List

Unit 9 Target Words

1. account
2. adverse
3. circulate
4. confederate
5. execute
6. expedition
7. fate
8. ferocious
9. gigantic
10. incredible
11. inherit
12. intention
13. invade
14. noble
15. objective
16. prevail
17. quality
18. scanty
19. substantial
20. vigorous

Unit 9 Related Words

1. accountable
2. accounting
3. adversity
4. circulation
5. confederacy
6. credible
7. execution
8. expeditious
9. fatal
10. fateful
11. inheritance
12. intend
13. intent
14. invasion
15. nobility
16. objection
17. prevalent
18. vigor

Unit 10 Target Words

1. accommodate
2. available
3. besiege
4. congregate
5. demolish
6. discount
7. domestic
8. hesitation
9. humiliate
10. incident
11. induce
12. meager
13. miraculous
14. morale
15. obvious
16. option
17. permeate
18. petrify
19. placid
20. smolder

Unit 10 Related Words

1. accommodation
2. avail
3. congregation
4. demolition
5. hesitate
6. humiliation
7. humility
8. incidence
9. incidental
10. inducement
11. induct
12. induction
13. miracle
14. moral
15. optional
16. permeation
17. siege

Unit 11 Target Words

1. appoint
2. bitterly
3. campaign
4. correspond
5. decency
6. dispose
7. engagement
8. institution
9. mortal
10. oust
11. parallel
12. percussion
13. practical
14. repercussion
15. resign
16. snipe
17. suite
18. sympathy
19. token
20. wage

Unit 11 Related Words

1. appointee
2. appointment
3. bittersweet
4. correspondence
5. correspondent
6. decent
7. disposition
8. engage
9. immortal
10. institute
11. percussive
12. practicality
13. resignation
14. sniper
15. sympathetic
16. sympathize
17. wager

Inferring Meaning from Context

For each sentence write the letter of the word or phrase that is closest in meaning to the word or words in italics.

_____ 1. Dan's *account* of the accident was somewhat unclear.
   a. development b. adaptation c. report d. execution

_____ 2. After Jane insulted Michael, he looked at her *bitterly*.
   a. ceaselessly b. carefully c. sweetly d. hatefully

_____ 3. Because Greg is known to stretch the truth, his friends *discount* most of the stories he tells.
   a. believe b. do not believe c. report d. are bored with

_____ 4. The officer was injured severely during the *engagement*.
   a. game b. drill c. battle d. occasion

_____ 5. The *expedition* into the forest required quite a bit of planning.
   a. vacation b. pursuit c. invitation d. exploration

_____ 6. The *incident* was so serious that the police were called.
   a. event b. injury c. disagreement d. loss

_____ 7. Allison's story about having lunch with the President of the United States is *incredible*.
   a. desperate b. too long c. unbelievable d. uneventful

_____ 8. My grandfather made a *miraculous* recovery from his illness.
   a. hazardous b. painful c. wondrous d. uneventful

_____ 9. Since he was only halfway through the work, it was *obvious* to Mr. Juarez that he would need more time to finish the project.
   a. confusing b. frustrating c. vague d. clear

_____ 10. Ms. Williams was offered two different jobs. She has the *option* of working as a computer programmer or as a research technician.
   a. fate b. intent c. objective d. choice

_____ 11. Lorraine's finest *quality* is her compassion toward others.
   a. trait b. reason c. intention d. accommodation

_____ 12. Ms. Tanaka was the director of the organization, but she *resigned* because it was taking up too much of her time.
   a. remained b. circulated c. quit d. hesitated

_____ 13. The charcoal on the grill continued to *smolder* long after we finished dinner.
   a. smoke b. cook c. smell d. linger

148

_____ 14. Mother tells us to stand up whenever an adult comes into the room. She says standing is *a token* act that shows respect.

     a. a fatal   b. an adverse   c. a credible   d. a symbolic

_____ 15. If we use new lumber instead of those cracked old boards, we will have a *substantial* cabin.

     a. solid   b. popular   c. vigorous   d. domestic

Number correct _____ (total 15)

Using Review Words in Context

Using context clues, determine which word from the list below best completes each sentence in the story. Write the word in the blank. Each word may be used only once.

available	gigantic	incredible	obvious	prevail
congregate	hesitation	meager	percussion	quality
fate	humiliate	objective	practical	smolder

Plan Your Work—Work Your Plan

Jeff's grandfather called himself Zolo the Magnificent. He was an amateur magician who performed _____ tricks of magic at schools, hospitals, or any other _____ place where an audience, large or small, could _____. Zolo made it a point to do every trick exactly according to plan so that each performance would be of the same high _____. He always said that it would _____ him to give a poor performance.

Zolo liked to begin his act with a pitch-black stage and the sound of a drum's _____. This created a feeling of suspense. Then a _____ flame would leap up from the middle of the stage, almost touching the ceiling. The flame would immediately die down but continue to _____, and out of its smoke would step Zolo! The success of this trick was dependent upon perfect timing. The slightest _____ on Zolo's part would cause the trick to fall flat, earning him only a _____ round of applause instead of a hearty welcome.

Zolo told Jeff that the _____ of any performance rested upon the performer's knowing exactly where he or she is taking the audience. "Remember, a magician's _____ is to build suspense by making the audience wonder what the outcome will be. The magician alone must know this; it must never be _____ to anyone else. This may seem unnecessary, but it is actually extremely _____. For only by building and holding suspense can a magician _____ in his or her battle of wits with the audience."

Here is a five-step trick that Zolo passed on to Jeff. Make sure that it is carried out step by step to build that uncertainty of outcome in your audience.

1. Ask someone to think of a number between one and ten.
2. Tell them to multiply that number by two.
3. Have them add ten.
4. Ask them to divide the result by two.
5. Tell them to subtract the original number.

Ask them if five is the number they ended up with. You know what they don't know—the answer will always be five.

Number correct _____ (total 15)

Part B   *Review Word Reinforcement*

Using Language and Thinking Skills

Homonyms Homonyms are words that are pronounced the same but have different meanings and spellings. Look up the words *suite, sweet, fate,* and *fete* in your dictionary. Then use context clues to complete the sentences with the correct homonym.

1. The furnished apartment had a living room _____ that included a couch, a coffee table, and two chairs.

2. It was a wonderful _____ with outdoor games, sidewalk dining, and a street dance in the evening.

3. Good luck seemed to be our _____.

4. The fudge tasted extra _____.

5. Amelia Earhart's plane disappeared during a flight across the ocean, but her _____ is still unknown.

Number correct _____ (total 5)

Practicing for Standardized Tests

Synonyms Write the letter of the word that is closest in meaning to the capitalized word.

_____ 1. ADVERSE: (A) unfavorable (B) moral (C) positive
(D) ineffective (E) satisfactory

_____ 2. BESIEGE: (A) circulate (B) release (C) demolish
(D) accommodate (E) encircle

_____ 3. GIGANTIC: (A) intense (B) huge (C) small
(D) miraculous (E) sheer

_____ 4. DEMOLISH: (A) humiliate (B) construct (C) destroy
(D) detect (E) alter

_____ 5. EXECUTE: (A) protect (B) suspend (C) kill (D) guard
(E) pursue

_____ 6. INVADE: (A) attack (B) permit (C) invite (D) snipe
(E) induce

_____ 7. PETRIFY: (A) cut (B) heal (C) thaw (D) paralyze
(E) strengthen

_____ 8. OBJECTIVE: (A) result (B) effort (C) goal (D) credit
(E) handicap

_____ 9. OUST: (A) invite (B) discount (C) find (D) appoint
(E) remove

_____ 10. OBVIOUS: (A) sheer (B) clear (C) invisible (D) peculiar
(E) vague

Number correct _____ (total 10)

Antonyms Write the letter of the word that is most nearly _opposite_ in meaning to the capitalized word or words.

_____ 1. BITTERLY: (A) angrily (B) stubbornly (C) lovingly
(D) carelessly (E) slowly

_____ 2. CONGREGATE: (A) circulate (B) sympathize (C) scatter
(D) accommodate (E) meet

_____ 3. DECENCY: (A) suitability (B) ineffectiveness (C) nobility
(D) fairness (E) improperness

_____ 4. SYMPATHY: (A) fear (B) curiosity (C) hope
(D) disapproval (E) sensitivity

_____ 5. FEROCIOUS: (A) vicious (B) bitter (C) frenzied (D) hazardous (E) gentle

_____ 6. SUBSTANTIAL: (A) large (B) suitable (C) shaky (D) solid (E) reliable

_____ 7. MEAGER: (A) plentiful (B) scanty (C) lean (D) efficient (E) impure

_____ 8. PLACID: (A) calm (B) inviting (C) awkward (D) wild (E) constant

_____ 9. DISPOSE OF: (A) like (B) keep (C) energetic (D) continue (E) predict

_____ 10. VIGOROUS: (A) weak (B) expeditious (C) energetic (D) common (E) fateful

Number correct _____ (total 10)

Analogies Determine the relationship between the pair of capitalized words. Then decide which other word pair expresses a similar relationship. Write the letter of this word pair.

_____ 1. ACCOUNT : REPORT :: (A) option : choice (B) friend : enemy (C) laboratory : chemist (D) veterinarian : animal (E) journalist : newspaper

_____ 2. EXPLOSION : REPERCUSSION :: (A) carelessness : errors (B) testimony : witness (C) table : wood (D) joy : sorrow (E) florist : flower

_____ 3. CIRCULATE : RUMOR :: (A) stumble : fall (B) compose : music (C) sleep : dream (D) prevail : loss (E) change : transformation

_____ 4. PERCUSSION : SOUND :: (A) fate : destiny (B) floor : ceiling (C) house : building (D) drums : drumsticks (E) advantage : disadvantage

_____ 5. INDUCE : PERSUADE :: (A) wage : end (B) accept : refuse (C) circulate : spread (D) grasp : release (E) come : go

Number correct _____ (total 5)

Spelling and Wordplay

Fill-ins Spell the review word correctly in the blanks to the right of its definition.

1. to choose or name: __ p p __ __ __ __

2. agreement: s __ __ __ __ __ h __

3. to attack in a sneaky way: __ __ __ p __

4. fierce: f __ __ __ __ __ __ u __

5. attitude: __ __ __ a __ __

6. to remove forcibly: __ __ s __

7. to write letters: __ __ r r __ __ __ __ __ __

8. result; effect: r __ __ __ __ c __ __ __ __ __ __

9. calm: __ __ __ c __ __

10. journey of exploration: __ x __ __ __ __ __ __ __ o n

11. choice: __ p __ __ __ __

12. useful: __ __ __ c __ __ c __ __

13. purpose; objective: __ n __ __ __ t __ __ __

14. wondrous: m __ __ __ c __ __ __ __ __

15. to carry on: __ __ g __

16. destiny; outcome: __ __ t __

17. not enought; scanty: m __ __ __ __ __

18. to spread throughout: p __ __ m __ __ __ __

19. to receive upon the death of someone: __ __ h __ r __ __

20. event: __ __ __ __ __ __ n __

Number correct _____ (total 20)

Part C Related Word Reinforcement

Using Related Words

Sentence Completion Write the related word from the list below that best completes the meaning of the sentence.

appointee   bittersweet   disposition   institute   sympathize
accommodation   decent   immortal   nobility   wager

_____ 1. When Winston Churchill was knighted, he joined the ? of England.

_____ 2. The members of the Student Council named Carmella as their ? to the homecoming committee.

_____ 3. Zona and Ben made a ? that whoever received the lowest grade on the test had to buy the refreshments.

_____ 4. Miguel never seems to be satisfied. He really has a sour ? .

_____ 5. Thank you for arranging the party to fit Terry's schedule. She and I both appreciate the ? .

_____ 6. The ancient Greeks worshiped Zeus, Athena, and other gods, and believed these gods were ? .

_____ 7. Grace wants to become an engineer. She plans on attending the Massachusetts ? of Technology after she graduates from high school.

_____ 8. At times, Gina and Lemuel are the best of friends; at other times they have angry fights. They really have a ? relationship.

_____ 9. Dad said that offering to lend Mr. Washington our car during the emergency was the ? thing to do.

_____ 10. I'll join you in your effort to change that law because I ? with your reasons.

Number correct _____ (total 10)

Reviewing Word Structures

Roots and Suffixes You have worked with the Latin roots *cred, greg,* and *duc,* and the suffixes *-ion* and *-ment.* Complete each of the sentences below with a word that contains one of these roots or suffixes. Choose the words from the Related Words in the Review Word List on page 147.

1. My dad's _____ to get me to clean the basement was a guarantee of a ticket to a baseball game.

2. After the worship service ended, the _____ stood outside the church and chatted about the week's events.

3. Do you think that story about Anton being a descendant of Robin Hood is actually _____?

4. If we don't hurry, we will be late for Tomas's _____ into the Organization of Honor Students.

5. When Kate's friends caught her in a lie, her _____ was obvious to everyone.

6. The Union Army general scheduled the spy's _____ for nine o'clock the next morning.

7. The defense attorney's _____ was based on the fact that the witness's testimony was hearsay—that is, that it could not be proved.

8. Can you make an _____ and have the dinner an hour earlier?

9. The _____ of a newspaper is the average number of copies of it that are distributed.

10. Rachel has to miss swimming practice on Thursday; she has a doctor's _____.

Number correct _____ (total 10)

Number correct in unit _____ (total 100)

Vocab Lab 3

FOCUS ON: *Forms of Literature*

The following words describe different types of literature.

allegory (al′ ə gôr′ ē) n. a story that uses animals, people, or things to represent ideas. ● *Pilgrim's Progress,* by John Bunyan, is an *allegory* about a man named Christian who meets Mr. Worldly Wiseman and the giant Despair.

autobiography (ôt′ ə bī äg′ rə fē, -bē-) n. the story of one's own life as told or written by oneself. ● Movie stars often write *autobiographies* in which they tell their life stories.

biography (bī äg′ rə fē, bē-) n. the story of a person's life as written by another. ● A new *biography* of Abraham Lincoln gives information that has never before been told.

epic (ep′ ik) n. a long narrative poem written in an elevated style and telling of the deeds of a hero. ● *The Iliad* is an *epic* telling of the heroics of Achilles.

essay (es′ ā) n. a short composition giving the writer's personal views of a subject. ● Thomas Paine wrote *essays* explaining his political ideas.

fable (fā′ b′l) n. a made-up story meant to teach a moral lesson. ● In the *fable* "The Ant and the Grasshopper," the ant, who prepares for winter, is better off than the grasshopper, who chooses to play instead of work.

folk tale (fōk tāl) a story or legend made up by ordinary people and handed down by word of mouth from generation to generation. ● Many *folk tales* have been told about the pioneer Johnny Appleseed, who planted apple trees all over Illinois, Indiana, Ohio, and Pennsylvania.

journal (jʉr′ n′l) n. a daily record of life's occurrences, as in a diary. ● *Journals* kept by early pioneers tell of the day-to-day hardships they experienced.

myth (mith) n. a traditional story explaining how something connected with nature of human life came to be. ● The Greek *myth* involving Demeter explains the origin of seasons.

novel (näv′′l) n. a book of fiction that is longer and more complex than a short story. ● The *novel* told the story of the main character from the time of her birth to the marriage of her first child.

play (plā) n. a story written to be acted out before an audience and told through the dialogue and actions of its characters. ● Most *plays* are divided into scenes, with each scene representing a different time or place.

poetry (pō′ ə trē) n. a form of literature that uses sounds, rhythm, and images to express emotion or opinion or to tell a story. ● Although some *poetry* rhymes and other poetry does not, most poetry is set in lines and divided into stanzas.

romance (rō mans′, rō′ mans) n. a novel of adventure, often including a love story. ● The stories about King Arthur and his Knights of the Roundtable are *romances.*

satire (sa′ tīr) n. a literary work that makes fun of foolish or immoral actions or customs of people. ● The *satire* in Swift's *Gulliver's Travels* pokes fun at people who give undue importance to insignificant things in daily life.

short story (shôrt stôr′ ē) a short fictional narrative often developed around a single incident. ● Most *short stories* can be read in one sitting.

Sentence Completion Write the focus word that best completes the meaning of the sentence.

_____ 1. Tanya kept a(n) ? in which she recorded what happened each day during her summer vacation.

_____ 2. Deborah wanted to become a doctor after reading a(n) ? written about Elizabeth Blackwell, the first woman doctor in the United States.

_____ 3. The ? became exciting when the actors faced off in the middle of the stage in a sword fight.

_____ 4. Adam's favorite fiction book is the ? *M.C. Higgins, the Great* by Virginia Hamilton. The book tells about mysterious places and curious people.

_____ 5. The first ? about Red Riding Hood was invented long ago by ordinary people who enjoyed telling stories.

_____ 6. Marty likes to write ? because she enjoys the rhythm and sounds of words.

_____ 7. The ambassador wrote a fascinating ? in which he described his experiences living in Asia.

_____ 8. Aesop made up the ? about the fox and the crow to teach a moral lesson about how greedy people act.

_____ 9. Frank's six-page ? tells about two fictitious brothers who explore a mysterious, haunted cave.

_____ 10. According to a Greek ? , Apollo drives his sun chariot across the sky to light the world.

_____ 11. Homer's *Odyssey* is a(n) ? that describes the adventures of the Greek hero Odysseus in a long narrative using formal poetic language.

_____ 12. Spenser's *The Faerie Queen* is a(n) ? in which the Red Cross Knight, representing humanity, must face the Beast of Scandal and the Dragon of Sin.

_____ 13. The paper published a(n) ? making fun of the decision to build a third parking lot in the town.

_____ 14. Yoshika wrote a(n) ? giving her view that logging should not be allowed in state forests.

_____ 15. The new novel is a(n) ? about a man and woman who are separated by war but who find each other after desperate adventures in wild places.

Number correct _____ (total 15)

FOCUS ON: *Going into a Word's Past*

Every word in the English language has a history, sometimes a very long one. Check a dictionary for word origins and you will find that most English words come originally from other languages, such as Greek, Latin, German, or French. The study of the origins and histories of words is called **etymology.** If you know something about etymology you can understand much better how words relate to one another. In fact, you can often figure out the meaning of a word you never saw before.

Etymology

For example, knowing that the word *visual* comes from the Latin *videre* helps you unlock many words related to *visual. Videre* means "to see." All English words that come from *videre* refer in some way to the act of seeing.

Again, take the word *mobile.* In both French and English it means "movable" and it comes from the Latin *movere,* "to move." Knowing this can help you learn such words as *immobile, mobilize,* and *mobility,* all of which have to do with movement. In French, *mobile* also came to suggest an emotional sensitivity—being "easily moved" to tears, laughter, or anger. This is the origin of the word *mob,* "a disorderly crowd," one that is too easily "moved" to action due to people's emotions.

Knowing something about word etymologies can give you interesting glimpses into how words change over time. You may know that the word *curfew* means a certain time when children, and occasionally adults as well, must be off the streets. But you probably didn't know that *curfew* comes from an old French word, *covrefeu,* meaning "cover fire." Since in wartime a burning fire could be a signal to the enemy, *curfew* in the Middle Ages referred to a time in the evening when people were supposed to cover fires, put out lights, and retire. Note how the ancient meaning of the word relates to the modern meaning and how the word has changed as time has passed.

Use the Dictionary

Most dictionaries include information about the origins and histories of words. Whenever you find yourself looking up the meaning of a word, check its etymology too. For example, look at the etymology for the word *chum.*

> *chum* (chum) n. [17th-c. slang; prob. <*chamber* in *chamber mate*] [Colloq.] a close friend

You would decipher the abbreviations in this etymology as follows: "Seventeenth century slang, probably coming from a clipped form of *chamber mate,* which meant *roommate.*"

158

Greek and Latin Roots Many present-day English words come from the following Greek and Latin words:

gramma—Greek word meaning "something written"
kyklos—Greek word meaning "a circle"
medius—Latin word meaning "middle" or "half"
norma—Latin word meaning "a rule"
pellere—Latin word meaning "to drive"
quaerere—Latin word meaning "to seek" or "to ask"
servare—Latin word meaning "to keep" or "to hold"

Choose the Greek or Latin word to which each of the following words is related.

1. medieval _____

2. request _____

3. abnormal _____

4. conserve _____

5. cycle _____

6. telegram _____

7. mediate _____

8. query _____

9. reservation _____

10. expel _____

11. inquiry _____

12. program _____

13. medium _____

14. norm _____

15. inquisitive _____

16. grammar _____

17. diagram _____

18. repellent _____

19. question _____

20. mediocre _____

21. quest _____

22. intermediate _____

23. compel _____

24. preserve _____

25. encyclopedia _____

26. bicycle _____

27. enormous _____

28. propeller _____

29. cyclical _____

30. observance _____

Number correct _____ (total 30)

Number correct in Vocab Lab _____ (total 45)

UNIT 13

Part A   *Target Words and Their Meanings*

1. ample (am′ p'l) adj.
2. anonymity (an′ ə nim′ ə tē) n.
3. consult (kən sult′) v.
4. contrary (kän′ trer ē) adj.
5. definite (def′ ə nit) adj.
6. dismal (diz′ m'l) adj.
7. duly (do͞o′ lē, dyo͞o′-) adv.
8. engineer (en′ jə nir′) n., v.
9. focus (fō′ kəs) v., n.
10. geologist (jē äl′ ə jist) n.
11. graduate (graj′ oo wit) n. (graj′ oo wāt′) v.
12. international (in′ ter nash′ ən 'l) adj.
13. ordain (ôr dān′) v.
14. previous (prē′ vē əs) adj.
15. purposefully (pur′ pəs fəl ē) adv.
16. systematically (sis′ tə mat′ i k'l ē, -klē) adv.
17. terrain (tə rān′, ter′ ān) n.
18. uncommonly (un käm′ ən lē) adv.
19. unheralded (un her′ əld id) adj.
20. unmindful (un mīnd′ f'l) adj.

Inferring Meaning from Context

For each sentence write the letter of the word or phrase that is closest in meaning to the word or words in italics. Use context clues to help you choose the correct answer. (For information about how context helps you understand vocabulary, see pages 1–6.)

_____ 1. With four sandwiches per person, we had *ample* food for the party.

a. scanty   b. quality   c. plentiful   d. fanciful

_____ 2. The real name of the author of the best-selling novel remains unknown. The writer seems to prefer *anonymity*.

a. namelessness   b. fame   c. credit   d. attention

_____ 3. If you are sick, you should *consult* a doctor about what to do.

a. talk to   b. seek payment from   c. pay   d. leave word with

_____ 4. Water running uphill is *contrary to* the laws of gravity.

a. opposite to   b. equal to   c. vital to   d. suitable for

_____ 5. The river gives a *definite* boundary to the desert. Sand and cactuses are on this side, while tall grass and trees are on the other side .

a. ferocious   b. impossible   c. vague   d. clear and unmistakable

_____ 6. The drizzle and dark clouds made the day seem quite *dismal*.
a. short   b. hopeful   c. miserable   d. soothing

_____ 7. After winning the election for state senator, Mr. Sentora was *duly* sworn into office by the standard legal process.
a. illegally   b. rightfully   c. unknowingly   d. specially

_____ 8. Mr. Dorset's job as *an engineer* involves designing automobile parts.
a. a practical scientist   b. a teacher   c. a business manager
d. a conductor

_____ 9. The room grew quiet as the students looked toward the teacher and *focused* their attention on her comments about the test.
a. divided   b. suspended   c. relaxed   d. concentrated

_____ 10. Diane enjoys studying rocks. She hopes to be *a geologist* one day.
a. an artist   b. an earth scientist   c. a doctor
d. a criminal lawyer

_____ 11. Miguel is *a graduate* of Thompson Junior High School. He now attends Kennedy High School.
a. a member   b. a person who is taking the courses
c. an outstanding student   d. a person who has a degree

_____ 12. Because two of our teammates are from Mexico and one is from Canada, we could call ourselves *an international team*.
a. a team with players from different countries   b. a team with players from one country   c. an exciting team   d. a powerful team

_____ 13. Our newly *ordained* minister studied at a college in Minnesota before being named our pastor and coming here.
a. released   b. conducted   c. appointed   d. detected

_____ 14. Mitsuho cried with joy when she broke the *previous* record of four minutes and eighteen seconds in the race.
a. permanent   b. old   c. eventual   d. easy

_____ 15. Joel lifted his chin, straightened his shoulders, and walked *purposefully* toward the gym, determined to find the coach and explain what had happened.
a. in a lazy way   b. with a goal in mind   c. in a sneaky way
d. oddly

_____ 16. Kit searched the room *systematically*, looking for her wallet. She carefully checked all the most likely places first, then the next most likely, and then the unlikely.
a. in a planned way   b. in a quick way   c. in a casual way
d. in a cheerful way

161

_____ 17. Be careful not to stumble. The *terrain* out here is quite rough.

      a. interior b. weather c. race d. ground

_____ 18. We go to that restaurant frequently; the food is *uncommonly* good.

      a. never b. rarely c. remarkably d. slightly

_____ 19. One English king had the habit of surprising common people by dropping in on them in their homes, *unheralded*.

      a. as planned b. against better judgment c. unannounced
      d. hurriedly

_____ 20. When Joan stepped off the end of the dock while reading a book, it proved that she was *unmindful* of what she was doing.

      a. not aware b. sure c. afraid d. doubtful

Number correct _____ (total 20)

Part B   *Target Words in Reading and Literature*

You should now have a general idea of the meaning of each target word. Sharpen your understanding by studying how these words are used in the following selection.

What Is Water Witching?

Howard V. Chambers

Water witching is a method of locating underground water supplies by using a forked stick. Some people are convinced water witching really works. They point to countless cases of witches finding water when all other efforts failed. Other people don't believe in it and think it's only luck when a water witch finds water. What do you think?

The three men sat in the truck, **unmindful** of the hot Nevada sun. Their attention was **focused** on a fourth man, middle-aged, tall, slender, and rather well dressed for the desertlike **terrain** of the Carson River Valley. He walked **purposefully** over the sandy soil, **systematically** covering the area of a gentle rise. In his outstretched hands was a Y-shaped tree branch. 5

"I feel silly about this," one of the men in the truck said. "What he's doing is **contrary** to all my beliefs."

"Just you wait," one of the other two told him. "Then you won't feel so silly anymore." 10

At length, the man with the branch stopped his walking. The stick he carried by the two ends of the Y no longer pointed toward the sky. Instead, it was pointing to the ground with a **definite** bobbing motion.

162

"That's it," one of the men in the truck called. He [15] vaulted over the side and ran toward the man with the stick. Within minutes, a stake had been driven into the ground at the point [20] where the forked stick was pointing. Early the next morning, a drilling rig lowered its bit[1] into the earth at the same point and mechan- [25] ical digging began. Less than twenty feet down, the drill struck something the man who said he felt silly had been seeking for months: water.

It had been an **uncommonly** dry summer, even for that part of [30] Nevada. One well had gone dry, and livestock were thirsty. **Previous** attempts at well drilling had failed. Government **geologists** and soil **engineers** had gone over the area with maps, testing equipment, and sounding devices. The best they could accomplish for the rancher was a **dismal** series of dry holes. All the rancher had to show for his faith in men of [35] science was a hefty drilling bill and a thirsty herd.

He had felt silly because he had been pushed by desperation into listening to some of his neighbors who suggested he try a water witch: the man with the forked stick.

After the well was completed and **ample** water flowed forth, the [40] rancher smiled nervously as he paid the water witch his twenty-five-dollar fee. "It seems so crazy to be doing this," he said. Perhaps part of the craziness came because the rancher was a university **graduate** and a teacher of science at a nearby high school. However, even odder was the water witch's request for **anonymity.** "I don't mind your telling people you [45]

---

[1] bit: the cutting part of a drill

163

had a well dowsed,"[2] the water witch had said, "but I'll be grateful to you if you don't mention my name in any way that gets into print. I don't think my boss would like it."

The water witch said this with a good-natured grin; his "boss" was a bishop of an **international** Christian religion, and the water witch himself was, among other things, a university graduate and **duly ordained** minister, licensed to practice in the state of Nevada. 50

His dowsing activities were strictly unlicensed, and **unheralded.** Although most of his customers were local ranchers or farmers, there had been some large businesses involved, too. And nearly ninety percent of these customers had gone first to governmental agencies or to specialists in the field of soil geology. They are all firm believers in water witching now, because they have seen it work. The other customers believed in water witching all along and count themselves as money and water to the good for not having **consulted** geologists first. 55

60

---

[2] doused: searched for water through the use of a Y-shaped stick called a divining rod

Refining Your Understanding

For each of the following items, consider how the target word is used in the passage. Write the letter of the word or phrase that best completes each sentence.

_____ 1. The author describes the men in the truck as being *"unmindful* of the hot Nevada sun" (line 1) to indicate that they   a. didn't know the sun was hot   b. were not paying much attention to the heat   c. were protected from the sun.

_____ 2. The author describes the water witch as walking *purposefully* over the ground (line 4) to show that he seemed to know   a. what he was doing   b. where the water would be   c. that someone was watching.

_____ 3. The summer is described as *uncommonly* dry (line 30) to indicate that there had been   a. the usual amount of rain   b. much less rain than usual   c. slightly less rain than usual.

_____ 4. The early attempts to drill for water are described as *dismal* holes (lines 34-35) to indicate that they   a. were unsuccessful efforts   b. made the rancher feel miserable   c. were made by miserable people.

_____ 5. The *anonymity* that the water witch desires (line 45) has to do with not having his name   a. known by anyone   b. known by other ranchers   c. come to his boss's attention.

Number correct _____ (total 5)

Part C   Ways To Make New Words Your Own

By now you are familiar with the target words and their meanings. This section presents activities that will help you make the words part of your permanent vocabulary.

Using Language and Thinking Skills

Sentence Completion Write the word from the list below that best completes the meaning of the sentence.

ample	contrary	engineer	graduate	previous
consult	dismal	geologist	international	systematically

_____ 1. The boating instructor wants us to _?_ with her about the weather before taking any of the sailboats out.

_____ 2. Sandra didn't think she'd do well on the test, but _?_ to her expectations, she got an A.

_____ 3. The _?_ spent weeks hiking in the nearby hills as she studied the rocks and structure of the land.

_____ 4. Our town's _?_ fair included displays and folk art from all over the world.

_____ 5. I always get up at least an hour before I have to leave for school so I will have _?_ time to eat breakfast.

_____ 6. The police _?_ searched for the thief in every building within four blocks of the crime scene.

_____ 7. Because he will soon be a _?_ of the state university, my brother is beginning to look for a job that requires the training he received during his education.

_____ 8. The _?_ news about the economy made us worry about being able to make a decent living.

_____ 9. Megan earned a perfect score on all of the _?_ tests, but she doesn't think she will do so well on this next one.

_____ 10. Without the skills of a talented _?_, we will never be able to build a safe bridge over the river.

Number correct _____ (total 10)

Finding the Unrelated Word Write the letter of the word that is not related in meaning to the other words in the set.

_____ 1. a. ignore b. consult c. discuss d. check

_____ 2. a. ground b. stamina c. land d. terrain

_____ 3. a. unusually b. regularly c. uncommonly d. rarely

_____ 4. a. popularity b. reputation c. anonymity d. fame

_____ 5. a. watchful b. unmindful c. aware d. alert

Number correct _____ (total 5)

Practicing for Standardized Tests

Synonyms Write the letter of the word that is closest in meaning to the capitalized word.

_____ 1. AMPLE: (A) placid (B) obvious (C) enough (D) impure (E) scanty

_____ 2. PREVIOUS: (A) earlier (B) prevalent (C) future (D) later (E) adverse

_____ 3. UNHERALDED: (A) unannounced (B) unfinished (C) excellent (D) uncommon (E) expected

_____ 4. ORDAIN: (A) forgive (B) prevail (C) resign (D) appoint (E) practice

_____ 5. DEFINITE: (A) effective (B) clear (C) vague (D) inexact (E) suitable

_____ 6. DULY: (A) properly (B) constantly (C) frequently (D) eventually (E) wrongly

_____ 7. CONTRARY: (A) undecided (B) together (C) effective (D) similar (E) opposite

_____ 8. DISMAL: (A) practical (B) decent (C) gloomy (D) cheery (E) endearing

_____ 9. FOCUS: (A) accommodate (B) govern (C) avail (D) concentrate (E) permeate

_____ 10. SYSTEMATICALLY: (A) objectively (B) orderly (C) vaguely (D) eventually (E) actually

Number correct _____ (total 10)

Spelling and Wordplay

Crossword Puzzle Read the clues and print the correct answer to each in the proper squares. There are a number of target words in this puzzle.

ACROSS

1. Recklessness caused by losing hope
6. Short for yonder
8. Standard distress signal
10. One who completes a course of study at a school
13. A coarse rug on which to wipe your feet
14. Plural present tense of *to be*
15. Slang for friend
16. A machine for grinding grain
17. The charge for riding on the bus
19. Abbr. England
21. Ground
22. That thing
23. Poor grades but not quite failing grades
24. To form into curd
26. To gash or wound
27. You and me
28. Slang for girl
29. State of being unknown

DOWN

1. Miserable
2. Adjective form of systematically
3. Abbr. post office
4. A scientist who plans and builds things
5. Abbr. American Medical Association
7. Person who studies the earth's crust, rocks, and fossils
9. A boat paddle
11. Precise
12. More than enough
18. To come back
20. To concentrate attention on
23. Rightfully or properly
25. Nickname for Donald
26. Feline
28. Another name for an American soldier

Word's Worth: dismal

Do you have bad days? For many people, a bad day is Friday the 13th. For some, any Monday is a bad day. That is what *dismal*, in its Latin roots, means: *dies*, "day," and *mal*, "bad." Bad days were taken quite seriously in the Middle Ages. On the calendar two days out of a month were sometimes marked unlucky. However the common meaning of dismal has changed; today we are more likely to think of dismal as "dreary" or "causing misery."

Part D Related Words

The words below are closely related to the target words. Use your knowledge of the target words and of word parts to determine the meanings of these words. (For information about word parts analysis, see pages 7–13.) Use your dictionary if necessary.

1. anonymous (ə năn′ ə məs) adj.
2. common (käm′ ən) adj.
3. consultant (kən sul′ t'nt) n.
4. consultation (kän′ s'l tā′ shən) n.
5. contrariness (kän′ trer ē nes, -nis) n.
6. definitely (def′ ə nit lē) adv.
7. engine (en′ jən) n.
8. engineering (en′ jə nir′ iŋ) n.
9. focal (fō′ k'l) adj.
10. geology (jē äl′ ə jē) n.
11. gradual (graj′ oo wəl) adj.
12. graduation (graj′ oo wā′ shən) n.
13. herald (her′ əld) n.
14. mindful (mīnd′ f'l) adj.
15. national (nash′ ə n'l) adj.
16. ordination (ôr′ d'n ā shən) n.
17. purposeful (pʉr′ pəs fəl) adj.
18. system (sis′ təm) n.

Understanding Related Words

Close Relatives Use one of these pairs of closely related words in each sentence below. Determine which word belongs in each blank. Use a dictionary to find the meaning of any word you do not know.

anonymity   consult   graduates   ordained   system
anonymous   consultants   graduation   ordination   systematically

1. During his work my father must often _____ with engineers, geologists, and other _____ who give him advice on how to do a certain job.

2. My entire family was invited to the _____ to watch my cousin Lee be _____ as a minister.

3. The reporter wanted to remain _____ in order to learn about the secret organization and he went to great lengths to protect his

_____.

4. The _____ will be called up individually to receive their diplomas during the _____.

5. Knowing there had to be a better _____ for studying, Katherine _____ reviewed her upcoming assignments and usual study habits.

Number correct _____ (total 10)

Using Context to Define Words Define each italicized word by examining its context, or how it is used in the sentence. Then check your definitions with those in the dictionary.

1. When beginning an exercise program, it is best to plan for *gradual* increases in exercise, adding a few minutes each day.

   _____

2. Brian made a *purposeful* attempt to lose weight by exercising an hour every day and eating less fat.

   _____

3. Because Leslie and I have so many *common* interests, such as bicycling, basketball, and popular music, we're almost always together.

   _____

4. Nobody knew who had written the letter; it was signed *"Anonymous."*

   _____

5. Because Sheila has an important test tomorrow, she *definitely* wants to go to sleep early tonight.

   _____

6. The *national* anthem of the United States is sung at the beginning of Major League baseball games.

   _____

7. The brightly colored flag served as the *focal* point of the painting.

   _____

8. Aunt Millie always cautioned us to be *mindful* of our manners and not to carelessly forget to be polite.

   _____

9. Jason's *contrariness* is getting out of hand; he disagrees with everything anyone says.

   _____

10. During her *consultation* with the homeowners, Mrs. Breton advised them to plant evergreen trees in back and flowering plants along the walk.

   _____

Number correct _____ (total 10)

Turn to **The Prefix *com-*** on page 222 of the **Spelling Handbook.** Read the rule and complete the exercise provided.

Analyzing Word Parts

The Latin Root *grad* The target word *graduate* comes from the Latin root *grad,* which means "a step" or "a degree." The related words *gradual* and *graduation* contain this root along with the words *grade* and *gradation.* Write the word from the list below that best completes the meaning of the sentences. Use your dictionary to check your work.

gradations   grade   gradual   graduate   graduation

_____ 1. Although the fabric was completely blue, ? of the color made it paler in some areas and darker in others.

_____ 2. We may not realize that spring is almost here because its approach is so ? .

_____ 3. Many students celebrate the day of their ? from high school with a special party.

_____ 4. The house, which is at the top of a steep ? , is difficult to reach when the road is icy.

_____ 5. A ? of a trade school has an easier time finding a job in his or her field than one who has no practical education.

Number correct _____ (total 5)

The Greek Root *geo* The target word *geologist* comes from two Greek words: *geo,* which means "earth," and *logy,* which means "word" or "speech." Literally, a geologist is someone who speaks about the earth. The root *geo* is also found in the related word *geology.* Using your knowledge of this root and other word parts, match each of the words below with the correct definition. Use your dictionary to check your work.

geocentric   geode   geography   geologist   geology

_____ 1. the study of the earth and how people use it

_____ 2. someone who studies the rocks, history, and structure of the earth

_____ 3. a round, hollow rock with crystals on the inside

_____ 4. having the earth at the center

_____ 5. the study of the history of how the earth was formed and its structure and rocks

Number correct _____ (total 5)

Number correct in unit _____ (total 80)

170

The Last Word

Writing

Choose one item from each of the three columns below. Then write a story based on these three items. Use your imagination.

Characters
- a *dismal geologist*
- an *ordained* minister
- a brilliant *engineer*
- an *anonymous* mechanic
- a *mindful* nurse
- a lazy *consultant*

Incidents
- *consulting* with the police
- *purposefully* avoiding one's friends
- *focusing* on a report
- hiking over rough *terrain*
- attending a *graduation*
- *graduating* with honors

Conditions
- with *ample* food and clothing
- keeping one's *anonymity*
- during the *previous* day
- in a *gradual* manner
- on the *national* news
- in an *unheralded* way

Speaking

Write a brief *anonymous* story. Your teacher should then collect the stories and pass them out randomly. Each student should read one of the stories aloud, while the class tries to guess the identity of the anonymous author.

Group Discussion

The earth's *terrain* has many different and interesting features, such as the Grand Canyon, Mississippi River, Great Plains, Everglades, and Great Salt Lake. Humans have often changed the terrain of an area. They have drained swamps so the land can be farmed. They've built dams to create huge lakes. Other smaller changes also affect the terrain, such as building roads, creating golf courses, and digging ponds. As a class, discuss some of the changes to the earth's terrain that you are familiar with. Consider these questions during your discussion: Are these changes always good? How much should people try to change the land? Who should decide whether a change is made to the land: the land's owner, the government, or the residents of the community or of the country?

UNIT 14

Part A Target Words and Their Meanings

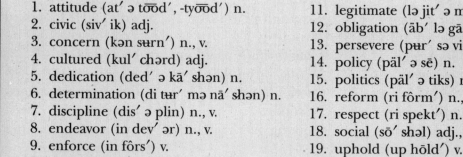

1. attitude (at′ ə tōōd′, -tyōōd′) n.
2. civic (siv′ ik) adj.
3. concern (kən surn′) n., v.
4. cultured (kul′ chərd) adj.
5. dedication (ded′ ə kā′ shən) n.
6. determination (di tur′ mə nā′ shən) n.
7. discipline (dis′ ə plin) n., v.
8. endeavor (in dev′ ər) n., v.
9. enforce (in fôrs′) v.
10. ignite (ig nīt′) v.

11. legitimate (lə jit′ ə mit) adj.
12. obligation (äb′ lə gā′ shən) n.
13. persevere (pur′ sə vir′) v.
14. policy (päl′ ə sē) n.
15. politics (päl′ ə tiks) n. pl.
16. reform (ri fôrm′) n., v.
17. respect (ri spekt′) n., v.
18. social (sō′ shəl) adj., n.
19. uphold (up hōld′) v.
20. versus (vur′ səs) prep.

Inferring Meaning from Context

For each sentence write the letter of the word or phrase that is closest in meaning to the word or words in italics. Use context clues to help you choose the correct answer. (For information about how context helps you understand vocabulary, see pages 1–6.)

_____ 1. Lee's success in school is due in part to his positive *attitude*. He approaches each task with the belief that he will do well.

 a. grades b. way of thinking c. teacher d. schedule

_____ 2. *Civic* responsibilities keep Alderwoman Burger busy day and night. As an elected official, she is always trying to solve problems that affect the citizens of her town.

 a. Technical b. Family and home c. Community d. Scientific

_____ 3. Because he loves animals, Julio has a *concern for* the decent treatment of stray dogs and cats.

 a. lack of feeling for b. complete inattention to
 c. disagreement with d. real interest in

_____ 4. Unlike Mr. Chase, who had a kind of rude, rough way of putting things, Ms. Upton spoke in a sophisticated, *cultured* way that impressed us.

 a. rude b. educated c. obvious d. abrupt

172

_____ 5. Cedric regularly volunteers at the shelter, and he frequently writes letters about the problem of homelessness to members of Congress. I admire his *dedication to* this cause.

a. devotion to   b. invitation to   c. formation of   d. hesitation about

_____ 6. In her physical therapy sessions, Rachel's *determination* is obvious. She works extremely hard to build strength in her injured leg.

a. fear   b. curiosity   c. purposefulness   d. sensitivity

_____ 7. When it comes to his music, Tom has a lot of *discipline*. Even though he sometimes wants to do other things, he spends most of his free time practicing the drums.

a. talent   b. betrayal   c. tricks   d. self-control

_____ 8. From mastering Spanish conversation to hiking the Appalachian Trail, Laura has been successful in most of *her endeavors*.

a. her friendships   b. the sports she has played   c. the things she has tried   d. the tests she has taken

_____ 9. Ms. Washington will *enforce* her rule about radios in school by patrolling the halls and taking any radios she finds to the office.

a. alter   b. suspend   c. make sure everyone obeys   d. ignore

_____ 10. When the fire was out, the firefighters tried to figure out what had *ignited* it, but they could not find the cause.

a. withstood   b. smothered   c. started   d. resisted

_____ 11. Will's teacher said that she didn't consider "I couldn't think of a good topic" to be a *legitimate* excuse for not doing the assignment but that "I was in the hospital" was.

a. reasonable   b. silly   c. strange   d. hopeless

_____ 12. A pet owner has many joys, but there are also *obligations,* such as providing the pet with food, water, shelter, and affection.

a. intentions   b. duties   c. conditions   d. choices

_____ 13. If you *persevere,* I believe you will eventually figure out how to solve the problem.

a. hesitate   b. keep trying   c. give up   d. guess

_____ 14. The town committee met to determine its *policy* on recycling, which will govern the way that garbage is collected and reused.

a. campaign   b. desire   c. safeguard   d. plan

_____ 15. Michael loves *politics;* in fact, he wants to become a senator or representative someday.

a. journalism   b. government affairs   c. military matters d. medical affairs

_____ 16. Mr. Cunningham does not think our tax system is as fair and efficient as it could be. He believes that the *reform* of tax laws is necessary.

a. improvement   b. circulation   c. withdrawal   d. end

_____ 17. Because Georgette has a great deal of *respect* for her Aunt Rita, she frequently asks her aunt for advice.

a. sympathy   b. admiration   c. dislike   d. bitterness

_____ 18. Our report must be about *a social issue,* such as poverty or crime. Can you think of any other issues that affect everyone?

a. an issue for people in general   b. an issue for lawyers
c. an easy problem   d. a matter of friendship

_____ 19. Even after others criticized him for it, the governor still *upheld* his original position on the housing problem.

a. revealed   b. denied   c. rejected   d. supported

_____ 20. Before the big game, we made a banner that said "The Victorious Vikings *versus* the Hawks. Goodbye, Hawks!"

a. against   b. for   c. at   d. from

Number correct _____   (total 20)

Part B   *Target Words in Reading and Literature*

You should now have a general idea of the meaning of each target word. Sharpen your understanding by studying how these words are used in the following selection.

A Winner

Howard Peet

Each of us should aspire to do and be the best we can. Congress-woman Barbara Jordan is an excellent example of someone who did just that.

Barbara Jordan's winning **attitude** has brought her success in her many **endeavors.** President Lyndon B. Johnson once said of Jordan, "She proved that black is beautiful before we knew what it meant." He described her as "the epitome[1] of the new **politics.**" Over the years Jordan's **dedication** to **social reform** has gained her the **respect** of not only government officials but also that of the American public.

[1] epitome: representative; model

The fact that Jordan was born in Houston, Texas, on February 21, 1936, to a poor, loving family helps explain her **legitimate concern** for social reform. However, it took **discipline** for Jordan to put her concern into action, a self-discipline learned from her father. He **ignited** her desire to seek out the best in herself. Jordan has said that her father, a Baptist minister, had three great loves—his family, his faith, and his language. It was from him that she learned the **cultured** way of speaking that has become her trademark.

Jordan's drive to achieve began to take shape early in her life. Hearing Edith Sampson, an African-American attorney, speak at Jordan's high school Career Day helped Jordan decide to become a lawyer. She graduated in 1956 from Texas Southern University, an all-black institution of higher learning. Pursuing her dream of becoming a lawyer, Jordan earned her LL.B.[2] degree at Boston University in 1959.

Eventually Jordan turned her attention toward government service. She showed her **determination**—and competitive spirit—by running for a seat in the Texas House of Representatives in 1962. She lost. She lost again in 1964. But Jordan **persevered,** and in 1966 she finally won a seat in the Texas Senate.

In the state senate, Jordan **upheld** her belief in the need for social reform. She saw to it that laws were passed to help "the really poor people—laundry workers, domestic [and] farm workers." She also used her influence to see that these laws were **enforced.** As a result of her efforts, she was named the outstanding new senator during her first year in office.

After several years in state government, Jordan directed her efforts toward the federal government. In 1972, it was Jordan **versus** Merritt for the United States Congress. Jordan won by more than 85,000 votes.

---

[2] LL.B.: Bachelor of Laws

Barbara Jordan became the first African-American woman from a Southern state to serve in the United States Congress.

175

Until her retirement from Congress at the end of 1978, her **policy** remained a simple one. She stated what she felt to be her **civic obligation** by saying, "I am here simply because all those people in the 18th District of Texas cannot get on planes and buses and come to Washington to speak for themselves. They have elected me as their spokesperson, nothing else, and my only job is to speak for them. That is the job of every one of the people's representatives." 40

Barbara Jordan is respected by Republicans and Democrats alike. However, what probably makes her a winner is that she respects herself. Following a glowing introduction from President Johnson's widow at the National Women's Conference in Houston in 1977, Jordan said, "Thank you, all of you, and thank you, Lady Bird Johnson, for an introduction of 45 which I am worthy."

Jordan currently holds The Lyndon B. Johnson Public Service Professorship at the L.B.J. School of Public Affairs, the University of Texas at Austin.

Refining Your Understanding

For each of the following items, consider how the target word is used in the passage. Write the letter of the word or phrase that best completes the sentence.

_____ 1. By using the word *social* (line 5), the author suggests that Jordan is interested in actions that involve   a. society as a whole   b. relaxation and recreation   c. government control.

_____ 2. The word *ignited,* as it is used in line 10, means   a. inspired   b. discouraged   c. stood in the way of.

_____ 3. By describing Jordan's *legitimate* concern (line 8), the author suggests that this concern is   a. legal   b. normal   c. reasonable under the circumstances.

_____ 4. An article describing Jordan's *policy* (line 34) would tell about   a. her supporters   b. the ideas that guide her actions   c. her success.

_____ 5. Jordan's *obligation* (lines 35–36) to the people of the 18th District included   a. thanking them   b. representing them   c. getting elected by them.

Number correct _____ (total 5)

Part C   *Ways to Make New Words Your Own*

By now you are familiar with the target words and their meanings. This section presents activities that will help you make the words part of your permanent vocabulary.

Using Language and Thinking Skills

True–False   Decide whether each statement is true (**T**) or false (**F**).

_____   1. A person who loves to read may have a *concern* about the library's closing down for three months while repairs are made.

_____   2. Throwing water on a fire will make it *ignite*.

_____   3. Ignoring a person is most often considered a sign of *respect*.

_____   4. Someone who likes *politics* would probably enjoy listening to speeches by people running for election.

_____   5. The town council's refusal to build more homes for the poor is a good example of *reform*.

_____   6. If Ms. Allen and Mr. Simon form a business partnership, they should put "Allen *versus* Simon" on their business cards.

_____   7. Grocery shopping for your family is a good example of a *civic* responsibility.

_____   8. Mountain climbers usually have a great deal of *determination*.

_____   9. A student arriving late to class is *enforcing* the rule against tardiness.

_____ 10. A group's statement about its *policy* would probably tell what its purpose and practices are.

Number correct _____ (total 10)

Matching Examples   Write the word from the list below that is most clearly related to the situation described in each sentence.

attitude   discipline   obligation   reform   versus

_____   1. After years of ignoring the needs of children with special problems, the school district finally set up classes that would help them learn.

_____   2. As Maria entered the testing room, she told herself that she would do well and that the test would be an opportunity to display her knowledge.

_____   3. Jim stayed on his diet even though he was often tempted by delicious but fattening foods.

_____ 4. Charles Allen sued Marilyn Hewitt for the damage done to his roof when her tree fell on it. The court battle took three days.

_____ 5. Mary Jo's mother told her that, even though she didn't want to, Mary Jo had to go to her cousin's party, because her cousin had done so many nice things for her.

Number correct _____ (total 5)

Practicing for Standardized Tests

Synonyms Write the letter of the word that is closest in meaning to the capitalized word.

____ 1. OBLIGATION: (A) option (B) objective (C) characteristic (D) development (E) responsibility

____ 2. ATTITUDE: (A) system (B) fate (C) outlook (D) advantage (E) logic

____ 3. VERSUS: (A) against (B) with (C) for (D) on (E) in

____ 4. UPHOLD (A) destroy (B) support (C) return (D) demolish (E) govern

____ 5. ENDEAVOR: (A) attempt (B) failure (C) habit (D) success (E) intention

Number correct _____ (total 5)

Antonyms Write the letter of the word that is most nearly *opposite* in meaning to the capitalized word.

____ 1. CULTURED: (A) crude (B) polite (C) refined (D) respectful (E) proud

____ 2. PERSEVERE: (A) stop (B) continue (C) change (D) ignore (E) relax

____ 3. IGNITE: (A) oust (B) smolder (C) douse (D) light (E) petrify

____ 4. LEGITIMATE: (A) civic (B) unreasonable (C) unhappy (D) practical (E) reliable

____ 5. CONCERN: (A) care (B) result (C) hope (D) disinterest (E) guarantee

Number correct _____ (total 5)

Spelling and Wordplay

Word Maze Find and circle each target word in this maze.

```
A C R D M N R E F O R M P Q Z
O D I S C I P L I N E M F E T
L E C I M A E H N D R T P O U
A T T I T U D E G F E P O B V
C E T G G V E R S U S O L L L
O R S E R N B I C P P L I I E
N M E I N T I J K H E I C G G
C I F N S F M T L O C T Y A I
E N D E A V O R E L T I G T T
R A O M L A C R B D R C H I I
N T S O C I A L C K S S T O M
T I C I V I C Q P E M N R N A
C O A B D E D I C A T I O N T
D N C U L T U R E D D I O T E
Y N P E R S E V E R E A C Y Y
```

attitude
civic
concern
cultured
dedication
determination
discipline
endeavor
enforce
ignite
legitimate
obligation
persevere
policy
politics
reform
respect
social
uphold
versus

Word's Worth: civic

Saving someone's life is one of the noblest things a person can do. In ancient Rome the *corona civica* was a crown bestowed upon a soldier who saved a citizen's life. Our word *civic* comes from the Latin *civis,* meaning "citizen." As you might guess, our word *city* also comes from *civis.* In a real sense, civic business is about citizens.

Part D   Related Words

The words below are closely related to the target words. Use your knowledge of the target words and of word parts to determine the meaning of these words. (For information about word parts analysis, see pages 7–13.) Use your dictionary if necessary.

1. civil (siv′′l) adj.
2. civilian (sə vil′ yən) n., adj.
3. civilize (siv′ ə līz′) v.
4. conform (kən fôrm′) v.
5. culture (kul′ chər) n., v.
6. deform (dē fôrm′) v.
7. enforcement (in fôrs′ mənt) n.
8. ignition (ig nish′ ən) n.
9. inform (in fôrm′) v.
10. obligate (äb′ lə gāt′) v.
11. political (pə lit′ i k'l) adj.
12. respectable (ri spek′ tə b'l) adj.
13. respectful (ri spekt′ fəl) adj.
14. socialize (sō′ shə līz′) v.
15. society (sə si′ ə tē) n.

Understanding Related Words

Using Context to Define Words Define each italicized word by examining its context, or how it is used in the sentence. Then check your definitions against those in the dictionary.

1. Because he wants to become a police officer, Phil will study law *enforcement* after high school.

_____

2. Tasting the free sample did not *obligate* us to buy the new brand of crackers, but we bought some because we liked them.

_____

3. Our drama teacher said our presentation was *respectable* but not excellent.

_____

4. Mom and Dad both enjoy parties because they like to *socialize*.

_____

5. You must *inform* Lillian of your decision. If she doesn't know, she will worry.

_____

6. Phoebe is writing an extra-credit report on Japanese *culture*. She will include information about Japanese customs, art, and religion.

_____

7. After Ben was discharged from the army, he said he was happy to be a *civilian* again.

_____

8. *Society* will not tolerate light punishments for people found guilty of serious crimes. People expect these criminals to receive stiff punishments.

_____

9. Ms. Vasquez said that gossiping during the guest speaker's lecture was not a *respectful* way for us to behave.

_____

10. In order to start the car, you first must put the key in the *ignition*.

_____

Number correct _____ (total 10)

Analyzing Word Parts

The Latin Root *form* This root comes from the Latin word *forma,* meaning "shape." The target word *reform* and the related words *conform, deform,* and *inform* all contain this root. Use your dictionary to learn the meanings of the words listed below. Then write the word from the list that best completes the meaning of each sentence.

conform   deformed   inform   transform

_____   1. Did anyone _?_ Li of the change in the schedule? If not, please make sure someone calls her.

_____   2. Drivers must _?_ to the speed limit restrictions.

_____   3. Picking up the clay pot before it was dry _?_ the shape of it.

_____   4. Tutoring sessions and a more positive attitude will help to _?_ Ken into a better student.

_____   5. If everyone else is wearing black this year, you can bet I'll wear purple. I hate the idea that everyone has to _?_.

Number correct _____ (total 5)

Number correct in unit _____ (total 65)

Turn to **The Letter** *c* on page 236 of the **Spelling Handbook.** Read the rule and complete the exercises provided.

The Last Word

Writing

Think of a time when you tried a difficult task or activity, and write a short description of the *endeavor*. Were you successful? What made the activity difficult? How did you go about completing the task?

Speaking

What change or *reform* would you like to see in your school or community? Choose a reform that you think is necessary and important. Prepare a short talk about the reform for your class. Explain the reform, how it could be carried out, and why you think it is important.

Group Discussion

What do you know about *politics* in your community? In a group, discuss the following questions: What are some important political issues that affect life in your neighborhood, city, or town? What political leaders seem to be most interested in issues that you, as a group, feel need attention? Should students become involved in politics? How could they do so?

UNIT 15

Part A Target Words and Their Meanings

1. apparel (ə per′ əl, -par′-) n.
2. bewitch (bi wich′) v.
3. compel (kəm pel′) v.
4. competitor (kəm pet′ ə tər) n.
5. considerable (kən sid′ ər ə b'l) adj.
6. contradict (kän′ trə dikt′) v.
7. decrease (di krēs′, dē′ krēs) v., n.
8. haven (hā′ vən) n.
9. insure (in shoor′) v.
10. isolate (ī′ sə lāt) v.
11. loathe (lōth) v.
12. lodge (läj) v., n.
13. mobile (mō′ b'l, -bīl) adj. (mō′ bēl) n.
14. proclaim (prō klām′, prə) v.
15. resent (ri zent′) v.
16. skirmish (skʉr′ mish) n.
17. toxic (täk′ sik) adj.
18. transmit (trans mit′) v.
19. veteran (vet′ ər ən, vet′ rən) n., adj.
20. violate (vī′ ə lāt′) v.

Inferring Meaning from Context

For each sentence write the letter of the word or phrase that is closest in meaning to the word or words in italics. Use context clues to help you choose the correct answer. (For information about how context helps you understand vocabulary, see pages 1–6.)

_____ 1. Members of the soccer team have to buy their own shirts, shorts, socks, and other *apparel*.

     a. clubs b. clothing c. accommodations d. awards

_____ 2. In the fairy tale the old hag was able to *bewitch* small children, making them believe she was a sweet young girl while she led them into the deep woods.

     a. put a spell over b. make fun of c. safeguard d. scold

_____ 3. We couldn't see through the heavy rain and so were *compelled* to stop the car and wait for the weather to clear.

     a. frightened b. helped c. forced d. unwilling

_____ 4. Diane and I are always trying to beat each other in sports. She has always been my greatest *competitor*.

     a. rival b. partner c. handicap d. coach

_____ 5. A robin has *a considerable* number of feathers—about three thousand.

     a. a constant b. a small c. an unknown d. a large

_____ 6. When Harry suddenly became very angry, he *contradicted* his previous statement that he never lost his temper.

a. reinforced   b. revealed   c. went against   d. continued

_____ 7. As Yolanda began to feel better, she started to *decrease* her dosage of medicine by taking one less pill each day.

a. add to   b. give up   c. overlook   d. lessen

_____ 8. The warm cabin was a welcome *haven* from the wet, snowy weather.

a. place of shelter   b. challenge   c. fantasy   d. hazard

_____ 9. The coach is trying to *insure* that she will have a winning team by making her players practice every day.

a. understand   b. predict   c. guarantee   d. find

_____ 10. The *isolated* patient was kept away from other people so her illness would not spread.

a. elderly   b. separated   c. miraculous   d. vigorous

_____ 11. Although Carla liked most vegetables, she *loathed* lima beans and refused to eat them.

a. hated   b. preferred   c. sniffed   d. liked

_____ 12. Squirrels usually *lodge* in nests made of twigs, but this one lived in the attic of a house.

a. have a home   b. grow   c. congregate   d. quarrel

_____ 13. Although the piano has wheels on its legs, no one would think of it as a very *mobile* instrument.

a. comfortable   b. movable   c. musical   d. heavy

_____ 14. Within an hour after the closing of the polls, the candidate for mayor *proclaimed* his victory with a joyful speech. His opponent thought the announcement was made too early.

a. gave up   b. forgot   c. demonstrated   d. declared

_____ 15. Everyone at school *resented* the Gopher football team. Not only did they beat our team regularly, but they made fun of our school.

a. admired   b. ignored   c. had bitter feelings toward
d. learned strategies from

_____ 16. The soldiers had a brief *skirmish* with an enemy patrol. They were lucky no one was hurt in the fight.

a. parade   b. battle   c. retreat   d. race

_____ 17. The scientist discovered that the fish were dying because *toxic* waste had been dumped in the river. The fish had little chance to survive in the deadly mixture.

a. transformed   b. useless   c. poisonous   d. floral

_____ 18. Although Walt could not speak the language, he could still _transmit_ his questions by using sign language and drawing pictures.

a. conceal   b. pass along   c. transform   d. understand

_____ 19. Because she has been an actress for over thirty years, Ms. Bloom is considered _a veteran_ of the Broadway stage.

a. an unknown member   b. a forgotten person   c. a first time performer   d. an experienced performer

_____ 20. The man believed that his rights as a citizen had been _violated_ when he was arrested but not told what he had done wrong.

a. transferred   b. guaranteed   c. disrespected   d. protected

Number correct _____ (total 20)

Part B   Target Words in Reading and Literature

You should now have a general idea of the meaning of each target word. Sharpen your understanding by studying how these words are used in the following selection.

Suppose a Rattlesnake Slithers into Your Life?

James Coomber

What would you do if you were suddenly face-to-face with a rattlesnake? This selection offers some helpful hints.

Many people **loathe** rattlesnakes. Years ago people commonly believed that these and other snakes had the power to **bewitch** people. Some people become frenzied at the thought of even seeing a rattler. Even nature lovers are **compelled** to look out for these creatures. However, knowing a little about these snakes and taking a few sensible precautions will **decrease** your chances of being struck by any poisonous snake.   5

Rattlers range in size—from about two feet in length to over six feet. At the end of the rattler's body is a set of rings. These make up the rattle. When the snake is alarmed, the rattle vibrates, causing a warning noise   10
to be **transmitted** a **considerable** distance.

Rattlers can be found in nearly all states and in some Canadian provinces. However, most rattlers prefer to live in arid places, such as the western United States and Mexico. Rocky, **isolated** areas are favorite places for rattlers to **lodge.** They may be seen mornings and evenings   15
sunning on rocky ledges. In the heat of mid-day they seek out a **haven** from the sun under rocks or in holes.

The rattlesnake is in many ways a friend to humans. Although this statement **contradicts** common opinion, the rattler is a big help in controlling the rodent population. The **toxic** venom[1] released by a rattler's bite kills small animals. Rattlers are **competitors** with owls and hawks for rodents such as mice, rats, and gophers. Rodents are often the losers in a **skirmish** with a hungry rattlesnake.

How can you avoid a rattlesnake bite? A few suggestions from **veterans** of the outdoors may help. First, do not run through high grass in areas well suited to rattlesnakes. You might surprise a snake that is otherwise minding its own business. Walking slowly **insures** ample time for the snake to slither away or **proclaim** its presence.

Although these snakes are very **mobile,** they will not chase you. If you hear a rattle, back up slowly and walk away. Do not run! The snake may have a friend or relative in the area who would **resent** being stepped on as you dash away.

Second, consider your **apparel,** particularly footwear. Snake fangs have occasionally pierced thick Western boots. However, such footgear offers much more protection than ordinary shoes.

Finally, when climbing, look before you reach or step. Rattlers like to lie on rocky ledges. Even if you intended to grab a rock rather than a rattler, the surprised snake might not understand.

Far from seeking a fight with a human, rattlers only strike to protect themselves or out of fear. Unless you **violate** the rules, you're not likely to have a painful meeting with a rattler.

---

[1] venom: the poison carried by some snakes, insects, and other animals, which they use to kill prey and to protect themselves.

Refining Your Understanding

For each of the following items, consider how the target word is used in the passage. Write the letter of the word or phrase that best completes the sentence.

_____ 1. The author's use of *compelled* (line 4) indicates that he   a. is a veteran hiker   b. believes people in the out-of-doors must be on the lookout for poisonous snakes   c. might discourage people from enjoying the outdoors.

_____ 2. A noise that is "*transmitted* a *considerable* distance" (line 11) is probably   a. loud   b. terrifying   c. hardly noticeable.

_____ 3. An example of a place where people typically *lodge* (line 15) would be a   a. restaurant   b. yard   c. motel.

_____ 4. A synonym of *contradict* (line 19) is   a. helps   b. denies   c. asserts.

_____ 5. A *haven* (line 16) for a lost child would make the child feel   a. frightened   b. safe   c. alone.

Number correct _____ (total 5)

Part C   Ways to Make New Words Your Own

By now you are familiar with the target words and their meanings. This section presents activities that will help you make the words part of your permanent vocabulary.

Using Language and Thinking Skills

Finding Examples Write the letter of the situation that best shows the meaning of the boldfaced word.

_____ 1. **apparel**
a. Carlos's parents are shopping for a stove.
b. Brendan is sure the answer to the mystery is something obvious.
c. Ann is looking for a new dress to wear to her friend's wedding.

_____ 2. **competitor**
a. An older club member is Jan's constant rival at swim meets.
b. A concert pianist is entertaining his friends at a recital.
c. Melina is someone who gives in easily.

_____ 3. **haven**
a. The captain of the boat looks for a safe harbor during a storm.
b. The street becomes very busy during rush hour.
c. The fishermen live in a large port city on the New England coast.

_____ 4. **skirmish**

    a. Andrew feels faint and dizzy on even a short boat trip.

    b. Two hockey players have a brief fight.

    c. A stream swirls over rocks as it nears the river.

_____ 5. **toxic**

    a. A doctor checks a patient for symptoms of a disease.

    b. A new medicine fails to cure a disease.

    c. A chemical waste poisons fish in a river.

_____ 6. **transmit**

    a. You've left your notebook on the school bus.

    b. You've used a shortwave radio to talk with someone in England.

    c. You've enrolled your dog in obedience school.

_____ 7. **veteran**

    a. Ms. Ryna has been a saleswoman for many years.

    b. Mr. Sylvester has just joined the army.

    c. Ms. Pirandello is studying to become an animal doctor.

_____ 8. **loathe**

    a. Jake is mildly upset about losing his pen.

    b. Mitch is willing to forgive Bob and to forget the whole incident.

    c. Meredith is disgusted with people who treat their pets badly.

_____ 9. **mobile**

    a. The Egyptian pyramids are the graves of ancient rulers.

    b. The Stevens took their family car on a vacation.

    c. Brian is very sick and must remain in bed.

_____ 10. **compel**

    a. Mrs. Smith makes Sandy eat his breakfast every day.

    b. Mike asks his friend to loan him his football.

    c. Leslie helps pick up the trash after a picnic.

Number correct _____ (total 10)

Word's Worth: toxic

The word _toxic_ comes from the Greek word _toxikos,_ which means "having to do with arrows used in archery." What, you might wonder, do arrows have to do with poison? Arrows could be poisonous, of course, if they were dipped in poison—which is what this word refers to. Poison-dipped arrows have been used as weapons for many centuries. When the Greek word moved into Latin as _toxicum,_ that's exactly what it meant, "poison for arrows."

Practicing for Standardized Tests

Antonyms Write the letter of the word that is most nearly *opposite* in meaning to the capitalized word.

_____ 1. TRANSMIT: (A) propel (B) receive (C) require
(D) announce (E) forgive

_____ 2. CONSIDERABLE: (A) sizable (B) suitable (C) large
(D) legitimate (E) small

_____ 3. CONTRADICT: (A) avail (B) oppose (C) agree
(D) detect (E) dispose

_____ 4. DECREASE: (A) propel (B) demolish (C) render
(D) distribute (E) expand

_____ 5. TOXIC: (A) repulsive (B) tasteful (C) poisonous
(D) healthy (E) shallow

_____ 6. MOBILE: (A) unmovable (B) movable (C) slow (D) fast
(E) plentiful

_____ 7. LOATHE: (A) hate (B) dislike (C) demolish (D) love
(E) neglect

_____ 8. VETERAN: (A) old-timer (B) beginner (C) soldier
(D) actor (E) doctor

_____ 9. RESENT: (A) frighten (B) hate (C) like (D) remember
(E) forget

_____ 10. VIOLATE: (A) disregard (B) offend (C) break (D) obey
(E) deny

Number correct _____ (total 10)

Spelling and Wordplay

Fill-ins Spell the target word correctly in the blanks to the right of its definition.

1. a brief fight: <u>s</u> __ __ __ __ __ <u>s</u> <u>h</u>

2. to break a law or rule: __ <u>i</u> __ __ __ __ <u>e</u>

3. clothing: __ <u>p</u> <u>p</u> __ __ __ __

4. experienced person: <u>v</u> __ __ __ <u>r</u> __ __

5. to send from one place to another: __ <u>r</u> __ __ <u>s</u> __ __ __

6. to force: __ __ <u>m</u> __ <u>e</u> __

7. poisonous: _ _ x _ c

8. to announce: _ _ _ _ _ a i _

9. to put a spell over, to enchant: _ e _ _ t _ _

10. able to be moved: _ _ b _ l _

11. rival: c _ m _ _ t _ _ _ _

12. to hate: _ _ _ t h _

13. to say the opposite: c _ _ _ r _ _ _ _ _

14. to live or remain in a place: _ _ d g _

15. to make less: d _ _ _ e a _ _

16. to guarantee: _ n _ _ r _

17. a safe shelter: h _ _ _ n

18. being apart or alone: _ s _ l _ _ _

19. very big: _ _ n s _ _ _ _ _ _ _

20. to feel anger toward: _ _ s _ _ t

Number correct _____ (total 20)

Part D *Related Words*

The words below are closely related to the target words. Use your knowledge of the target words and of word parts to determine the meanings of these words. (For information about word parts analysis, see pages 7–13.) Use your dictionary if necessary.

1. assure (ə shoͬor′) v.
2. claim (klām′) n., v.
3. clamor (klam′ ə r) n., v.
4. compete (kəm pēt′) v.
5. competition (käm′ pə tish′ ən) n.
6. compulsion (kəm pul′ shən) n.
7. consider (kən sid′ ər) v.
8. contradiction (kän′ trə dik′ shən) n.
9. contradictory (kän′ trə dik′ tər ē) adj.
10. ensure (in shoͬor′) v.
11. exclaim (iks klām′) v.
12. exclamation (eks′ klə mā′ shən) n.
13. increase (in′ krēs) n. (in krēs′, in′ krēs) v.
14. insurance (in shoͬor′ əns) n.
15. isolation (ī sə lā′ shən) n.
16. mobility (mō bil′ ə tē) n.
17. proclamation (präk′ lə mā′ shən) n.
18. resentment (ri zent′ mənt) n.
19. transmission (trans mish′ ən) n.
20. violation (vī′ ə lā′ shən) n.

Understanding Related Words

True–False Decide whether each statement is true (**T**) or false (**F**).

_____ 1. A traffic *violation* is within the law.

_____ 2. You can *assure* yourself of not doing poorly in school by studying hard.

_____ 3. Doctors are not interested in preventing the *transmission* of disease.

_____ 4. If you have health *insurance,* you would probably expect your medical bills to be paid for you when you are ill.

_____ 5. A prisoner in *isolation* will have other prisoners for company.

_____ 6. Good friends usually have *resentment* for each other.

_____ 7. Voters approved a tax *increase,* so people will be paying less in taxes.

_____ 8. If a crowd raises a *clamor,* you would expect the noise to be loud.

_____ 9. An athlete who has just begun walking again after recovering from a broken leg probably enjoys his new *mobility.*

_____ 10. Rival schools with outstanding teams often *compete* for championship trophies.

Number correct _____ (total 10)

Sentence Writing Write one sentence for each pair of words below. You may change the form of the words if necessary. **Answers will vary.**

1. assure/competition: _____

_____

2. contradictory/exclaim: _____

_____

3. isolation/mobility: _____

_____

4. resentment/violation: _____

_____

5. ensure/transmission: _____

_____

Turn to **The Prefix *ex-*** on page 224 of the **Spelling Handbook.** Read the rule and complete the exercise provided.

6. insurance/hospital: _____

_____

7. exclamation/increase: _____

_____

8. proclamation/consider: _____

_____

9. contradiction/assure: _____

_____

10. compete/compulsion: _____

_____

Number correct _____ (total 10)

Analyzing Word Parts

The Latin Root *clam* The target word *proclaim* comes from the Latin word *clamare,* meaning "to shout" or "to cry out." The following related words come from this same Latin word:

claim   clamor   exclaim   exclamation   proclamation

Look up the meaning of each word in your dictionary. Then use the words to complete the following sentences.

_____ 1. The king made a __?__ that all of his subjects would be treated equally.

_____ 2. Sheila will attend the court hearing and __?__ her share of the estate.

_____ 3. "Thank goodness you are here at last!" __?__ed Jack's worried mother.

_____ 4. Surprised by the sudden appearance of a detective with a pair of handcuffs, Robert's loud __?__ could be heard throughout the theater.

_____ 5. A fierce __?__ arose among the Russians crowding the streets when they thought the Soviet tanks were attacking.

Number correct _____ (total 5)

Number correct in unit _____ (total 90)

The Last Word

Writing

Choose one item from each of the columns below. Then write a story based on these three items. Use your imagination.

Characters	Incidents	Conditions
• a fierce *competitor*	• *transmitting* messages in secret code	• for a ladies' *apparel* store
• the owner of a *toxic* waste dump	• *contradicting* everything that was said	• without any *decrease* in skill
• the participants in a brief *skirmish*	• *loathing* the present conditions	• toward a quiet *haven*
• a *veteran* sports writer	• *proclaiming* the news	• with a *clamor* of activity
• a person with a *bewitching* smile	• *compelled* to respond	• with an *increase* in responsibility
• an *isolated* prisoner on an island	• *violating* the rules	• near a remote hunting *lodge*

Speaking

Interview family and friends about *apparel* worn in the 1960's, 1970's, and 1980's. Ask them to describe the clothing and to explain how it reflected what happened in each decade. Prepare a speech relating what you learned from the interviews. Include in the speech your own description of apparel worn in the 1990's and tell how it might reflect the events and attitudes of this decade.

Group Discussion

Think about athletes, political leaders, and other people who are good *competitors*. Take a few minutes to list the qualities of a good competitor. Then share your list with the rest of your class. As a class, decide which qualities are found in most good competitors. Discuss why each quality is a good one for a competitor to have.

UNIT 16: Review of Units 13–15

Part A Review Word List

Unit 13 Target Words

1. ample
2. anonymity
3. consult
4. contrary
5. definite
6. dismal
7. duly
8. engineer
9. focus
10. geologist
11. graduate
12. international
13. ordain
14. previous
15. purposefully
16. systematically
17. terrain
18. uncommonly
19. unheralded
20. unmindful

Unit 13 Related Words

1. anonymous
2. common
3. consultant
4. consultation
5. contrariness
6. definitely
7. engine
8. engineering
9. focal
10. geology
11. gradual
12. graduation
13. herald
14. mindful
15. national
16. ordination
17. purposeful
18. system

Unit 14 Target Words

1. attitude
2. civic
3. concern
4. cultured
5. dedication
6. determination
7. discipline
8. endeavor
9. enforce
10. ignite
11. legitimate
12. obligation
13. persevere
14. policy
15. politics
16. reform
17. respect
18. social
19. uphold
20. versus

Unit 14 Related Words

1. civil
2. civilian
3. civilize
4. conform
5. culture
6. deform
7. enforcement
8. ignition
9. inform
10. obligate
11. political
12. respectable
13. respectful
14. socialize
15. society

Unit 15 Target Words

1. apparel
2. bewitch
3. compel
4. competitor
5. considerable
6. contradict
7. decrease
8. haven
9. insure
10. isolate
11. loathe
12. lodge
13. mobile
14. proclaim
15. resent
16. skirmish
17. toxic
18. transmit
19. veteran
20. violate

Unit 15 Related Words

1. assure
2. claim
3. clamor
4. compete
5. competition
6. compulsion
7. consider
8. contradiction
9. contradictory
10. ensure
11. exclaim
12. exclamation
13. increase
14. insurance
15. isolation
16. mobility
17. proclamation
18. resentment
19. transmission
20. violation

Inferring Meaning from Context

For each sentence write the letter of the word or phrase that is closest in meaning to the word or words in italics.

_____ 1. Georgette's warm winter *apparel was* unsuitable for the climate in Atlanta.
   a. clothing was   b. boots were   c. gloves were   d. heater was

_____ 2. Rachel has a bad *attitude about* the party, so she will probably not have a good time.
   a. objection to   b. observation of   c. way of thinking about
   d. way of traveling to

_____ 3. The twins have always been *competitors,* continually trying to outdo each other.
   a. friends   b. enemies   c. rivals   d. teammates

_____ 4. Because of his *concern about* the environment, Rich has joined a group that works to protect the forests.
   a. knowledge of   b. lack of feeling for   c. happiness about
   d. real interest in

_____ 5. *Contrary to* the way she acted today, Michiko is really a nice person.
   a. Opposite to   b. Characteristic of   c. Similar to   d. Vital to

_____ 6. Randy's parents gave her *a definite* time to be home.
   a. an obvious   b. an early   c. a precise   d. a vague

_____ 7. It takes great *determination* to finish medical school.
   a. intelligence   b. purposefulness   c. fear   d. curiosity

_____ 8. "If you want to become a good hitter," Bob's baseball coach said, "you have to learn *discipline* in waiting for the right pitch to hit."
   a. self-confidence   b. relaxation   c. self-control   d. stamina

_____ 9. After double-checking scores from each contest, the judge *duly* awarded the trophy to the team from Roosevelt Middle School.
   a. rightfully   b. respectfully   c. stubbornly   d. incorrectly

_____ 10. Our principal strictly *enforces* the attendance rules by notifying our parents whenever we are absent.
   a. ignores   b. makes sure everyone obeys   c. changes
   d. tries to discuss

_____ 11. The auditorium was so hot that it was difficult to *focus* our attention on the speaker.
   a. fuse   b. relax   c. concentrate   d. develop

_____ 12. The doorway of the grocery store provided _a haven_ for Sally during the brief downpour.

a. a hazard   b. a meal   c. an umbrella   d. a place of shelter

_____ 13. The _isolated_ cabin sat on the edge of a lake miles from the nearest town.

a. safe   b. separated   c. unheated   d. crowded

_____ 14. The man walked _purposefully_ over to the clerk and asked for his money back.

a. in a hasty manner   b. in a relaxed manner
c. in a determined manner   d. with great anger

_____ 15. Cindy does not _respect_ people who do not stand up for themselves.

a. think highly of   b. remain friends with   c. reform   d. dislike

_____ 16. Residents of the community were evacuated because of the _toxic_ fumes.

a. unpleasant   b. poisonous   c. dirty   d. smoky

_____ 17. The boys used walkie-talkies to _transmit_ their messages.

a. listen to   b. accumulate   c. pass along   d. mute

_____ 18. School was canceled due to the _uncommonly_ heavy snowfall.

a. normally   b. occasionally   c. frequently   d. unusually

_____ 19. As they splashed around in the lake, the children were _unmindful of_ the storm clouds overhead.

a. thinking of   b. unconcerned about   c. afraid of
d. watchful of

_____ 20. Barbara Jordan was determined to _uphold_ social reform by backing legislation to give more rights to the disadvantaged.

a. support   b. violate   c. write about   d. suspend

Number correct _____ (total 20)

Using Review Words in Context

Using context clues, determine which word from the list below best completes each sentence in the story that follows. Write the word in the blank. Each word will be used only once.

ample	considerable	endeavor	insure	toxic
attitude	contrary	enforced	policy	unmindful
civic	duly	focus	systematically	violate

A Good Drink of Water

It's true that the world has an _____ supply of water. However, _____ to general opinion, our supply of *fresh* water is limited. That's because so much of our water is the salty kind found in oceans. In addition, some fresh water becomes unusable because of _____ chemicals that get into it from industry and farming. Although there are laws to protect our water, these laws are not always _____. As citizens, however, we can no longer take our supply of clean water for granted. Some people believe we need a new national _____ on water usage, as follows:

They believe we should begin by requiring our governments to identify those industries that _____ sound water practices by dumping dangerous chemicals into rivers or streams or by wasting water. Then we should _____ punish those that break the law. Just as importantly, we need to teach people that having clean water is their _____ right and their responsibility.

People should develop a positive _____ toward water conservation. They should _____ to use water wisely.

One thing each person can do is to _____ attention on the ways we use water. When we realize that the average American uses 110 gallons of water every day, it may be time to _____ examine and correct some of the careless and _____ uses. Did you know, for instance, that a leaky faucet can waste 25 to 30 gallons of water a day? This alone adds up to a _____ amount of waste that should compel us to fix broken faucets. Another example is the 180 gallons of water people waste when they let the hose run while they're washing the car.

Look around you. Think about what you can do to help _____ that there will be plenty of fresh, clean water in the future.

Number correct _____ (total 15)

Part B Review Word Reinforcement

Using Language and Thinking Skills

Finding Examples Write the letter of the situation that best shows the meaning of the boldfaced word.

_____ 1. **anonymity**

    a. William Faulkner, one of the best-known American writers, won the Nobel Prize for literature.

    b. Andrew, who wants to become a professional dancer, practices every day for four hours.

    c. Michelle, who is very shy, writes short stories but never signs her real name to them.

_____ 2. **persevere**

    a. Phillip likes building models, but he gives up if they're too difficult.

    b. Sara wants to make the basketball team, so she practices every day.

    c. Melissa likes politics and wants to become a member of the student council next year.

_____ 3. **loathe**

    a. Hector loves swimming and surfing.

    b. Richard hates any kind of sports.

    c. Barbara is good at softball, but it's not her favorite sport.

_____ 4. **geologist**

    a. Chris has a rock collection and knows how each rock was formed.

    b. Allison wants to design and build bridges.

    c. Sam has a telescope and can tell you all about the solar system.

_____ 5. **reform**

    a. The state senator announced he wants to serve another term.

    b. The newspaper is calling for a change in how people pay taxes to support education.

    c. The scientist is seeking a cure for the common cold.

_____ 6. **versus**

    a. Mark and John are good team players.

    b. Mr. and Mrs. Sanchez want to eat dinner at the new restaurant.

    c. Michiko and Bev are playing each other in tennis.

_____ 7. **ignite**

    a. Ron gathered wood and then struck a match to start a fire.

    b. The truck driver pulled into the restaurant for lunch.

    c. The lake overflowed and flooded the valley.

_____ 8. **terrain**

    a. The wind blew violently all night.

    b. The bear went all winter without eating.

    c. The pioneers took a week to cross the rugged mountains.

_____ 9. **international**

    a. Brian's family has lived in the United States for four generations.

    b. Julie's class includes students from Mexico, Jamaica, and Germany.

    c. Diane's family is traveling to New Hampshire this summer.

_____ 10. **decrease**

    a. Less rain has fallen this year than last year.

    b. More corn is grown in Iowa than in Indiana.

    c. Long winters prevent farmers from planting their fields early.

Number correct _____ (total 10)

Practicing for Standardized Tests

Antonyms Write the letter of the word that is most nearly _opposite_ in meaning to the capitalized word.

_____ 1. ANONYMITY: (A) graduate (B) fame (C) obscurity
(D) competitor (E) namelessness

_____ 2. CONTRADICT: (A) agree (B) deny (C) dispute
(D) reform (E) correct

_____ 3. CULTURED: (A) literate (B) respected (C) unrefined
(D) adaptable (E) polished

_____ 4. DECREASE: (A) intend (B) reduce (C) increase
(D) recede (E) alter

_____ 5. DISMAL: (A) gloomy (B) petrifying (C) solemn
(D) joyous (E) fateful

_____ 6. IGNITE: (A) douse (B) induce (C) light (D) resign
(E) enforce

_____ 7. LEGITIMATE: (A) normal (B) lawful (C) toxic
(D) unjustified (E) legal

_____ 8. LOATHE: (A) besiege (B) ordain (C) love (D) isolate
(E) hate

_____ 9. MOBILE: (A) transitional (B) movable (C) reliable
(D) continuous (E) immovable

_____ 10. PREVIOUS: (A) formative (B) next (C) prevalent
(D) earlier (E) placid

Number correct _____ (total 10)

Synonyms Write the letter of the word that is closest in meaning to the capitalized word.

_____ 1. AMPLE: (A) streamlined (B) scanty (C) nutritious (D) meager (E) plenty

_____ 2. COMPEL: (A) bewitch (B) consult (C) force (D) allow (E) induce

_____ 3. ENDEAVOR: (A) effort (B) siege (C) neglect (D) situation (E) development

_____ 4. LODGE: (A) oust (B) dwell (C) travel (D) invade (E) leave

_____ 5. OBLIGATION: (A) option (B) desire (C) choice (D) duty (E) determination

_____ 6. ORDAIN: (A) bless (B) reject (C) appoint (D) focus (E) enforce

_____ 7. REFORM: (A) improvement (B) politics (C) repercussion (D) endeavor (E) reason

_____ 8. SKIRMISH: (A) objective (B) battle (C) haven (D) fantasy (E) retreat

_____ 9. SYSTEMATIC: (A) competitive (B) mindless (C) noble (D) disorganized (E) planned

_____ 10. PROCLAIM: (A) declare (B) prevail (C) maintain (D) decide (E) establish

Number correct _____ (total 10)

Analogies Determine the relationship between the pair of capitalized words. Then decide which other pair expresses a similar relationship. Write the letter of this word pair.

_____ 1. APPAREL : SHIRT :: (A) heat : fire (B) fruit : orange (C) rage : anger (D) socks : shoes (E) summer : winter

_____ 2. GEOLOGIST : ROCK :: (A) mountain : valley (B) writer : pencil (C) boat : vessel (D) yesterday : tomorrow (E) astronaut : space

_____ 3. ANONYMITY : FAME :: (A) joy : happiness (B) proclamation : announcement (C) war : peace (D) soldier : battlefield (E) resentment : anger

_____ 4. DETERMINATION : SUCCESS ::   (A) obligation : duty
   (B) city : country   (C) teamwork : victory   (D) farmer : field
   (E) graduate : high school

_____ 5. DISCIPLINE : SELF-CONTROL ::   (A) tennis : sports
   (B) rain : weather   (C) student : school   (D) choice : option
   (E) explorer : expedition

Number correct _____ (total 5)

Spelling and Wordplay

Copy Editor Find the misspelled words in the news item below. Write the corrected words in the blanks in the order they appear in the item.

A Single Drop Will Do

The chief witness for the defense was Dr. John Oaks, a geeolajust. He is also a gradjuet engjunear with an intinnashunel reputation who has won reespekt in both subjects.

The fokus of the lawsuit was public konsern over toxick dumping. The dispute involved protecting the environment vursis profit.

Mr. White, attorney for the state, sistimattecally indevored to trick Dr. Oaks into contradicing himself. Dr. Oaks insisted, however, that the company's dumping did not vyolat any law. He said that the state would not be able to inforce the law against dumping nor would it be able to kompell the company not to dump. He said the company had a ligitimat right to do everything within the law to make a profit. He added that it was not a civik duty of the company to work for reefarm because from a strict technical standpoint the company was not breaking the law. Dr. Oaks said the company had no oblegation to protect public health.

Mr. White accused Dr. Oaks and the company of seeking a haeven in a legal loophole.

A tense hush settled over the courtroom when Mr. White asked Dr. Oaks to drink a glass of water taken from a well near the dumping site. Dr. Oaks refused.

1. _____	6. _____	11. _____	16. _____
2. _____	7. _____	12. _____	17. _____
3. _____	8. _____	13. _____	18. _____
4. _____	9. _____	14. _____	19. _____
5. _____	10. _____	15. _____	20. _____

Number correct _____ (total 20)

Part C   Related Word Reinforcement

Using Related Words

Matching Definitions Use your knowledge of the meaning of the target words to match the following definitions with the related words listed below. Write the related word in the blank.

anonymous	compulsion	exclaim	ignition	proclamation
assure	contradiction	isolation	geology	socialize
common	deform	inform	political	transmission

_____ 1. shared by all

_____ 2. separation from others

_____ 3. to mix with other people

_____ 4. the study of the earth, its structure, and how it was formed

_____ 5. without the name being known

_____ 6. to damage the shape

_____ 7. an inner drive forcing someone to act

_____ 8. to cry out suddenly in surprise

_____ 9. a public announcement

_____ 10. the passing or sending of something from one person to another

_____ 11. to seek to convince

_____ 12. being interested in or involved with government

_____ 13. a device for starting a car

_____ 14. to provide knowledge about

_____ 15. a statement in opposition to another statement

Number correct _____ (total 15)

Reviewing Word Structures

The Word Parts *clamare, forma, geo,* and *gradus* Complete each of the following sentences with a word from the Review List (page 194). Follow the directions in parentheses, using a word with a *clamare, forma, geo,* or *gradus* root.

_____ 1. After my sister's _?_ from high school, she enrolled in junior college to study graphic arts. (Use a word with the root *gradus*.).

_____ 2. The governor made a _?_ on television designating that the month of May be used as a time to honor the state's teachers. (Use a word with the root *clamare*.)

_____ 3. Kate is fascinated by _?_. She took a trip to the Grand Canyon just so she could see the rock formations and how the Colorado River had cut through the earth. (Use a word with the root *geo*.)

_____ 4. After the apple had sat on the counter for several days without being eaten, it began to dry out, shrivel, and _?_. (Use a word with the root *forma*.)

_____ 5. As the crowd grew larger, the _?_ became louder as more people joined in the shouting. (Use a word with the root *clamare*.)

_____ 6. The agency decided the best way to _?_ the public about a possible water shortage was through an announcement on radio and television. (Use a word with the root *forma*.)

_____ 7. After the furnace stopped working, we noticed a _?_ loss of heat as the cold air found its way through the poorly fitting windows and doors. (Use a word with the root *gradus*.)

_____ 8. "If you want to play on a winning team," the coach barked out, "you must _?_ to the rules I will teach you about team play." (Use a word with the root *forma*.)

_____ 9. Meredith walked up to the stage to _?_ her trophy as the outstanding tennis player in the district. (Use a word with the root *clamare*.)

_____ 10. The actor's _?_ of surprise brought roars of laughter from the audience. They enjoyed the character's look of complete joy as much as his shout of surprise. (Use a word with the root *clamare*.)

Number correct _____ (total 10)

Number correct in unit _____ (total 115)

Vocab Lab 4

FOCUS ON: Cinema

The words and phrases below are used in the motion picture industry. Knowing them will make it easier for you to talk about movies you have seen.

animation (an′ ə ma′ shən) n. the process of preparing motion picture cartoons. ● Artists creating *animation* must produce thousands of drawings in order to show movement when the pictures are projected on a screen.

casting (kas′ tiŋ) n. the choosing of actors to play the roles in a play or film. ● Because the *casting* of the lead characters was weak, the film wasn't effective.

cinematography (sin′ ə mə täg′ rə fē) n. the art of motion-picture photography. ● The movie *Dances with Wolves* is known for its beautiful *cinematography*.

close-up (klōs′ up′) n. a scene in which the subject is shown very near to the camera. ● In the *close-up* we could see tiny scratches on the deer's antlers.

costume designer (käs′ to͞om, -tyo͞om di zī′ nər) the person who prepares the costumes, or clothing, for a theatrical or film production. ● The *costume designer* wanted the actors' clothes to be exactly like those worn in the eighteenth century.

director (di rek′ tər) n. The person who plans and supervises the action and characters of a play or film. ● The *director* of a film is in some ways like the conductor of an orchestra.

documentary (däk′ yə men′ tə rē) n. a film that dramatizes real conditions or actual events rather than fictional ones. ● The class watched a *documentary* based on the life of the Plains Indians.

editor (ed′ i tər) n. the person who prepares a motion picture for presentation by cutting, splicing, and rearranging the film footage. ● The film *editor* has one of the most important jobs in the making of a movie.

pan (pan) v. to rotate the camera horizontally so as to follow a moving object or show a wide, sweeping view of a location. ● The director told the cameraman to *pan* slowly across the faces of the audience in the stadium.

producer (prə do͞os′ ər, -dyo͞os′) n. a person who supervises and finances the making of a play or film. ● The *producer* was happy when she finally had enough money to make the movie.

sneak preview (snēk prē′ vyo͞o) the showing of a film in advance of its official release in order to observe audience reaction or increase interest in the film. ● The audience was excited when they learned they were about to see a *sneak preview* of the new movie.

sound track (sound trak) a narrow strip along one side of a film, carrying its recorded sound. ● Steve bought a recording of the *sound track* of the new musical.

special effects (spesh′ əl ə fekts′) ways of making strange or spectacular events in a movie look real even though they are faked. ● The *special effects* in the movie *E.T.* made the fantastic occurrences seem very convincing.

storyboard (stôr′ ē bōrd′) n. a series of sketches arranged to show the sequence of shots or scenes in a film being planned. ● The director used a *storyboard* to present an overview of the movie to the cast.

stunt person (stunt pur′ s'n) a person who substitutes for an actor in scenes that involve special athletic ability or possible danger. ● A good *stunt person* needs special training and nerves of steel.

Matching Ideas Write the focus word that is most clearly related to each of the descriptions below.

_____ 1. to swing the camera in order to get a wide shot of a landscape

_____ 2. filming a model ship being blown up in a swimming pool

_____ 3. someone looking for a particular kind of coat worn in the 1930's

_____ 4. unexpectedly getting to see a new movie before it is even out

_____ 5. cartoons children watch on Saturday morning

_____ 6. someone who may cut some scenes from a film or rearrange their order

_____ 7. a film that tries to show the reality of a historical event

_____ 8. the art of using the camera effectively in movie making

_____ 9. matching the characters' lip movements with their voices

_____ 10. the way that actors, in what they call a "cattle call," might get chosen for parts in a movie

_____ 11. what the camera sees when it zooms up to within feet or inches of its subject

_____ 12. the person who makes all the arrangements so that a movie can be made

_____ 13. someone who can jump out of a speeding car without getting hurt

_____ 14. the person who suggests to the actors how they should play the next scene

_____ 15. a way you can sketch out the sequence of scenes before you shoot a movie

Number correct _____ (total 15)

FOCUS ON: *Word Games*

Playing word games is a good way to stretch your vocabulary. Although pencil and paper are needed for many of the games, some require nothing more than an active imagination and a good vocabulary.

Below are examples of a few common word games from which many other word games have sprung. Look over each game, work the sample exercise, and then make up your own game.

Categories

In this game players are given a list of categories—such as flowers, foods, or states—and a word like *chair*. The idea is to name one item in each category whose first letter is one of the letters in the word. An example follows.

Category	C	H	A	I	R
Animal	cow	horse	antelope	ibex	rabbit
Flower	carnation	heather	aster	iris	rose
Sport	cycling	hockey	archery	ice skating	rugby
Country	China	Hungary	Austria	India	Russia
State capital	Concord	Helena	Austin	Indianapolis	Raleigh

Exercise A Work out the puzzle below.

Category	F	I	L	M
Animal				
State				
Food				
City				
Country				

Number correct _____ (total 20)

Rebus

A rebus uses letters, numbers, symbols, or pictures that suggest words or phrases. A rebus known to all is the familiar IOU that stands for "I Owe You." Rebuses are frequently used on personalized auto license plates. Examples include IMB4U (I am before you) or ICUR (I see you are).

Here are some single-word rebuses:

4C	foresee	NE1	anyone
DK	decay	SA	essay

Exercise B Make up a rebus for your personalized license plate.

Words Within Words

Choose a fairly long word. Find as many words as you can from the letters of the chosen word, using each letter of the word only once. The winner of the game is the one who can produce the longest list of words. You can make the game as difficult or as easy as you want by setting up rules that exclude such items as two-letter words, three-letter words, proper nouns, foreign words, abbreviations, plurals, and so on. For example, below is a selection of words of three or more letters that can be made from *birthday*.

aid, air, bar, bard, bat, bath, bay, bid, bird, birth, bit, brad, brat, bray, dab, dart, day, dirt, drab, drat, dray, dry, habit, had, hat, hit, raid, rat, ray, rib, rid, tab, tad, tar, Thai, third, tray, triad, yah, yard

Exercise C Find at least ten words within the word *wordskills*.

1. _____   6. _____

2. _____   7. _____

3. _____   8. _____

4. _____   9. _____

5. _____   10. _____

Number correct _____ (total 10)

Word Squares

A word square is made of words with an equal number of letters that read the same across and down. Words with two or three letters are fairly easy to use in making a word square. The more letters you use, the more difficult it becomes.

Here are some examples:

| Two-letter words | A N | I T |
| | N O | T O |

Three-letter words	T I E	B I D
	I V Y	I C Y
	E Y E	D Y E

Four-letter words	S A L E	S A N E
	A R E A	A R E A
	L E E R	N E A T
	E A R S	E A T S

Exercise D Create a two-letter-word word square and then see if you can work your way up to a four-letter-word word square or beyond.

Number correct in Vocab Lab _____ (total 45)

Units 1–8 *Standardized Vocabulary Test*

The following questions test your comprehension of words studied in the first half of the book. Test questions have been written in a way that will familiarize you with the typical standardized test format. The questions are divided into the following categories: **synonyms, sentence completion, antonyms,** and **analogies.**

Synonyms

Each question below consists of a word in capital letters followed by five lettered words. In the blank, write the letter of the word that is closest in meaning to the word in capital letters. Because some of the questions require you to distinguish fine shades of meaning, consider all the choices before deciding which is best.

_____ 1. ESTABLISH: (A) create   (B) grow   (C) expand
(D) demolish   (E) stand

_____ 2. ADAPT: (A) add   (B) develop   (C) adjust   (D) loosen
(E) admit

_____ 3. MERGE: (A) submerge   (B) combine   (C) release
(D) separate   (E) enjoy

_____ 4. DOUSE: (A) boil   (B) lurk   (C) melt   (D) drench
(E) praise

_____ 5. TRAIT: (A) friend   (B) handicap   (C) family
(D) characteristic   (E) bait

_____ 6. GUARANTEE: (A) zeal   (B) situation   (C) pledge
(D) license   (E) advantage

_____ 7. REPULSIVE: (A) effective   (B) disgusting   (C) smelly
(D) legal   (E) delightful

_____ 8. CONSTANT: (A) untimely   (B) seasonal   (C) extinct
(D) brief   (E) continuous

_____ 9. AWKWARD: (A) rigid   (B) desperate   (C) clumsy   (D) awful
(E) harmful

_____ 10. FUSE: (A) transfer   (B) involve   (C) divide   (D) join
(E) use

_____ 11. MAGNIFICENT: (A) massive   (B) tall   (C) splendid
(D) awful   (E) abnormal

____ 12. VITAL: (A) necessary (B) continuous (C) interesting
(D) special (E) delicious

____ 13. SHEER: (A) desperate (B) short (C) free (D) pure
(E) finished

____ 14. IMPURE: (A) suitable (B) clean (C) dirty (D) drinkable
(E) immediate

____ 15. PECULIARLY: (A) warmly (B) smartly (C) normally
(D) quietly (E) strangely

____ 16. OBSERVE: (A) see (B) think (C) break (D) show
(E) disclose

____ 17. MUTE: (A) talkative (B) afraid (C) silent (D) changeable
(E) resistant

____ 18. FANTASY: (A) mission (B) reality (C) contest (D) dream
(E) movie

____ 19. HAZARDOUS: (A) intense (B) dangerous (C) laborious
(D) repulsive (E) desperate

____ 20. INTENSE: (A) vague (B) infrequent (C) weak (D) vocal
(E) strong

Number correct _____ (total 20)

Sentence Completion

Each sentence below has one or two blanks. Each blank indicates that a
word has been omitted. Beneath the sentence are five lettered words or pairs
of words. In the blank to the left of each sentence, write the letter of the word
or pair of words that *best* fits the meaning of the sentence.

____ 1. Because Bill had experience in directing plays, he offered to _?_
the rehearsal.
(A) forget (B) return (C) conduct (D) regain
(E) accumulate

____ 2. The discussion was so _?_ that I took notes continuously.
(A) informative (B) boring (C) fanciful (D) distinct
(E) simple

____ 3. Numerous police officers were on duty at the rock concert to _?_
the many spectators.
(A) ignore (B) suspend (C) harass (D) safeguard
(E) enrage

_____ 4. The __?__ child felt it was his __?__ to examine the contents of every cabinet in the kitchen.

(A) seasonal . . . testimony   (B) silly . . . guarantee
(C) curious . . . mission   (D) sleepy . . . advantage
(E) angry . . . application

_____ 5. The __?__ in the mystery movie made my heart pound.

(A) comedy   (B) magnification   (C) sensitivity
(D) intermission   (E) suspense

_____ 6. Nicole's __?__ into the lawn-maintenance business was successful; in three months she earned $800.

(A) venture   (B) possibility   (C) myth   (D) visit   (E) intrigue

_____ 7. Because the baby was born with a birth defect, he had to undergo __?__ surgery.

(A) brief   (B) fanciful   (C) educated   (D) inviting
(E) corrective

_____ 8. A __?__ in __?__ took an X-ray of Leslie's broken arm.

(A) florist . . . formation   (B) specialist . . . radiology
(C) writer . . . Latin   (D) zealot . . . alteration
(E) governess . . . pursuit

_____ 9. The photograph __?__ that Sam had undergone a(n) __?__. He was no longer fat, but quite thin!

(A) detected . . . involvement   (B) revealed . . . transformation
(C) composed . . . hazard   (D) guaranteed . . . character
(E) hindered . . . stamina

_____ 10. Brent does not let his __?__ __?__ him; he tries to do most of the things other children do.

(A) credit . . . govern   (B) testimony . . . involve
(C) handicap . . . hinder   (D) cycle . . . regain
(E) poise . . . propel

_____ 11. One of Miguel's best __?__ is his __?__ toward the feelings of others.

(A) quests . . . suspension   (B) characteristics . . . sensitivity
(C) traits . . . development   (D) habits . . . wealth
(E) invitations . . . coldness

_____ 12. With no school, no camp plans, and no job, Margie was __?__ during the summer.

(A) busy   (B) friendly   (C) idle   (D) vital   (E) seasonal

_____ 13. The ? continued her ? of the president, hoping the president would give her an interview.

(A) senator . . . zeal   (B) police officer . . . myth
(C) journalist . . . pursuit   (D) lecturer . . . adaptation
(E) cook . . . detection

_____ 14. Because of the ? noise from the party next door, Mr. Canfield ? called the police.

(A) continuous . . . eventually   (B) pleasant . . . temporarily
(C) attractive . . . invitingly   (D) scheduled . . . sleepily
(E) infrequent . . . hazardously

_____ 15. Doris ? remembered meeting the man last year, but she could not think of his name.

(A) jointly   (B) ceaselessly   (C) lately   (D) vaguely
(E) solemnly

Number correct _____ (total 15)

Antonyms

Each test item below consists of a word in capital letters followed by five lettered words. In the blank, write the letter of the word that is most nearly _opposite_ in meaning to the word in capital letters. Because some of the questions require you to distinguish fine shades of meaning, consider all the choices before deciding which is best.

_____ 1. FREQUENTLY: (A) rarely (B) regularly (C) often
(D) sometimes   (E) thirstily

_____ 2. RECALL: (A) telephone (B) remember (C) forget
(D) memorize   (E) read

_____ 3. EFFICIENT: (A) ready (B) ineffective (C) organized
(D) effective   (E) inviting

_____ 4. LINGER: (A) remain (B) eat (C) leave (D) hurry
(E) stop

_____ 5. FRENZIED: (A) crazy (B) tired (C) confused (D) friendly
(E) calm

_____ 6. EFFECTIVENESS: (A) efficiency (B) uselessness
(C) punctuality (D) loneliness (E) dullness

_____ 7. ACCOMPLISHMENT: (A) achievement (B) quest
(C) desperation (D) accident (E) failure

_____ 8. DISTRIBUTE: (A) present (B) call (C) collect (D) sell
(E) disclose

_____ 9. ACTUAL: (A) active (B) real (C) silly (D) timely (E) fanciful

_____ 10. ABNORMAL: (A) unusual (B) abstract (C) lengthy (D) typical (E) risky

Number correct _____ (total 10)

Analogies

Each question below consists of a pair of capitalized words followed by five pairs of words that are lettered. Determine the relationship between the pair of capitalized words. Then decide which lettered word pair expresses a similar relationship. In the blank, write the letter of the word pair.

_____ 1. FLORIST : FLOWERS :: (A) journalist : writer
(B) teacher : students (C) orthopedist : doctor
(D) baby : infant (E) boy : girl

_____ 2. ZEAL : INTEREST :: (A) satisfaction : dissatisfaction
(B) photograph : album (C) window : glass
(D) telephone : communication (E) hatred : dislike

_____ 3. DETERMINED : COMMITTED :: (A) inviting : appealing
(B) generous : stingy (C) early : late (D) warm : cool
(E) interesting : boring

_____ 4. INSEPARABLE : DIVISIBLE :: (A) solemn : serious
(B) afraid : scared (C) straight : crooked (D) awful : terrible
(E) messy : sloppy

_____ 5. VERTICAL : TOWER :: (A) magnificent : splendor
(B) frenzied : frenzy (C) actual : reality
(D) horizontal : tabletop (E) bossy : characteristic

Number correct _____ (total 5)

Number correct in Units 1–8 Test _____ (total 50)

Units 9–16 *Standardized Vocabulary Test*

The following questions test your comprehension of words studied in the second half of the book. Test questions have been written in a way that will familiarize you with the typical standardized test format. The questions are divided into the following categories: **synonyms, sentence completion, antonyms,** and **analogies.**

Synonyms

Each question below consists of a word in capital letters followed by five lettered words. In the blank, write the letter of the word that is closest in meaning to the word in capital letters. Because some of the questions require you to distinguish fine shades of meaning, consider all the choices before deciding which is best.

____ 1. CIRCULATE: (A) spread (B) draw (C) lie (D) type (E) enforce

____ 2. OBJECTIVE: (A) lesson (B) obligation (C) goal (D) right (E) option

____ 3. INCREDIBLE: (A) incidental (B) believable (C) humorous (D) fantastic (E) unbelievable

____ 4. EXPEDITION: (A) vacation (B) journey (C) race (D) accommodation (E) expressway

____ 5. OPTION: (A) choice (B) obligation (C) risk (D) operation (E) intention

____ 6. HUMILIATE: (A) prevail (B) embarrass (C) beg (D) resign (E) loathe

____ 7. INCIDENT: (A) accident (B) event (C) engagement (D) fear (E) identification

____ 8. MEAGER: (A) sheer (B) gigantic (C) scanty (D) regular (E) substantial

____ 9. CONGREGATE: (A) listen (B) pray (C) disperse (D) locate (E) gather

____ 10. PLACID: (A) calm (B) decent (C) dismal (D) vigorous (E) intense

____ 11. DISMAL: (A) cloudy (B) gloomy (C) happy (D) fatal (E) sympathetic

_____ 12. TERRAIN: (A) ground (B) train (C) invasion (D) desert
(E) map

_____ 13. ENDEAVOR: (A) resignation (B) report (C) engine
(D) undertaking (E) loss

_____ 14. APPAREL: (A) suitcase (B) clothing (C) closet (D) ghost
(E) fruit

_____ 15. TOXIC: (A) smelly (B) sweet (C) poisonous (D) indirect
(E) harmful

_____ 16. PRACTICAL: (A) useful (B) useless (C) substantial
(D) rightful (E) daily

_____ 17. ORDAIN: (A) oust (B) preach (C) appoint (D) organize
(E) elect

_____ 18. CONCERN: (A) knowledge (B) condition (C) objective
(D) quantity (E) interest

_____ 19. REFORM: (A) fate (B) law (C) information (D) change
(E) resistance

_____ 20. ENGAGEMENT: (A) battle (B) incident (C) encouragement
(D) consultation (E) race

Number correct _____ (total 20)

Sentence Completion

Each sentence below has one or two blanks. Each blank indicates that a word has been omitted. Beneath the sentence are five lettered words or pairs of words. In the blank to the left of the sentence, write the letter of the word or pair of words that _best_ fits the meaning of the sentence.

_____ 1. Although the pair of jeans was more   ? , I purchased the red silk dress because it was more attractive.
(A) placid (B) colorful (C) practical (D) useless
(E) definite

_____ 2. The way the coach lifted the team's   ?   after the defeat was   ? .
(A) morale ... miraculous (B) lockers ... mobile
(C) football ... fatal (D) spirit ... orthopedic
(E) curfew ... considerable

_____ 3. ? material in the water has a(n)   ?   effect on those who drink the water.
(A) Mortal ... good (B) Toxic ... adverse
(C) Bittersweet ... political (D) Cultured ... vigorous
(E) Optional ... fateful

_____ 4. It is my ? to return the gift because I don't like it.
  (A) concern (B) surprise (C) induction (D) intention
  (E) repercussion

_____ 5. The old, rickety house was set to be ? by the wrecking crew.
  (A) purchased (B) decreased (C) ousted (D) decorated
  (E) demolished

_____ 6. When the king dies, his son will ? the kingdom.
  (A) inherit (B) resign (C) destroy (D) ignite (E) visit

_____ 7. As the smoke ? the Wilson's house, it was ? that they had to
  escape.
  (A) filled . . . incredible (B) permeated . . . obvious
  (C) extinguished . . . vague (D) ignited . . . miraculous
  (E) invaded . . . humorous

_____ 8. With the storm less than an hour away, we must try to find a ?
  that is ? .
  (A) shelter . . . meager (B) blizzard . . . decent
  (C) decision . . . common (D) policy . . . anonymous
  (E) haven . . . substantial

_____ 9. ? to David's report that the food at the restaurant was awful, I
  found it to be ? good.
  (A) True . . . frequently (B) Special . . . purposefully
  (C) Contrary . . . uncommonly (D) Counter . . . tastelessly
  (E) Opposite . . . bitterly

_____ 10. Police officers are dedicated to ? the law.
  (A) breaking (B) inducing (C) violating (D) discussing
  (E) upholding

_____ 11. Chris was ? because she had not met her ? of losing ten
  pounds.
  (A) ferocious . . . repercussion (B) decent . . . option
  (C) wonderful . . . endeavor (D) dismal . . . objective
  (E) legitimate . . . campaign

_____ 12. During the ? test in this class, I did not have ? time to answer
  all the questions, but I will finish today's test early.
  (A) long . . . brief (B) previous . . . ample (C) next . . . enough
  (D) prevalent . . . respectable (E) ferocious . . . same

_____ 13. Because Mario is such a strong ? , I must spend ? time
  practicing so I can beat him.
  (A) competitor . . . considerable (B) confederate . . . scanty
  (C) athlete . . . optional (D) appointee . . . little
  (E) engineer . . . much

215

_____ 14. The winning team loudly ⎯?⎯ its victory.
  (A) denied (B) ordained (C) challenged (D) explained
  (E) proclaimed

_____ 15. People like Carlos because his ⎯?⎯ toward others is one of ⎯?⎯.
  (A) attitude . . . respect (B) fate . . . humility
  (C) feeling . . . hatred (D) desire . . . selfishness
  (E) trait . . . competition

Number correct _____ (total 15)

Antonyms

Each question below consists of a word in capital letters followed by five lettered words. In the blank, write the letter of the word that is most nearly *opposite* in meaning to the word in capital letters. Because some of the questions require you to distinguish fine shades of meaning, consider all the choices before deciding which is best.

_____ 1. PREVAIL: (A) win (B) compete (C) find (D) lose
  (E) predict

_____ 2. UNMINDFUL: (A) unaware (B) placid (C) fateful
  (D) contradictory (E) aware

_____ 3. DEFINITE: (A) ineffective (B) vague (C) ready
  (D) specific (E) meager

_____ 4. DECREASE: (A) shorten (B) increase (C) enforce (D) die
  (E) lessen

_____ 5. UNHERALDED: (A) unobserved (B) credible
  (C) proclaimed (D) observed (E) hazardous

_____ 6. GIGANTIC: (A) tiny (B) huge (C) domestic (D) fat
  (E) hidden

_____ 7. WAGE: (A) prevail (B) hesitate (C) end (D) play
  (E) decrease

_____ 8. PERSEVERE: (A) permeate (B) contradict (C) focus
  (D) rest (E) quit

_____ 9. ANONYMITY: (A) reliability (B) shyness (C) knowledge
  (D) fame (E) nobility

_____ 10. LOATHE: (A) loaf (B) love (C) like (D) dislike
  (E) tolerate

Number correct _____ (total 10)

Analogies

Each question below consists of a pair of capitalized words followed by five pairs of words that are lettered. Determine the relationship between the pair of capitalized words. Then decide which lettered word pair expresses a similar relationship. In the blank, write the letter of this word pair.

_____ 1. SKIRMISH : DEATH ::   (A) gift : pleasure   (B) apparel : clothing
(C) correspondent : newspaper   (D) respect : disrespect
(E) execution : prison

_____ 2. GEOLOGIST : SCIENTIST ::   (A) veteran : experience
(B) sniper : gun   (C) worker : paycheck   (D) pilot : airplane
(E) runner : athlete

_____ 3. ENGAGEMENT : SOLDIER ::   (A) engine : car
(B) game : competitor   (C) nurse : patient   (D) janitor : mop
(E) keys : purse

_____ 4. VIOLATE : DISOBEY ::   (A) start : stop   (B) inform : deform
(C) appoint : choose   (D) lose : find   (E) resign : begin

_____ 5. ADVERSE : FAVORABLE ::   (A) cultured : refined
(B) mobile : movable   (C) meager : ample
(D) legitimate : reasonable   (E) miraculous : wondrous

Number correct _____ (total 5)

Number correct in Units 9–16 Test _____ (total 50)

217

SPELLING HANDBOOK

Knowing the meanings of words is essential to using language correctly. However, another important skill is knowing how to spell the words you use.

Almost everyone has at least some problems with spelling. If you have trouble spelling, you might be encouraged to know that many others like you have learned to avoid spelling errors by following these suggestions:

1. **Proofread everything you write.** Everyone occasionally makes errors through carelessness or haste. By carefully reading through what you have written, you will catch many of your errors.

2. **Look up difficult words in a dictionary.** If you are not sure about the spelling of a word, don't guess at it. Take the time to look up the word.

3. **Learn to look at the letters in a word.** Learn to spell a word by examining various letter combinations contained in the word. Note the prefix, suffix, or double letters. Close your eyes and visualize the word. Then write the word from memory. Look at the word again to check your spelling.

4. **Pronounce words carefully.** It may be that you misspell certain words because you do not pronounce them correctly. For example, if you write *probly* instead of *probably,* it is likely that you are mispronouncing the word. Learning how to pronounce words and memorizing the letter combinations that create the sounds will improve your spelling.

5. **Keep a list of your "spelling demons."** Although you may not think about it, you *do* correctly spell most of the words you use. It is usually a few specific words that give you the most trouble. Keep a list of the words you have trouble spelling, and concentrate on learning them. Also, look for patterns in the words you misspell and learn those patterns.

6. **Use memory helps, called mnemonic devices, for words that give you trouble.** *Stationery* has *er* as in *letter;* there is *a rat* in *separate; Wednesday* contains *wed.*

7. **Learn and apply the rules given in this section.** Make sure you understand these rules. Then practice using them until they become automatic.

Words with Prefixes

The Addition of Prefixes

A prefix is a group of letters added to the beginning of a word to change its meaning. When a prefix is added to a base word, the spelling of the base word remains the same. (For further information about word parts, see pages 7–13.)

in- + form = inform   *ob-* + serve = observe

in- + separable = inseparable   *ab-* + normal = abnormal

dis- + lodge = dislodge   *un-* + timely = untimely

A prefix can be added to a root as well as to a base word. A root is a word part that cannot stand alone; it must be joined to other parts to form a word. A root can be joined with many different prefixes to form words with different meanings. **However, the spelling of the prefix and the root remains the same.**

de- + tect = detect   *in-* + ject = inject

pro- + tect = protect   *re-* + ject = reject

Exercise A Add the prefixes as indicated, and write the new word.

1. *re-* + call = _____

2. *trans-* + form = _____

3. *per-* + form = _____

4. *in-* + effective = _____

5. *un-* + accountable = _____

6. *de-* + cease = _____

7. *pro-* + claim = _____

8. *con-* + form = _____

9. *in-* + sure = _____

10. *re-* + cycle = _____

Number correct _____ (total 10)

Exercise B Using words from the following list, complete each sentence with two words that have the same root.

applying	corrected	dispose	maintaining	resist
assigned	decreased	increase	persistent	resulted
composition	depending	instantly	reply	retain
constant	directions	insults	resigned	suspend

1. After _____ for a job as a stockroom worker, Gerri

   anxiously awaited a(an) _____ from the manager.

2. The conflict between the two teams _____ in an

   exchange of _____, with even the managers
   trading angry words.

3. The puppy gave _____ attention to its new owner but

   _____ retreated at the approach of its owner's friend.

4. It was difficult to _____ Jonathan's _____
   offer to share his bag of peanuts, but Sheila kept saying no.

5. Although her fever had _____ considerably, going down

   to 99.7°, Roxanne's thirst continued to _____.

6. When Mr. Lamont _____ as the company's accountant
   after twenty years in the position, his work was temporarily

   _____ to Mr. Gonzales.

7. Vince wanted to _____ his heavyweight wrestling title, so

   he worked hard at _____ his excellent physical condition.

8. Nuclear waste is difficult to _____ of because of its

   radioactive _____.

9. Because the Washingtons provided the wrong _____ to
   the party on the invitation, they had to cross them out and write a

   _____ version.

10. _____ on how bad the weather becomes on the Fourth of

    July, the mayor might _____ the scheduled parade and
    fireworks.

Number correct _____ (total 20)

The Prefix *ad-*

When some prefixes are added to certain words, the spelling of the prefix changes. The prefix *ad-* changes in the following cases to create a double consonant:

ac- before *c*   *ag-* before *g*   *an-* before *n*   *ar-* before *r*   *at-* before *t*

af- before *f*   *al-* before *l*   *ap-* before *p*   *as-* before *s*

Examples:

ad- + counting = accounting   *ad-* + pease = appease

ad- + fix = affix   *ad-* + range = arrange

ad- + gression = aggression   *ad-* + sist = assist

ad- + locate = allocate   *ad-* + tend = attend

ad- + nounce = announce

Exercise Add the prefix *ad-* to each of the roots or base words below. Change the spelling of the prefix as appropriate, and write the word.

1. *ad-* + commodation = _____

2. *ad-* + firm = _____

3. *ad-* + versity = _____

4. *ad-* + here = _____

5. *ad-* + cumulate = _____

6. *ad-* + sure = _____

7. *ad-* + mire = _____

8. *ad-* + test = _____

9. *ad-* + nex = _____

10. *ad-* + join = _____

11. *ad-* + parel = _____

12. *ad-* + apt = _____

13. *ad-* + complish = _____

14. *ad-* + plication = _____

15. *ad-* + flict = _____

Number correct _____ (total 15)

The Prefix com-

The spelling of the prefix *com-* does not change when it is added to roots or words that begin with the letter *m, p,* or *b.*

com- + mon = common   com- + ponent = component
com- + mit = commit   com- + bine = combine

The prefix *com-* changes to *con-* when added to roots or words that begin with the letter *c, d, g, j, n, q, s, t,* or *v.*

com- + current = concurrent   com- + trary = contrary
com- + sult = consult   com- + vince = convince

The prefix *com-* changes to *col-* when added to roots or words that begin with the letter *l,* to create a double consonant.

com- + lect = collect   com- + lide = collide

The prefix *com-* changes to *cor-* when added to roots or words that begin with the letter *r,* to create a double consonant.

com- + relation = correlation   com- + rupt = corrupt

Exercise Add the prefix *com-* to each of the roots or base words below. Change the spelling of the prefix as appropriate, and write the word.

1. *com-* + cern = _____

2. *com-* + ductor = _____

3. *com-* + respond = _____

4. *com-* + stant = _____

5. *com-* + tain = _____

6. *com-* + cept = _____

7. *com-* + nect = _____

8. *com-* + gregate = _____

9. *com-* + league = _____

10. *com-* + bustion = _____

11. *com-* + pete = _____

12. *com-* + vention = _____

13. *com-* + pel = _____

14. *com-* + prehend = _____

15. *com-* + rect = _____

Number correct _____ (total 15)

The Prefix *in-*

The spelling of the prefix *in-* does not change, except in the following cases:

(a) The prefix *in-* changes to *im-* when added to roots or words beginning with *m, p,* or *b.*

in- + possible = impossible   in- + purity = impurity
in- + mature = immature   in- + balance = imbalance

(b) The prefix *in-* changes to *il-* when added to roots or words beginning with *l,* to create a double consonant.

in- + legal = illegal   in- + lusion = illusion

(c) The prefix *in-* changes to *ir-* when added to roots or words beginning with *r,* to create a double consonant.

in- + regular = irregular   in- + rational = irrational

Exercise Find the misspelled word in each group. Write the word correctly.

_____ 1. inprobable
    illustrate
    irreverent
    immediate

_____ 2. immodest
    imperceptible
    inept
    inbecile

_____ 3. innovation
    imhuman
    immovable
    inhale

_____ 4. invitation
    imcredible
    immaculate
    immortal

_____ 5. insure
    inherit
    intention
    imform

_____ 6. imcrease
    implement
    imply
    impersonal

_____ 7. instinct
    ingenuity
    inject
    inmune

_____ 8. invade
    incident
    induct
    inpeach

_____ 9. illusion
    illefficient
    illegible
    illiterate

_____ 10. irresponsible
    irresistible
    irvariable
    irreversible

Number correct _____ (total 10)

The Prefix ex-

The spelling of the prefix *ex-* does not change when it is added to roots or words beginning with vowels or with the consonant *p, t, h,* or *c.*

ex- + pert = expert   ex- + claim = exclaim
ex- + tend = extend   ex- + it = exit
ex- + hale = exhale   ex- + ample = example

Exception: *Ex-* becomes *ec-* before *c* in the word *eccentric.*

The prefix *ex-* changes to *ef-* when added to roots or words beginning with *f.*

ex- + fort = effort   ex- + fect = effect

The prefix *ex-* changes to *e-* before most other consonants.

ex- + ject = eject   ex- + rase = erase
ex- + merge = emerge   ex- + lection = election

No common English words begin with the letters *exs.* When the prefix *ex-* is joined to roots that begin with the letter *s,* the *s* is dropped.

ex- + sert = exert   ex- + sist = exist

Exercise Find the misspelled word in each group. Write the word correctly.

_____ 1. excuse
excite
exibit
exhaust

_____ 2. event
elude
eternal
ellevate

_____ 3. erode
exficient
effort
exasperate

_____ 4. exceed
exxaggerate
expend
expand

_____ 5. examine
exxecute
exorbitant
extra

_____ 6. exept
exclude
exchange
excel

_____ 7. extreme
exponent
excess
exlate

_____ 8. extract
ectreme
extinguish
eccentric

_____ 9. eftra
effervesce
effort
effusive

_____ 10. elaborate
evolve
evaporate
errupt

Number correct _____ (total 10)

224

Words with Suffixes

Words Ending in *y*

A suffix is a group of letters added to the end of a word that changes the word's meaning.

When a suffix is added to a word ending in *y* preceded by a consonant, the *y* is usually changed to *i*.

laboratory + *-es* = laboratories   apply + *-es* = applies
frenzy + *-ed* = frenzied   fancy + *-ful* = fanciful

Exceptions:

(a) When *-ing* is added, the *y* does not change.

apply + *-ing* = applying   deny + *-ing* = denying
try + *-ing* = trying   carry + *-ing* = carrying

(b) In some one-syllable words, the *y* does not change.

dry + *-ness* = dryness   shy + *-ness* = shyness

When a suffix is added to a word ending in *y* preceded by a vowel, the *y* usually does not change.

delay + *-ed* = delayed   play + *-ful* = playful
enjoy + *-able* = enjoyable   joy + *-less* = joyless

Exceptions: day + *-ly* = daily   gay + *-ly* = gaily

Exercise A In these sentences, find each misspelled word, and write the correct spelling on the line following the sentence. There may be more than one misspelled word in a sentence.

1. Taro displaied little sensitivity when the class bully was caught red-handed.

   _____

2. "I cannot stress too strongly," our coach said, "the necessity of your relyance on your teammates."

   _____

3. Tony and Sam were petrifyed by the monster, whose image was magnifyed twenty times.

   _____

4. The crowd's sympathyes toward the candidates were mixed.

   _____

5. As a camp counselor, I enjoied helping kids acquire new talents and abilitys.

   _____

6. The suspense intensifyed as the hero of the story encountered many adversityes.

_____

7. During colonyal days the seeds of democracy were planted.

_____

Number correct _____ (total 10)

Exercise B Add the suffixes indicated, and write the word in the blank.

1. society + -es = _____

2. silly + -ness = _____

3. joy + -ous = _____

4. say + -ing = _____

5. policy + -es = _____

6. pay + -ment = _____

7. try + -ing = _____

8. mutiny + -es = _____

9. dignify + -ed = _____

10. study + -ous = _____

11. contrary + -ness = _____

12. dirty + -ed = _____

13. beauty + -ful = _____

14. busy + -est = _____

15. frequency + -es = _____

16. defy + -ing = _____

17. qualify + -ed = _____

18. easy + -ly = _____

19. abnormality + -es = _____

20. employ + -ment = _____

21. pray + -ing = _____

22. ugly + -er = _____

23. timely + -ness = _____

24. nasty + -ly = _____

25. thirsty + -est = _____

26. impurity + -es = _____

27. gray + -ish = _____

28. thirty + -es = _____

29. supply + -es = _____

30. testimony + -al = _____

Number correct _____ (total 30)

The Final Silent *e*

When a suffix beginning with a vowel is added to a word ending in a silent *e*, the *e* is usually dropped.

create + *-ion* = creation   observe + *-able* = observable
translate + *-ed* = translated   desperate + *-ion* = desperation
stole + *-en* = stolen   examine + *-ing* = examining

When a suffix beginning with a consonant is added to a word ending in a silent *e*, the *e* is usually retained.

suspense + *-ful* = suspenseful   involve + *-ment* = involvement
extreme + *-ly* = extremely   cease + *-less* = ceaseless
entire + *-ty* = entirety   mute + *-ness* = muteness

Exceptions:

true + *-ly* = truly   whole + *-ly* = wholly
argue + *-ment* = argument   awe + *-ful* = awful

Exercise A In these sentences, find each misspelled word, and write the correct spelling on the line following the sentence. There may be more than one misspelled word in a sentence.

1. The doctor questioned the effectivness of providing a smaller nursing staff to treat the patients in intenseive care.

   _____

2. From the observeation deck, Jack could see a congregation of people.

   _____

3. The actress's embarrassment over forgetting her lines made it difficult for her to keep her composeure.

   _____

4. During the suspensful climax of the horror film, the people were poisd on the edge of their seats.

_____

5. Martin was definitly bewildered by our idleness.

_____

6. We were determind not to get involved in other people's affairs.

_____

7. Ms. Aronson lodgd a legitimate complaint with the careless company.

_____

8. The president's awarness of the grave threat posed by declining food supplies prompted her to declare a state of national emergency.

_____

9. The police officer warned that another violateion of the law would require the issuing of a fine.

_____

10. The blueish chemical permeated the thin plastic container, spilled onto the floor, and began eating through the tile.

_____

11. Although our savings had decreaseed, the bank officer assurd us that we would receive a loan.

_____

12. The play was vaguly familiar to Anna, but she was completly unable to recall when she may have seen it.

_____

13. Several schools in the metropolitan area competd in the track meet, which was held five days before graduateion.

_____

14. It did not require much inducment for Sherry to admit her involvement in the desperately planned scheme.

_____

15. Maria hesitated, but then scraped the leftover food into the disposeal.

_____

Number correct _____ (total 20)

Exercise B Add the suffixes indicated, and write the new word in the blank.

1. guarantee + -ed = _____

2. accumulate + -ion = _____

3. humiliate + -ing = _____

4. mobile + -ity = _____

5. culture + -ed = _____

6. change + -ing = _____

7. engage + -ment = _____

8. arrange + -ed = _____

9. purpose + -ful = _____

10. endure + -ance = _____

11. recline + -er = _____

12. extreme + -ity = _____

13. douse + -ing = _____

14. sensitive + -ly = _____

15. fate + -ful = _____

16. decease + -ed = _____

17. definite + -ly = _____

18. subtle + -ty = _____

19. same + -ness = _____

20. assure + -ance = _____

21. impure + -ity = _____

22. rage + -ing = _____

23. congregate + -ed = _____

24. blame + -ing = _____

25. execute + -ion = _____

26. pierce + -ing = _____

27. grad + -ed = _____

28. intrigue + -ed = _____

29. enforce + -ment = _____

30. circulate + -ion = _____

Number correct _____ (total 30)

Doubling the Final Consonant

In one-syllable words that end with a single consonant preceded by a single vowel, double the final consonant before adding a suffix beginning with a vowel.

pin + -ing = pinning   fat + -er = fatter

Before adding a suffix beginning with a vowel to a word of two or more syllables, double the final consonant only if both of the following conditions exist:
1. The word ends with a single consonant preceded by a single vowel.
2. The word is accented on the last syllable.

pro pel′ + -ed = pro pelled′   re fer′ + -al = re fer′ ral

pro pel′ + -er = pro pel′ ler   per mit′ + -ing = per mit′ ting

com mit′ + -ed = com mit′ ted   de ter′ + -ence = de ter′ rence

Note in the examples above that the syllable accented in the new word is the same syllable that was accented before adding the suffix.

If the newly formed word is accented on a different syllable, the final consonant is not doubled.

re fer′ + -ence = ref′ er ence   pre fer′ + -ence = pref′ er ence

Exercise Each word below is divided into syllables. Determine which syllable in each word is accented, and insert the accent mark. Then add the suffix indicated, writing the new word in the blank. Repeat this procedure with the second suffix indicated.

Example: e mit′ + -ed = emitted + -ing = emitting

1. de mol′ish + -ed   = _____ + -ing   = _____

2. al′ter + -ed   = _____ + -ing   = _____

3. trans mit′ + -ed   = _____ + -ance = _____

4. ad mit′ + -ed   = _____ + -ing   = _____

5. cor re spond′ + -ed   = _____ + -ence = _____

6. be gin′ + -er   = _____ + -ing   = _____

7. gov′ern + -ed   = _____ + -ing   = _____

8. trans fer′ + -ed   = _____ + -ence = _____

9. ex hib′it + -ed   = _____ + -ing   = _____

10. cor rupt´ + -ed   = _____   + -ing   = _____

11. cor ral´ + -ed   = _____   + -ing   = _____

12. e quip´ + -ed   = _____   + -ing   = _____

13. in fer´ + -ed   = _____   + -ence   = _____

14. de liv´ er + -ed   = _____   + -ing   = _____

15. at tend´ + -ed   = _____   + -ance   = _____

Number correct _____ (total 30)

Words Ending in *-ize* or *-ise*

The suffix *-ize* is usually added to base words to form verbs meaning "to make" or "to become."

special + *-ize* = specialize (to make special)
memory + *-ize* = memorize (to make into a memory)

The *-ise* ending is less common. It is usually part of the base word itself rather than a suffix.

advertise   surprise   televise   devise   revise

Exercise Decide whether *-ize* or *-ise* should be added to each word or letter group. Then write the complete word in the blank.

1. merchand   _____   11. modern   _____

2. telev   _____   12. adv   _____

3. general   _____   13. conc   _____

4. civil   _____   14. organ   _____

5. exerc   _____   15. neutral   _____

6. superv   _____   16. comprom   _____

7. desp   _____   17. symbol   _____

8. idol   _____   18. compr   _____

9. critic   _____   19. social   _____

10. formal   _____   20. disgu   _____

Number correct _____ (total 20)

231

The Suffix *-ion*

The suffix *-ion* changes verbs to nouns.

rotate + *-ion* = rotation   confuse + *-ion* = confusion
distribute + *-ion* = distribution   discuss + *-ion* = discussion

In the examples above, *-ion* is either added directly to the verb form, or the final *e* is dropped before *-ion* is added.

Some verbs when made into nouns have irregular spellings.

compose + *-ion* = composition   adapt + *-ion* = adaptation
solve + *-ion* = solution   continue + *-ion* = continuation

In the case of words that do not follow regular spelling patterns, you must memorize their spellings.

Exercise A Add *-ion* to each of the following words. Then write the new word.

1. gravitate _____   9. express _____
2. contradict _____   10. violate _____
3. detect _____   11. graduate _____
4. object _____   12. correct _____
5. situate _____   13. compensate _____
6. quest _____   14. ignite _____
7. isolate _____   15. obligate _____
8. separate _____

Number correct _____ (total 15)

Exercise B Each of the following nouns is formed by adding the *-ion* suffix to a verb. Write the verb from which the word was formed. Use a dictionary when needed.

1. provision _____   9. revelation _____
2. disposition _____ 10. transmission _____
3. invitation _____   11. proclamation _____
4. competition _____ 12. invasion _____
5. application _____ 13. information _____
6. suspension _____   14. exclamation _____
7. qualification _____ 15. compulsion _____
8. seclusion _____

Number correct _____ (total 15)

Other Spelling Problems

Words with *ie* and *ei*

When the sound is long *e* (ē), it is spelled *ie*, except after *c*. If the vowel combination sounds like a long *a* (ā), spell it *ei*.

i before e

believe	brief	chief
fierce	grief	niece
siege	thief	yield

except after c

ceiling	perceive	deceit
deceive	receive	receipt

or when sounded as a

neighbor	weigh	reign

Exceptions:

either	weird	seize	financier
neither	species	leisure	

You can remember these words by combining them into the following sentence: *Neither financier seized either weird species of leisure.*

Exercise A In these sentences, find each misspelled word, and write the correct spelling on the line following the sentence.

1. Our chief reason for leaving the old nieghborhood was to seek a quieter spot.

   _____

2. His little neice seized the candy from his hand and gobbled it greedily.

   _____

3. The boxer's weight was decieving for a person of his enormous strength.

   _____

4. It was the tennis player's beleif that he would someday reign as world champion.

   _____

5. Sally received niether a receipt nor a verbal acknowledgment of her purchase.

   _____

6. Timothy will yeild the right of way to his fierce competitor.

   _____

7. The shadows cast upon the ceiling had a wierd appearance.

   _____

8. During the leisurely trip the Lopez family paid a breif visit to the home of friends.

   _____

9. The theif smuggled an unusual species of parrot into the country.

   _____

10. Dana was asked to retreive the financier's umbrella, which had blown across the street.

   _____

Number correct _____ (total 10)

Exercise B Fill in the blanks with *ie* or *ei*.

1. f __i__ __e__ ld
2. rel __i__ __e__ f
3. handkerch __i__ __e__ f
4. sl __e__ __i__ gh
5. conc __e__ __i__ ve
6. dec __e__ __i__ t
7. p __i__ __e__ r
8. bes __i__ __e__ ge

9. gr __i__ __e__ f
10. shr __i__ __e__ k
11. perc __e__ __i__ ve
12. sh __i__ __e__ ld
13. s __i__ __e__ ge
14. gr __i__ __e__ vous
15. financ __i__ __e__ r

Number correct _____ (total 15)

Words with the "Seed" Sound

One English word ends in *sede:*
supersede

Three words end in *ceed:*
exceed   proceed   succeed

All other words ending in the sound of *seed* are spelled with *cede:*
accede   concede   precede   recede   secede

Exercise In these sentences, find each misspelled word, and write the correct spelling on the line following the sentence.

1. Lonnie succeeded in learning the game quickly and before long had proceded to the most difficult level.

   _____

2. Mr. Barnes acceeded to his customer's demands and proceeded to reduce the price of the new car.

   _____

3. Julio learned that it was exceedingly easy to succede in school if he took his homework seriously.

   _____

4. In 1991, the Republic of the Ukraine seceeded from the Soviet Union and proceeded to set up an independent government.

   _____

5. The senator conceeded that her opponent's reasoning was correct and agreed to vote for the law.

   _____

6. Judge Stone announced his intention to proceed with the trial because the new federal law superceded state law.

   _____

7. As the flood waters began to receed, it became obvious that the damage far exceeded everyone's expectations.

   _____

8. After lengthy training, Jan succeeded in exceding her previous record in the 100-yard dash by almost one-half second.

   _____

9. Julia conceded that everything in her preceeding statement had been based on inaccurate information.

   _____

10. The committee chairperson interseded in our debate and suggested that we proceed with the next topic.

    _____

Number correct _____ (total 10)

The Letter c

When the letter c has a k sound, it is usually followed by the vowel a, o, or u, or by any consonant except y.

calendar   conform   culture   predict

When the letter c has an s sound, it is usually followed by an e, an i, or a y.

descent   difference   civil   bicycle

Exercise A Decide if the c in each word below has a k or an s sound. Write k or s in the blank.

1. accumulate _____
2. objection _____
3. chaos _____
4. ceremony _____
5. execution _____
6. necessity _____
7. picture _____
8. projection _____
9. incidental _____
10. policy _____

11. conductor _____
12. performance _____
13. cinema _____
14. indicate _____
15. continuous _____
16. miracle _____
17. colony _____
18. scissors _____
19. distinct _____
20. campaign _____

Number correct _____ (total 20)

Exercise B Write the missing letter or letters in each word.

1. soc __ ety
2. c __ mpete
3. disc __ pline
4. foc __ s
5. c __ emist
6. ac __ uality
7. c __ mpose
8. logic __ l
9. c __ riosity
10. inc __ ease

11. respec __ ful
12. proc __ amation
13. relianc __
14. mec __ anic
15. handic __ p
16. c __ editable
17. c __ amor
18. ac __ nowledgment
19. c __ rrec __ ion
20. c __ mmon

Number correct _____ (total 20)

The Letter *g*

When the letter *g* has a hard sound, as in the word *go*, it is usually followed by the vowel *a*, *o*, or *u*, or by any consonant except *y*.

engage   govern   gulf   neglect

When the letter *g* has a *j* sound, it is usually followed by an *e*, an *i*, or a *y*.

genuine   merge   rigid   gymnasium

Exceptions: giggle   gill   girl   give

Exercise A Decide if the *g* in each word has a *j* sound or a hard sound, as in the word *go*. Write *j* or *go* in the blank.

1. guide	____	11. goal	____
2. merge	____	12. ghost	____
3. graduate	____	13. generous	____
4. besiege	____	14. gather	____
5. golf	____	15. gravitate	____
6. gramaphone	____	16. germ	____
7. gypsy	____	17. glacier	____
8. original	____	18. golden	____
9. gently	____	19. general	____
10. glass	____	20. linger	____

Number correct _____ (total 20)

Exercise B Write the missing letter or letters in each word.

1. resig __ ation	11. mytholog __
2. vig __ r	12. intrig __ e
3. cong __ eg __ tion	13. g __ arantee
4. lodg __	14. ig __ ition
5. g __ adual	15. neg __ ig __ nt
6. radiolog __	16. g __ asp
7. eng __ neer	17. log __ cal
8. sieg __	18. safeg __ ard
9. oblig __ tion	19. mag __ ificent
10. vag __ e	20. g __ g __ ntic

Number correct _____ (total 20)

Spelling Review

Exercise A Add the prefix or suffix indicated, and write the new word.

1. lazy + -ly = _____
2. culture + -ed = _____
3. ad- + pear = _____
4. civil + -ize = _____
5. frequency + -es = _____
6. con- + mitment = _____
7. mute + -ness = _____
8. transmit + -ion = _____
9. in- + possible = _____
10. enforce + ment = _____
11. pre- + serve = _____
12. con- + nect = _____
13. ad- + sure = _____
14. graduate + -ion = _____
15. ex- + pel = _____
16. rely + -ance = _____
17. time + -ly = _____
18. in- + credible = _____
19. re- + call = _____
20. ex- + lection = _____

Number correct _____ (total 20)

Exercise B Three of the words in each row follow the same spelling pattern.
Circle the word that does not follow that pattern.

1. vaguely   inviting   awareness   ceaseless
2. correspond   correction   confederacy   corrupt
3. perceive   deceit   siege   receipt
4. goal   geology   neglect   gravity

5. excuse   elude   erode   erase

6. mobilize   devise   characterize   realize

7. observable   insured   impurity   idleness

8. peculiar   contrary   corrupt   civilize

9. deceased   situation   decreased   strangely

10. disposition   engaging   recycled   gravitation

Number correct _____ (total 10)

Exercise C Find the misspelled words in these sentences, and spell them correctly on the line after the sentence. There may be more than one misspelled word in a sentence.

1. Lisa's brother is interested in becoming an adcountant.

   _____

2. The final ecsamination was more difficult than the preceeding test.

   _____

3. The biology class observeed slides of microscopic animals magnifyed 5,000 times.

   _____

4. The geologist made a purposful attempt at dislodgeing the large rock.

   _____

5. Hilary's comstant involvment in club activities made her very popular.

   _____

6. The rocket propeled the spacecraft into a perfect orbit.

   _____

7. The theif did not perceive the presence of the law enforcment officers.

   _____

8. The feirce lion played gentley with the quizzical cub.

   _____

9. Suspention of the baseball game disadpointed many devoted fans.

   _____

10. The ecstremely tired runner had little energy left by the end of the race.

    _____

11. The teacher assigned a breif English compostion to be completed by Friday.

    _____

12. The arguement between the players ended quickly, and competition continueed.

_____

13. Even highly advanceed animals like monkeys have trouble adaptting to changes in their surroundings.

_____

14. Joel's untimly illness cost his team a chance at winning the championship title.

_____

15. It was inpossible to comvince Tess of her friend's seriousness.

_____

16. The excentric old lady was determind to rob the savings and loan.

_____

17. Everyone came to rely on Marcia's logic and well-constructed statments to help the debate club win its victoryes.

_____

18. The suspensful performance left the audience speechless.

_____

19. The leader of the lost expedition adsured the explorers that they could still succede in their mission.

_____

20. When Johns' inprobable story finally ended, the echausted campers doused the fire and went to sleep.

_____

Number correct _____ (total 35)

Number correct in Spelling Handbook _____ (total 430)

Commonly Misspelled Words

abbreviate	description	intelligence	realize
accidentally	desirable	knowledge	recognize
achievement	despair	laboratory	recommend
all right	desperate	lightning	reference
altogether	dictionary	literature	referred
amateur	different	loneliness	rehearse
analyze	disappear	marriage	repetition
anonymous	disappoint	mathematics	representative
answer	discipline	medicine	restaurant
apologize	dissatisfied	minimum	rhythm
appearance	efficient	mischievous	ridiculous
appreciate	eighth	missile	sandwich
appropriate	eligible	mortgage	scissors
arrangement	embarrass	municipal	separate
associate	emphasize	necessary	sergeant
awkward	enthusiastic	nickel	similar
bargain	environment	ninety	sincerely
beginning	especially	noticeable	sophomore
believe	exaggerate	nuclear	souvenir
bicycle	exhaust	nuisance	specifically
bookkeeper	experience	obstacle	success
bulletin	familiar	occasionally	syllable
bureau	fascinating	occur	sympathy
business	February	opinion	symptom
calendar	financial	opportunity	temperature
campaign	foreign	outrageous	thorough
candidate	fourth	parallel	throughout
certain	fragile	particularly	together
changeable	generally	permanent	tomorrow
characteristic	government	permissible	traffic
column	grammar	persuade	tragedy
committee	guarantee	pleasant	transferred
courageous	guard	pneumonia	truly
courteous	gymnasium	politics	Tuesday
criticize	handkerchief	possess	twelfth
curiosity	height	possibility	undoubtedly
cylinder	humorous	prejudice	unnecessary
dealt	imaginary	privilege	vacuum
decision	immediately	probably	vicinity
definitely	incredible	pronunciation	village
dependent	influence	psychology	weird

Commonly Confused Words

The following section lists words that are commonly confused and misused. Some of these words are homonyms, words that sound similar but have different meanings. Study the words in this list and learn how to use them correctly.

accent (ak′sent) n.—emphasis in speech or writing
ascent (ə sent′) n.—act of going up
assent (ə sent′) n.—consent; v.—to accept or agree

accept (ək sept′, ak-) v.—to agree to something or receive something willingly
except (ik sept′) v.—to omit or exclude; prep.—other than; but

adapt (ə dapt′) v.—to adjust; make fitting or appropriate
adept (ə dept′) adj.—skillful
adopt (ə däpt′) v.—to choose as one's own; accept

affect (ə fekt′) v.—to influence; pretend
affect (af′ekt) n.—feeling
effect (ə fekt′, i-) n.—result of an action
effect (ə fekt′, i-) v.—to accomplish or produce a result

all ready adv. (all) and adj. (ready)—completely prepared
already (ôl red′ē) adv.—even now; before the given time

any way adj. (any) and n. (way)—in whatever manner
anyway (en′ē wa′) adv.—regardless

appraise (ə prāz′) v.—to set a value on
apprise (ə prīz′) v.—to inform

bibliography (bib′lē äg′rə fē) n.—list of writings on a particular topic
biography (bī äg′ rə fē, bē-) n.—written history of a person's life

bazaar (bə zär′) n.—market; fair
bizarre (bi zär′) adj.—odd

coarse (kôrs) adj.—rough; crude
course (kôrs) n.—route; progression; part of a meal; class or unit of instruction in a subject

costume (käs′tōōm, -tyōōm) n.—special way of dressing
custom (kus′təm) n.—usual practice or habit

decent (dē′s'nt) adj.—proper
descent (di sent′) n.—a fall; a coming down
dissent (di sent′) n.—disagreement; v.—to disagree

desert (dez′ərt) n.—dry region
desert (di zʉrt′) v.—to abandon
dessert (di zʉrt′) n.—sweet course served at the end of a meal

device (di vīs′) n.—a tool or machine
devise (di vīz′) v.—to plan

elusive (i lo͞o′siv) adj.—hard to catch or understand
illusive (i lo͞o′siv) adj.—misleading; unreal

emigrate (em′ə grāt′) v.—to leave a country and take up residence elsewhere
immigrate (im′ə grāt′) v.—to enter a country and take up residence

farther (fär′thər) adj.—more distant (refers to space)
further (fʉr′thər) adj.—additional (refers to time, quantity, or degree)

flair (fler) n.—natural ability; knack; sense of style
flare (fler) v.—to flame; erupt; n.—a blaze of light

lay (lā) v.—to set something down or place something
lie (lī) v.—to recline; tell untruths; n.—an untruth

moral (môr′əl, mär′-) n.—lesson; adj.—relating to right and wrong
morale (mə ral′, mô-) n.—mental state of confidence, enthusiasm

personal (pʉr′s'n əl) adj.—private
personnel (pʉr′sə nel′) n.—persons employed in an organization

precede (pri sēd′) v.—to go before
proceed (prə sēd′, prō-) v.—to advance; continue

profit (präf′it) v.—to gain earnings; n.—financial gain on investments
prophet (präf′it) n.—predictor, fortuneteller

quiet (kwī′ ət) adj.—not noisy; n.—a sense of calm; v.—to soothe
quit (kwit) v.—to stop
quite (kwīt) adv.—very

step (step) n.—footfall; dance movement; one of a series of acts; v.—to move
the foot as in walking
steppe (step) n.—large, treeless plain

team (tēm) n.—group of people working together on a project
teem (tēm) v.—to swarm or be full of

than (*than, then; unstressed th*ən, *th*n) conj.—word used in comparison
then (*th*en) adv.—at that time, next in order of time; n.—that time

thorough (thʉr′ ō, -ə) adj.—complete
through (thro͞o) prep.—by means of; from beginning to end; adv.—in one
side and out the other

Glossary

A

abnormal (adj.) unusual; unnatural; p. 24. *Related word:* abnormality; p. 32.

accommodate (v.) to make room for; take care of; make fit; adapt; p. 124. *Related word:* accommodation; p. 131.

accomplishment (n.) achievement; completion; p. 35. *Related word:* accomplish; p. 43.

account (n.) explanation or report; credit arrangement with a bank or business; reckoning of money received or paid out; (v.) to give acceptable reasons or an explanation; p. 112. *Related words:* accountable, accounting; p. 121.

accumulate (v.) to collect; pile up; p. 24. *Related word:* accumulation; p. 32.

acknowledge (v.) to admit; recognize; p. 70. *Related word:* acknowledgment; p. 77.

actual (adj.) real; true; p. 70. *Related word:* actuality; p. 77.

adapt (v.) to adjust in order to fit different circumstances or fill a need; p. 58. *Related words:* adaptable, adaptation; p. 66.

advantage (n.) a more favorable position; superiority or a better chance; p.35

adverse (adj.) unfavorable; opposed to; negative; p. 112. *Related word:* adversity; p. 121.

alter (v.) to make different; modify; p. 14. *Related words:* alteration, alternate; p. 21.

ample (adj.) more than enough; abundant; plenty; p. 160.

anonymity (n.) namelessness; the state of not having one's name known; p. 160. *Related word:* anonymous; p. 168.

apparel (n.) clothing; p. 183.

apply (v.) to be suitable or relevant; use practically; put on; p. 82. *Related word:* application; p. 90.

appoint (v.) to name for an office or other position; p. 135. *Related words:* appointee, appointment; p. 144.

attitude (n.) point of view; way of thinking; p. 172.

available (adj.) that can be used; accessible; p. 124. *Related word:* avail; p. 131.

awkward (adj.) clumsy; unskilled; p. 58.

B

besiege (v.) to surround with armed forces; overwhelm; p. 124. *Related word:* siege; p. 131.

bewitch (v.) to attract as if by the power of witchcraft or magic; cast a spell on; p. 183.

bitterly (adv.) in a manner characterized by hatred or resentment; p. 135. *Related word:* bittersweet; p. 144.

C

campaign (n.) actions undertaken to achieve a political, social, or financial goal; (v.) to engage in a campaign; p. 135.

ceaselessly (adv.) nonstop; unendingly; p. 82. *Related word:* deceased; p. 90.

characteristic (n.) noticeable feature or trait; (adj.) distinctive; typical of an individual, group, or situation; p. 58. *Related word:* character; p. 66.

chemist (n.) an expert in chemistry; p. 14. *Related word:* nonchemical; p. 21.

circulate (v.) to spread; pass from person to person or from place to place; p. 112. *Related word:* circulation; p. 121.

civic (adj.) of or relating to a citizen, citizenship, or governmental affairs; p. 172. *Related words:* civil, civilian, civilize; p. 180.

cluster (n.) a number of things or persons gathered together; bunch; (v.) to gather or grow together; p. 24.

compel (v.) force; p. 183. *Related word:* compulsion; p. 190.

competitor (n.) one who strives for an object, prize, or position; a rival; p. 183. *Related words:* compete, competition; p. 190.

compose (v.) to make by combining different elements or parts; create through artistic or mental effort; quiet or make calm; p. 58.

concern (n.) special interest or regard arising through a personal tie or relationship; a worry; (v.) to relate to; be a care of; care about; p. 172.

condition (n.) manner or state of being; state of health; social rank; anything called for as a requirement; (v.) to bring into desired form; p. 14.

conduct (v.) to carry on; manage; lead; (n.) behavior; management; p. 14. *Related word:* conductor; p. 21.

confederate (n.) ally; associate; p. 112. *Related word:* confederacy; p. 121.

congregate (v.) to gather together; assemble; (adj.) gathered; assembled; p. 124. *Related word:* congregation; p. 131.

considerable (adj.) worth thinking about; important; much or large; p. 183. *Related word:* consider; p. 190.

constant (adj.) regular; uninterrupted; (n.) something unchanging, as a mathematical quantity; p. 35. *Related word:* constantly; p. 43.

consult (v.) to ask the advice of; confer; p. 160. *Related words:* consultant; consultation; p. 168.

continuous (adj.) unbroken; uninterrupted; regular; p. 58. *Related word:* continuity; p. 66.

contradict (v.) to resist or oppose in argument; deny the truth of; p. 183. *Related words:* contradiction, contradictory; p. 190.

contrary (adj.) opposite; p. 160. *Related word:* contrariness; p. 168.

cope (v.) to deal with problems or troubles; fight or contend with successfully or on equal terms; p. 58.

corrective (adj.) tending to improve a defect or weakness; p. 35. *Related word:* correction; p. 43.

correspond (v.) to exchange letters; p. 135. *Related words:* correspondence, correspondent; p. 144.

credit (n.) recognition; honor; praise; (v.) to believe; give recognition or praise; p. 35. *Related word:* creditable; p. 43.

cultured (adj.) refined; educated; knowledgeable about literary and artistic works; p. 172. *Related word:* culture; p. 180.

curious (adj.) questioning; eager for information; p. 24. *Related word:* curiosity; p. 32.

cycle (n.) series of regularly repeated events; (v.) to occur repeatedly at regular intervals; go through a cycle; p. 58. *Related words:* cyclical, recycle; p. 66.

D

decency (n.) proper behavior; socially proper actions; p. 135. *Related word:* decent; p. 144.

decrease (v.) to lessen; diminish; (n.) a reduction; p. 183. *Related word:* increase; p. 190.

dedication (n.) wholehearted devotion; commitment; p. 172.

definite (adj.) precise; exact; certain; p. 160. *Related word:* definitely; p. 168.

demolish (v.) to destroy completely; p. 124. *Related word:* demolition; p. 131.

desperate (adj.) extremely dangerous or serious; hopeless; p. 24. *Related word:* desperation; p. 32.

detect (v.) to discover the existence or presence of; p. 14. *Related words:* detection; detector; p. 21.

determination (n.) act of deciding firmly and purposefully; resolve; p. 172.

determined (adj.) decided; firm; settled; p. 35. *Related words:* determinant, determination, determine; p. 43.

development (n.) growth; an event or happening; p. 14. *Related word:* develop; p. 21.

discipline (n.) training that develops self-control or orderliness; the result of such training; (v.) to punish or penalize; train or develop by instruction; p. 172.

disclose (v.) to bring into view; uncover; make known; p. 70. *Related word:* disclosure; p. 77.

discount (v.) to disregard completely or believe only part of a story; reduce the regular price; (n.) a reduction from the regular price; p. 124.

dismal (adj.) gloomy; depressing; p. 160.

dispose (v.) to deal with; get rid of; eliminate; p. 135. *Related word:* disposition; p. 144.

distribute (v.) to spread out; divide among many; hand out; p. 58. *Related word:* distribution; p. 66.

domestic (adj.) of the home or family; of or relating to one's own country; (n.) a servant in the home; p. 124.

douse (v.) to pour liquid over; drench; soak; p. 70.

duly (adv.) properly; in due manner or time; p. 160.

E

effectiveness (n.) usefulness; forcefulness; p. 24. *Related words:* effective, ineffective; p. 32.

efficient (adj.) producing much with little waste; productive; p. 58. *Related word:* efficiency; p. 66.

endear (v.) to make beloved; p. 24. *Related word:* endearing; p. 32.

endeavor (n.) serious effort; undertaking; (v.) to attempt; undertake; p. 172.

enforce (v.) to carry out effectively; strengthen; p. 172. *Related word:* enforcement; p. 180.

engagement (n.) an encounter between opposing forces; an appointment; a pledge to marry; p. 135. *Related word:* engage; p. 144.

engineer (n.) one trained to apply scientific principles to practical needs; (v.) to construct or manage; guide the course of; p. 160. *Related words:* engine, engineering; p. 168.

establish (v.) to start; organize; p. 14. *Related word:* reestablish; p. 21.

eventually (adv.) finally; at an unspecified later time; p. 58. *Related words:* event, eventual; p. 66.

execute (v.) to put to death by capital punishment; carry out a plan or order; p. 112. *Related word:* execution; p. 121.

expedition (n.) journey undertaken for a specific purpose, such as exploration or battle; p. 112. *Related word:* expeditious; p. 121.

F

fanciful (adj.) imaginary; unreal; p. 82. *Related word:* fancy; p. 90.

fantasy (n.) an imaginative story; a dream; p. 82.

fate (n.) final outcome; destiny; p. 112. *Related words:* fatal, fateful; p. 121.

ferocious (adj.) fierce; savage; violent; p. 112.

florist (n.) one who sells flowers; one who grows flowers for sale; p. 14. *Related word:* floral; p. 21.

focus (v.) to concentrate; give one's full attention to; (n.) center of activity or attraction; p. 160. *Related word:* focal; p. 168.

formation (n.) a thing formed; the way in which something is arranged; structure; p. 14.

frenzied (adj.) wildly excited; frantic; p. 82. *Related word:* frenzy; p. 90.

frequently (adv.) often; usually; p. 14. *Related words:* frequency; infrequent; p. 21.

fuse (v.) to join or blend together, possibly by heating or melting; (n.) electrical safety device that prevents overloading a circuit; strip of combustible material, such as string or cloth, used to set off an explosive charge; p. 58.

G

geologist (n.) a scientist trained in the study of rocks and other earth formations; p. 160. *Related word:* geology; p. 168.

gigantic (adj.) huge; enormous; p. 112.

govern (v.) to rule; regulate or control; p. 82. *Related words:* governess, government; p. 90.

graduate (n.) one who receives a diploma or degree after completing a required course of study; (v.) to receive an academic degree; p. 160. *Related words:* gradual, graduation; p. 168.

grasp (v.) to take or seize; clutch; (n.) hold; control; understanding; p. 35.

guarantee (n.) a promise regarding the satisfactory performance of a product or satisfactory outcome of an event; a pledge; (v.) to promise; to pledge; p. 14.

H

handicap (n.) a disability or limitation; drawback; (v.) to put at a disadvantage; p. 14. *Related word:* handicapped; p. 21.

haven (n.) a place of shelter or safety; p. 183.

hazardous (adj.) dangerous; risky; p. 70. *Related word:* hazard; p. 77.

hesitation (n.) a halting or pausing for a moment; an unsureness; p. 124. *Related word:* hesitate; p. 131.

hinder (v.) to hold back; slow the progress of; p. 70. *Related word:* hindrance; p. 77.

horizontally (adv.) across, in a position parallel to the horizon; p. 58. *Related word:* horizontal; p. 66.

humiliate (v.) to hurt the pride or dignity of by causing to appear foolish; degrade; p. 124. *Related words:* humiliation, humility; p. 131.

I

idle (adj.) useless; inactive; (v.) to be or make inactive; p. 82.

ignite (v.) to excite; set afire; p. 172. *Related word:* ignition; p. 180.

impure (adj.) improper; unclean; dirty; p. 70. *Related word:* impurity; p. 77.

incident (n.) an event; a definite occurrence; p. 124. *Related words:* incidence, incidental; p. 131.

incredible (adj.) unbelievable; p. 112. *Related word:* credible; p. 121.

induce (v.) to move by persuasion or influence; cause; lead on; p. 124. *Related words:* inducement, induct, induction; p. 131.

informative (adj.) instructive; educational; p. 14.

inherit (v.) to come into possession of, often through a legal will; p. 112. *Related word:* inheritance; p. 121.

inseparable (adj.) unable to be parted; joined very closely; p. 14.

institution (n.) an established law, practice, or custom; an organization; the building housing such an organization; p. 135. *Related word:* institute; p. 144.

insure (v.) to make certain by taking necessary precautions; to guarantee; p. 183. *Related words:* assure, ensure, insurance; p. 190.

intense (adj.) to an extreme degree; considerable; deeply felt; p. 35. *Related words:* intensify, intensive; p. 43.

intention (n.) determination to do a specified thing; purpose; p. 112. *Related words:* intend, intent; p. 121.

international (adj.) of, relating to, or by various countries or the people of various countries; p. 160. *Related word:* national; p. 168.

intrigue (n.) secret plot; conspiracy; (v.) to arouse interest; plot or scheme; p. 70. *Related word:* intriguing; p. 77.

invade (v.) to enter by force in order to conquer; p. 112. *Related word:* invasion; p. 121.

inviting (adj.) appealing; tempting; p. 70. *Related word:* invitation; p. 77.

involve (v.) to include; participate in; p. 35. *Related word:* involvement; p. 43.

isolate (v.) to set apart from others; p. 183. *Related word:* isolation; p. 190.

J

journalist (n.) a person who reports or edits news for a television newscast, newspaper, or other type of media; p. 70. *Related word:* journalism; p. 77.

L

laboratory (n.) a place for scientific research and experimentation; p. 82. *Related word:* laborious; p. 90.

legitimate (adj.) reasonable; justifiable; genuine; p. 172.

linger (v.) to be slow in leaving; delay; p. 70.

loathe (v.) to dislike greatly; hate; p. 183.

lodge (v.) to occupy a place temporarily; come to rest and remain firmly fixed; (n.) a house set apart for some special use, such as a hunting lodge; p. 183.

logic (n.) clear, sensible reasoning; p. 82. *Related word:* logistics; p. 90.

lurk (v.) to lie hidden; move secretively; p. 82.

M

magnificent (adj.) splendid; extremely impressive; p. 14. *Related words:* magnification; magnificence; magnify; p. 21.

maintain (v.) to keep up; hold on to; p. 58. *Related word:* maintenance; p. 66.

maneuver (n.) a skillful movement or shrewd action; (v.) to scheme or plot; move in a controlled manner; manage skillfully; p. 70.

massive (adj.) big; larger than normal; imposing or impressive; p. 35.

meager (adj.) thin; emaciated; of poor quality or amount; p. 124.

merge (v.) to combine or blend into one; p. 58.

metropolitan (adj.) relating to a central city and its surrounding communities; p. 70.

miraculous (adj.) wondrous; awe-inspiring; p. 124. *Related word:* miracle; p. 131.

mission (n.) the special duty that a person or group is sent to do; a group of persons sent by a church or government to perform a special duty; p. 24.

mobile (adj.) capable of movement or of being moved; (n.) an abstract hanging sculpture with moving parts; p. 183. *Related word:* mobility; p. 190.

morale (n.) confidence; spirit; p. 124. *Related word:* moral; p. 131.

mortal (adj.) very intense; subject to death; human; (n.) a human being; p. 135. *Related word:* immortal; p. 144.

mute (adj.) silent; unable to speak; (v.) to reduce the sound of; silence; p. 24.

mutiny (n.) revolt against authority (especially by soldiers or sailors against their officers); (v.) to rebel; disobey; p. 24.

mythical (adj.) imaginary; existing only in myths or unreal stories; p. 82. *Related words:* myth, mythology; p. 90.

N

noble (n.) one possessing a title in a country ruled by royalty; a person of high birth or rank; (adj.) heroic; dignified; being a member of nobility; p. 112. *Related word:* nobility; p. 121.

O

objective (n.) something someone is trying to achieve or capture; a goal; (adj.) open-minded; not influenced by personal feelings; p. 112. *Related word:* objection; p. 121.

obligation (n.) duty; commitment; p. 172. *Related word:* obligate; p. 180.

observe (v.) to look at closely; examine; watch; p. 14. *Related words:* observation; unobserved; p. 21.

obvious (adj.) readily apparent; easily seen; p. 124.

option (n.) a choice; the act of choosing; p. 124. *Related word:* optional; p. 131.

ordain (v.) to establish or order by appointment or law; issue an order; p. 160. *Related word:* ordination; p. 168.

orthopedic (adj.) of or relating to the study and treatment of bones and joints; p. 35. *Related word:* orthopedist; p. 43.

oust (v.) to force out; expel; p. 135.

P

parallel (adj.) extending in the same direction, everywhere equally distant; on the same line as; (n.) something equal or similar in all important details; (v.) to make one thing parallel to another; p. 135.

peculiarly (adv.) distinctively; strangely; p. 82. *Related words:* peculiar, peculiarity; p. 90.

percussion (n.) the hitting of one object against another; a musical instrument that produces sound by being tapped or struck, such as a drum; p. 135. *Related word:* percussive; p. 144.

permeate (v.) to spread throughout; p. 124. *Related word:* permeation; p. 131.

persevere (v.) to continue in some effort or course of action in spite of difficulty; persist; p. 172.

petrify (v.) to stun or paralyze with fear; turn into, or as if into, stone; become rigid; p. 124.

placid (adj.) calm; free of interruption or disturbance; p. 124.

poise (v.) to balance; suspend; (n.) self-assurance; balance; p. 82.

policy (n.) a principle that guides action; definite course or plan of action; p. 172.

politics (n.) the art or science of government; governmental actions or practices; p. 172. *Related word:* political; p. 180.

practical (adj.) useful; realistic; p. 135. *Related word:* practicality; p. 144.

prediction (n.) a statement of what one thinks will happen; p. 14.

prevail (v.) to win out; be greater in strength or influence; p. 112. *Related word:* prevalent; p. 121.

previous (adj.) going before in time or order; p. 160.

proclaim (v.) to show; announce; state publicly; p. 183. *Related words:* claim, clamor, exclaim, exclamation, proclamation, p. 190.

propel (v.) to force into forward motion; push ahead; p. 58. *Related word:* propeller; p. 66.

purposefully (adv.) in a determined way; decisively; p. 160. *Related word:* purposeful; p. 168.

pursuit (n.) the act of chasing or seeking; the act of following; an occupation or hobby; p. 70. *Related word:* pursue; p. 77.

Q

quality (n.) excellence; a character trait; noticeable feature; p. 112.

quantity (n.) an amount; a portion; a great amount or number; p. 35.

quest (n.) a search; (v.) to go in search or pursuit of; p. 24.

R

radiology (n.) the science dealing with the use of X-rays in the diagnosis and treatment of disease; p. 35. *Related word:* radiologist; p. 43.

recall (v.) to bring back to mind; remember; call back; (n.) the ability to remember information; memory; p. 35.

reform (n.) removal or correction of faults or errors; (v.) to improve; become better; p. 172. *Related words:* conform, deform, inform; p. 180.

regain (v.) to recover; get back again; p. 82.

reliable (adj.) dependable; p. 70. *Related words:* reliability, reliance, rely; p. 77.

render (v.) to deliver; to present; p. 14.

repercussion (n.) after-effect of an action or event; result; consequence; p. 135.

repulsive (adj.) disgusting; upsetting; p. 24.

resent (v.) to feel or show bitter hurt or anger at or toward someone; p. 183. *Related word:* resentment; p. 190.

resign (v.) to give up deliberately; p. 135; *Related word:* resignation; p. 144.

resistant (adj.) opposing; unaccepting; p. 58. *Related word:* resistance; p. 66.

respect (n.) high or special regard; (v.) to admire; regard highly; p. 172. *Related words:* respectable, respectful; p. 180.

reveal (v.) to show; p. 82.

rotate (v.) to move around a central point; take turns when performing an action; p. 58. *Related word:* rotation; p. 66.

S

safeguard (n.) protection; a precaution; (v.) to protect against; keep secure; p. 14.

scanty (adj.) barely enough or not enough; insufficient; p. 112.

seasonal (adj.) dependent upon the seasons or time of year; p. 14. *Related word:* unseasonable; p. 21.

sensitivity (n.) responsiveness to outside conditions and stimulations; responsiveness to others' feelings; p. 35. *Related word:* sensitive; p. 43.

sheer (adj.) absolute; pure; easily seen through, as applied to cloth; p. 35.

situation (n.) condition; circumstance; location; p. 82. *Related word:* situate; p. 90.

skirmish (n.) a minor dispute between opposing forces; a minor fight; p. 183.

smolder (v.) to burn slowly, without flame and with much smoke; p. 124.

snipe (v.) to attack slyly; shoot from hiding; p.135. *Related word:* sniper; p. 144.

social (adj.) of or relating to human communities; (n.) an informal gathering; a party; p. 172. *Related words:* socialize, society; p. 180.

solemn (adj.) serious, deeply earnest; p. 70. *Related word:* solemnity; p. 77.

specialist (n.) an expert in a specific field; p. 35. *Related word:* specialty; p. 43.

stamina (n.) endurance; the physical or mental ability to continue an undertaking in spite of difficulties; p. 35.

streamline (v.) to shape for smooth movement; update and modernize; p. 58.

substantial (adj.) real; solid; large; important; p. 112.

suitable (adj.) appropriate; acceptable; p. 58. *Related word:* suit; p. 66.

suite (n.) a matched set of furniture; a series of connecting rooms; p. 135.

suspend (v.) to stop or remove temporarily; hang freely, except at the point of support; p. 82. *Related word:* suspension; p. 90.

suspense (n.) mental uncertainty; state of excitement regarding the outcome of an event; p. 24. *Related words:* suspend, suspenseful; p. 32.

sympathy (n.) feeling of sorrow for another person's situation; p. 135. *Related words:* sympathetic, sympathize; p. 144.

systematically (adv.) in an organized, orderly manner; p. 160. *Related word:* system; p. 168.

T

technician (n.) one having special scientific or mechanical skills; p. 24. *Related word:* technical; p. 32.

terrain (n.) physical features of the earth, such as mountains, cliffs, and valleys; p. 160.

testimony (n.) any form of evidence; a statement made by a witness under oath in a court of law; p. 24.

token (adj.) slight; symbolic; done as an indication or a pledge; (n.) an outward sign or expression; a sign or a symbol; a small metal object used in place of a coin; p. 135.

toxic (adj.) poisonous; p. 183.

trait (n.) identifying feature; characteristic; p. 82.

tranquilize (v.) to calm through the use of medication; cause to relax; p. 35. *Related words:* tranquil, tranquillity; p. 43.

transformation (n.) change in shape, size, appearance, or character; p. 24. *Related words:* transfer, transform, translate, transparent, transplant; p. 32.

transition (n.) connection; change from one state or place to another or the period of this change; p. 82. *Related words:* transit, transmission; p. 90.

transmit (v.) to send; transfer; p. 183. *Related word:* transmission; p. 190.

U

unaccountable (adj.) not responsible for; unexplainable; p. 70. *Related word:* accountable; p. 77.

unaware (adj.) unknowing; not conscious of; p. 70. *Related words:* aware, awareness; p. 77.

uncommonly (adv.) unusually; remarkably; exceptionally; p. 160. *Related word:* common; p. 168.

unheralded (adj.) not expected or announced; not well-known; p. 160. *Related word:* herald; p. 168.

unmindful (adj.) unaware; careless; p. 160. *Related word:* mindful; p. 168.

untimely (adj.) occurring at the wrong time; (adv.) before the natural or proper time; p. 24.

uphold (v.) to give support to, especially emotional support; p. 172.

V

vaguely (adv.) unclearly; indistinctly; p. 82. *Related word:* vague; p. 90.

venture (n.) a risky undertaking, particularly in a business or financial sense; (v.) to risk; dare; p. 24.

version (n.) a description or retelling related from one person's point of view; an interpretation; p. 70.

versus (prep.) against; p. 172.

vertical (adj.) straight up and down; p. 58.

veteran (n.) one with long experience in a particular field; (adj.) experienced; p. 183.

veterinarian (n.) medical doctor specializing in the treatment of animals; p. 35.

vigorous (adj.) energetic; strong; lively; p. 112. *Related word:* vigor; p. 121.

violate (v.) to break or disregard; treat with disrespect; p. 183. *Related word:* violation; p. 190.

vital (adj.) essential; necessary; full of life; p. 24. *Related word:* vitality; p. 32.

vivid (adj.) lively; bright; lifelike; p. 70. *Related word:* vividness; p. 77.

W

wage (n.) money paid for work done; (v.) to take part in or carry on; p. 135. *Related word:* wager; p. 144.

Z

zeal (n.) enthusiasm; p. 24. *Related words:* zealot, zealous; p. 32.

Pronunciation Key

Symbol	Key Words
a	ask, fat, parrot
ā	ape, date, play
ä	ah, car, father
e	elf, ten, berry
ē	even, meet, money
i	is, hit, mirror
ī	ice, bite, high
ō	open, tone, go
ô	all, horn, law
o͞o	ooze, tool, crew
oo	look pull, moor
yo͞o	use, cute, few
yoo	united, cure, globule
oi	oil, point, toy
ou	out, crowd, plow
u	up, cut, color
ur	urn, fur, deter
ə	a in ago e in agent i in sanity o in comply u in focus
ər	perhaps, murder

Symbol	Key Words
b	bed, fable, dub
d	dip, beadle, had
f	fall, after, off
g	get, haggle, dog
h	he, ahead, hotel
j	joy, agile, badge
k	kill, tackle, bake
l	let, hellow, ball
m	met, camel, trim
n	not, flannel, ton
p	put, apple, tap
r	red, port, dear
s	sell, castle, pass
t	top, cattle hat
v	vat, hovel, have
w	will, always, swear
y	yet, onion, yard
z	zebra, dazzle, haze
ch	chin, catcher, arch
sh	she, cushion, dash
th	thin, nothing, truth
th	then, father, lathe
zh	azure, leisure
ŋ	ring, anger, drink
′	able (a′ b'l)
′ ′	expedition (ek′ spə dish′ ən)

Pronunciation key and some glossary entries reprinted from *Webster's New World Dictionary*, Student Edition. Copyright © 1981, 1976 Simon & Schuster. Used by permission.

Inventory Test

These are all the target words in the book. Why not see how many you think you already know . . . or don't know?

- If you're sure *you know the word*, mark the **Y** *("yes") circle.*
- If you think you *might know it*, mark the **?** *(question mark) circle.*
- If you have no idea *what it means*, mark the **N** *("no") circle.*

Y	?	N	
O	O	O	abnormal
O	O	O	accommodate
O	O	O	accomplishment
O	O	O	account
O	O	O	accumulate
O	O	O	acknowledge
O	O	O	actual
O	O	O	adapt
O	O	O	advantage
O	O	O	adverse
O	O	O	alter
O	O	O	ample
O	O	O	anonymity
O	O	O	apparel
O	O	O	apply
O	O	O	appoint
O	O	O	attitude
O	O	O	available
O	O	O	awkward
O	O	O	besiege
O	O	O	bewitch
O	O	O	bitterly
O	O	O	campaign
O	O	O	ceaselessly
O	O	O	characteristic
O	O	O	chemist
O	O	O	circulate
O	O	O	civic
O	O	O	cluster
O	O	O	compel
O	O	O	competitor
O	O	O	compose
O	O	O	concern
O	O	O	condition
O	O	O	conduct
O	O	O	confederate
O	O	O	congregate
O	O	O	considerable
O	O	O	constant
O	O	O	consult

That's the first 40.

Y	?	N	
O	O	O	continuous
O	O	O	contradict
O	O	O	contrary
O	O	O	cope
O	O	O	corrective
O	O	O	correspond
O	O	O	credit
O	O	O	cultured
O	O	O	curious
O	O	O	cycle
O	O	O	decency
O	O	O	decrease
O	O	O	dedication
O	O	O	definite
O	O	O	demolish
O	O	O	desperate
O	O	O	detect
O	O	O	determination
O	O	O	determined
O	O	O	development

You're making progress.

Y	?	N	
O	O	O	discipline
O	O	O	disclose
O	O	O	discount
O	O	O	dismal
O	O	O	dispose
O	O	O	distribute
O	O	O	domestic
O	O	O	douse
O	O	O	duly
O	O	O	effectiveness
O	O	O	efficient
O	O	O	endear
O	O	O	endeavor
O	O	O	enforce
O	O	O	engagement
O	O	O	engineer
O	O	O	establish
O	O	O	eventually
O	O	O	execute
O	O	O	expedition

Y	?	N	
O	O	O	fanciful
O	O	O	fantasy
O	O	O	fate
O	O	O	ferocious
O	O	O	florist
O	O	O	focus
O	O	O	formation
O	O	O	frenzied
O	O	O	frequently
O	O	O	fuse
O	O	O	geologist
O	O	O	gigantic
O	O	O	govern
O	O	O	graduate
O	O	O	grasp
O	O	O	guarantee
O	O	O	handicap
O	O	O	haven
O	O	O	hazardous
O	O	O	hesitation
O	O	O	hinder
O	O	O	horizontally
O	O	O	humiliate
O	O	O	idle
O	O	O	ignite
O	O	O	impure
O	O	O	incident
O	O	O	incredible
O	O	O	induce
O	O	O	informative
O	O	O	inherit
O	O	O	inseparable
O	O	O	institution
O	O	O	insure
O	O	O	intense
O	O	O	intention
O	O	O	international
O	O	O	intrigue
O	O	O	invade
O	O	O	inviting

Take a break!

Y	?	N		Y	?	N		Y	?	N	
○	○	○	involve	○	○	○	placid	○	○	○	specialist
○	○	○	isolate	○	○	○	poise	○	○	○	stamina
○	○	○	journalist	○	○	○	policy	○	○	○	streamline
○	○	○	laboratory	○	○	○	politics	○	○	○	substantial
○	○	○	legitimate	○	○	○	practical	○	○	○	suitable
○	○	○	linger	○	○	○	prediction	○	○	○	suite
○	○	○	loathe	○	○	○	prevail	○	○	○	suspend
○	○	○	lodge	○	○	○	previous	○	○	○	suspense
○	○	○	logic	○	○	○	proclaim	○	○	○	sympathy
○	○	○	lurk	○	○	○	propel	○	○	○	systematically
○	○	○	magnificent	○	○	○	purposefully	○	○	○	technician
○	○	○	maintain	○	○	○	pursuit	○	○	○	terrain
○	○	○	maneuver	○	○	○	quality	○	○	○	testimony
○	○	○	massive	○	○	○	quantity	○	○	○	token
○	○	○	meager	○	○	○	quest	○	○	○	toxic
○	○	○	merge	○	○	○	radiology	○	○	○	trait
○	○	○	metropolitan	○	○	○	recall	○	○	○	tranquilize
○	○	○	miraculous	○	○	○	reform	○	○	○	transformation
○	○	○	mission	○	○	○	regain	○	○	○	transition
○	○	○	mobile	○	○	○	reliable	○	○	○	transmit
○	○	○	morale	○	○	○	render				*Only 20 more.*
○	○	○	mortal	○	○	○	repercussion	○	○	○	unaccountable
○	○	○	mute	○	○	○	repulsive	○	○	○	unaware
○	○	○	mutiny	○	○	○	resent	○	○	○	uncommonly
○	○	○	mythical	○	○	○	resign	○	○	○	unheralded
			Half the alphabet.	○	○	○	resistant	○	○	○	unmindful
○	○	○	noble	○	○	○	respect	○	○	○	untimely
○	○	○	objective	○	○	○	reveal	○	○	○	uphold
○	○	○	obligation	○	○	○	rotate	○	○	○	vaguely
○	○	○	observe	○	○	○	safeguard	○	○	○	venture
○	○	○	obvious	○	○	○	scanty	○	○	○	version
○	○	○	option	○	○	○	seasonal	○	○	○	versus
○	○	○	ordain	○	○	○	sensitivity	○	○	○	vertical
○	○	○	orthopedic	○	○	○	sheer	○	○	○	veteran
○	○	○	oust	○	○	○	situation	○	○	○	veterinarian
○	○	○	parallel	○	○	○	skirmish	○	○	○	vigorous
○	○	○	peculiarly	○	○	○	smolder	○	○	○	violate
○	○	○	percussion				*This list will end soon.*	○	○	○	vital
○	○	○	permeate	○	○	○	snipe	○	○	○	vivid
○	○	○	persevere	○	○	○	social	○	○	○	wage
○	○	○	petrify	○	○	○	solemn	○	○	○	zeal

Congratulations!

That was 240 words. How many of them *don't* you know? Highlight any words you marked **N**, write them on the Personal Vocabulary Log pages provided (beginning on page 270), and pay special attention to them as you work through the book. You'll soon know them all!

Pretest Strategies

Use What You Already Know

There are many ways to figure out what a word you don't know might mean.

- It may contain a familiar **whole word**.
- It may be a **compound** of familiar words put together.
- You may recognize the **root**.
- You may recognize a **prefix** or **suffix**.
- There may be **context clues** to the meaning.

Try Everything

When you see an unfamiliar word, use every trick you can think of. You may be surprised to discover how useful what you already know can be. Take a look at how this can work with the word *malodorous* in the sentence "What a malodorous plant!"

	THOUGHT PROCESS	
malodorous	It describes a plant. Must be an adjective.	**a context clue**
mal•*odorous*	What does *mal-* do? Let's see. A malfunction is bad. Malnutrition is bad. So *mal-* is probably "bad."	**a familiar prefix**
*mal•*odor*•ous*	I see *odor* in there.	**a whole word**
*malodor•*ous	I've seen *-ous* at the end of lots of words, like *famous*. Hmm . . . *fame, famous . . . humor, humorous.*	**a familiar suffix**
	Adjective. Bad. Odor. . . . What a bad-smelling plant!	

Try It Yourself

_____ 1. falsity (think about *false* and *captivity*)
   a. kindness   b. dishonesty   c. carelessness

_____ 2. readmit (think about *reread* and *admit*)
   a. to look at   b. to do over   c. to let in again

_____ 3. decolorize (think about *defrost*, *color*, and *alphabetize*)
   a. to bleach   b. to stain   c. to paint

_____ 4. disallow (think about *disappear* and *allow*)
   a. to forbid   b. to scold   c. to bring back

_____ 5. purposeless (think about *purpose* and *hopeless*)
   a. not real   b. deliberate   c. without a goal

Part A   Recognizing Meaning

Write the letter of the word or phrase that is closest in meaning to the word in italics.

_____ 1. to *safeguard* a treasure
    a. buy   c. protect
    b. find   d. appreciate

_____ 2. the *magnificent* painting
    a. huge   c. expensive
    b. wonderful   d. very colorful

_____ 3. to *observe* someone
    a. watch   c. arrest
    b. enjoy   d. try to meet

_____ 4. friends who are *inseparable*
    a. loyal   c. the same size
    b. cheerful   d. always together

_____ 5. to *establish* rules
    a. make   c. break
    b. need   d. dislike

_____ 6. to *detect* mice
    a. fear   c. notice
    b. chase   d. strongly dislike

_____ 7. a question asked *frequently*
    a. often   c. rudely
    b. slowly   d. with confusion

_____ 8. to see a *florist*
    a. bakery   c. carpet seller
    b. blossom   d. flower seller

_____ 9. to *conduct* a meeting
    a. plan   c. go to
    b. have   d. interrupt

_____ 10. to *alter* a jacket
    a. buy   c. change
    b. need   d. borrow

Part B   Matching Definitions

Match each word on the left with its definition on the right. Write the letter of the definition in the blank.

_____ 11. condition   a. limited to a certain time of year

_____ 12. seasonal   b. a promise that a product will work

_____ 13. render   c. something told beforehand

_____ 14. prediction   d. state of being or health; requirement

_____ 15. handicap   e. growth; an event or happening

_____ 16. informative   f. a disadvantage or disability

_____ 17. development   g. containing facts or giving knowledge

_____ 18. formation   h. to provide or give; present

_____ 19. chemist   i. a structure or shape; arrangement

_____ 20. guarantee   j. a person who works with chemicals

UNIT 2 Test Yourself

Part A Applying Meaning
Write the letter of the best answer.

_____ 1. A <u>curious</u> person is likely to often say,
   a. "No!"   b. "Go away!"   c. "Why?"   d. "Let's eat."

_____ 2. When you are in <u>suspense</u>, you feel
   a. glad.   b. sorry.   c. proud.   d. nervous.

_____ 3. Who would be most worried about a <u>mutiny</u>?
   a. a cook   b. a firefighter   c. a dogcatcher   d. a ship's captain

_____ 4. If I <u>endear</u> myself to you, you will be sure to
   a. pay me.   b. like me.   c. copy me.   d. be mad at me.

_____ 5. An <u>untimely</u> event is one that happens
   a. very slowly.   b. at the wrong time.   c. much too fast.   d. over and over
                                                                      again.

Part B Synonyms
Write the letter of the word that is closest in meaning to the capitalized word.

_____ 6. MUTE: (A) sad   (B) sweet   (C) silent   (D) grouchy

_____ 7. REPULSIVE: (A) clumsy   (B) difficult (C) illegal   (D) disgusting

_____ 8. ABNORMAL: (A) unusual   (B) unhealthy (C) regular   (D) upsetting

_____ 9. ACCUMULATE: (A) gather   (B) change   (C) welcome   (D) count

_____ 10. TRANSFORMATION: (A) growth   (B) change   (C) collection (D) surprise

_____ 11. DESPERATE: (A) angry   (B) sure   (C) hopeless   (D) final

_____ 12. CLUSTER: (A) noise   (B) group   (C) mistake   (D) hint

_____ 13. VITAL: (A) real   (B) loud   (C) convenient (D) necessary

_____ 14. QUEST: (A) search   (B) complaint (C) answer   (D) trip

_____ 15. MISSION: (A) duty   (B) absence   (C) error   (D) victory

_____ 16. TESTIMONY: (A) sadness   (B) support   (C) assignment (D) evidence

_____ 17. VENTURE: (A) attack   (B) risk   (C) enjoy   (D) win

_____ 18. TECHNICIAN: (A) worker   (B) puzzle   (C) expert   (D) assistant

_____ 19. EFFECTIVENESS: (A) fondness   (B) experience (C) bravery   (D) usefulness

_____ 20. ZEAL: (A) anger   (B) strictness (C) speed   (D) enthusiasm

---

Score Yourself!   _The answers are on page 268._   Number correct: _____   Part A: _____   Part B: _____

UNIT 3 Test Yourself

Part A Matching Definitions

Match each word on the left with its definition on the right. Write the letter of the definition in the blank.

_____ 1. constant   a. to remember

_____ 2. tranquilize   b. a number, amount, or portion

_____ 3. sensitivity   c. the ability to be affected

_____ 4. quantity   d. to make calm or relaxed

_____ 5. credit   e. continuing; not changing

_____ 6. involve   f. the ability to continue doing something difficult

_____ 7. stamina   g. extreme; deeply felt

_____ 8. specialist   h. something that helps; benefit

_____ 9. corrective   i. meant to improve

_____ 10. intense   j. an expert in some job or skill

_____ 11. accomplishment   k. having one's mind made up; firm

_____ 12. sheer   l. honor, praise, or special notice

_____ 13. advantage   m. something done successfully

_____ 14. recall   n. to include; require as part of

_____ 15. determined   o. not mixed with anything else; pure

Part B Applying Meaning

Write the letter of the best answer.

_____ 16. The science of <u>radiology</u> helps people see
a. a long distance.   b. inside the body.   c. invisible things.   d. in the dark.

_____ 17. During a baseball game, you must <u>grasp</u> the ball if you are the
a. pitcher.   b. umpire.   c. batter.   d. scorekeeper.

_____ 18. One animal that is known for being <u>massive</u> is a
a. fox.   b. pigeon.   c. whale.   d. rattlesnake.

_____ 19. A <u>veterinarian</u> would have to know a lot about
a. dogs.   b. babies.   c. insects.   d. old people.

_____ 20. You might need to see an <u>orthopedic</u> expert if you had
a. poor eyesight.   b. a headache.   c. a chipped tooth.   d. a broken arm.

UNIT 5   Test Yourself

Part A   Synonyms

Write the letter of the word that is closest in meaning to the capitalized word.

_____ 1. SUITABLE: (A) proper   (B) needed   (C) clever   (D) matching

_____ 2. CONTINUOUS: (A) recent   (B) noisy   (C) tiring   (D) lasting

_____ 3. PROPEL: (A) change   (B) push   (C) improve   (D) explode

_____ 4. AWKWARD: (A) lonely   (B) mean   (C) clumsy   (D) dangerous

_____ 5. EVENTUALLY: (A) quickly   (B) later   (C) soon   (D) especially

_____ 6. MERGE: (A) blend   (B) collide   (C) subtract (D) assist

_____ 7. ADAPT: (A) take   (B) succeed   (C) argue   (D) adjust

_____ 8. EFFICIENT: (A) kind   (B) dainty   (C) able   (D) hard

_____ 9. VERTICAL: (A) distant   (B) upright   (C) long   (D) thin

_____ 10. ROTATE: (A) spoil   (B) list   (C) turn   (D) begin

Part B   Recognizing Meaning

Write the letter of the word or phrase that is closest in meaning to the word in italics.

_____ 11. to *maintain* your concentration
    a. lose   c. keep
    b. interrupt   d. be proud of

_____ 12. stripes that ran *horizontally*
    a. across   c. narrowly
    b. crookedly d. up and down

_____ 13. to *cope* with the children
    a. talk   c. have fun
    b. deal well   d. be pleased

_____ 14. an odd *characteristic*
    a. person   c. feature
    b. response   d. movement

_____ 15. to *streamline* mail delivery
    a. expect   c. interrupt
    b. speed up   d. charge for

_____ 16. to be *resistant*
    a. unhappy   c. bouncy
    b. far away   d. not accepting

_____ 17. to *fuse* the pieces
    a. join   c. mix up
    b. locate   d. separate

_____ 18. to *compose* a song
    a. sing   c. listen to
    b. make up   d. recognize

_____ 19. an endless *cycle*
    a. problem   c. change
    b. dizziness d. repeated series

_____ 20. to *distribute* the tests
    a. take   c. pass out
    b. not enjoy d. do well on

Score Yourself!   *The answers are on page 268.*   Number correct: _____   Part A: _____   Part B: _____

UNIT 6   Test Yourself

Part A   Recognizing Meaning

Write the letter of the word or phrase that is closest in meaning to the word in italics.

_____ 1. some *hazardous* activities
  a. unsafe   c. difficult
  b. peaceful   d. interesting

_____ 2. to *hinder* walking
  a. dislike   c. encourage
  b. succeed at   d. make difficult

_____ 3. to *acknowledge* the truth
  a. defend   c. admit
  b. believe   d. investigate

_____ 4. a *solemn* look
  a. serious   c. lonely
  b. threatening d. strange

_____ 5. to *linger* at the playground
  a. talk   c. be active
  b. stay on   d. cause trouble

_____ 6. the *pursuit* of rabbits
  a. habits   c. description
  b. chasing   d. living place

_____ 7. *unaware* that we were there
  a. very glad   c. not happy
  b. not afraid   d. not realizing

_____ 8. to be *unaccountable*
  a. left out   c. very poor
  b. not to blame d. not affected

_____ 9. to *disclose* a plan
  a. try to hide c. make
  b. make known   d. want to know

_____ 10. to be *impure*
  a. plain   c. not clean
  b. angry   d. not selfish

_____ 11. the *actual* event
  a. big   c. noticeable
  b. real   d. long-lasting

_____ 12. to *maneuver* the car
  a. repair   c. quickly stop
  b. get into   d. skillfully move

_____ 13. a *vivid* tale
  a. lively   c. short
  b. frightening d. believable

_____ 14. get *reliable* information
  a. too much   c. repeated
  b. interesting d. trustworthy

Part B   Applying Meaning

Write the letter of the best answer.

_____ 15. In large <u>metropolitan</u> areas, you would expect to find
  a. farms.   b. traffic jams.   c. ships.   d. forests.

_____ 16. You could <u>douse</u> a fire with
  a. water.   b. small sticks.   c. a blanket.   d. a fireplace.

_____ 17. A job that calls for a great deal of <u>intrigue</u> is that of a
  a. spy.   b. banker.   c. doctor.   d. musician.

_____ 18. Any <u>journalist</u> needs to be able to
  a. draw.   b. teach.   c. write.   d. be amusing.

_____ 19. Three <u>versions</u> of the same story probably have three different
  a. plots.   b. endings.   c. authors.   d. characters.

_____ 20. If a path looked <u>inviting</u>, people would want to
  a. avoid it.   b. walk down it.   c. make it wider.   d. be very careful.

Score Yourself!   *The answers are on page 268.*   Number correct: _____   Part A: _____   Part B: _____

UNIT 7 Test Yourself

Part A Matching Definitions

Match each word on the left with its definition on the right. Write the letter of the definition in the blank.

_____ 1. poise   a. unclearly

_____ 2. trait   b. to wait out of sight

_____ 3. lurk   c. to control or rule

_____ 4. fantasy   d. a product of the imagination

_____ 5. logic   e. clear, sensible thinking

_____ 6. vaguely   f. to balance; hang without moving

_____ 7. mythical   g. wildly excited; upset and frantic

_____ 8. govern   h. a condition; combination of facts or events

_____ 9. laboratory   i. a passage or period of change

_____ 10. transition   j. having to do with myths; imaginary

_____ 11. frenzied   k. a place for doing science research and experiments

_____ 12. situation   l. a characteristic; whatever allows something to be identified

Part B Recognizing Meaning

Write the letter of the word or phrase that is closest in meaning to the word in italics.

_____ 13. to be made *peculiarly*
    a. carefully   c. long ago
    b. strangely   d. in a new way

_____ 14. to *suspend* our efforts
    a. ignore   c. take pride in
    b. substitute for d. stop for awhile

_____ 15. directions that *apply*
    a. are clear   c. are difficult
    b. are useful   d. cause problems

_____ 16. moving *ceaselessly*
    a. quickly   c. safely
    b. foolishly   d. without stopping

_____ 17. during *idle* moments
    a. pleasant   c. special
    b. not busy   d. ordinary

_____ 18. to *reveal* your feelings
    a. show   c. calm
    b. be sure of   d. try to hide

_____ 19. to *regain* our home
    a. sell   c. get back
    b. fix up   d. move out of

_____ 20. a *fanciful* story
    a. long   c. interesting
    b. believable   d. full of imagination

UNIT 9   Test Yourself

Part A   Synonyms

Write the letter of the word that is closest in meaning to the capitalized word.

_____ 1. CONFEDERATE: (A) associate (B) nation (C) trick (D) argument

_____ 2. GIGANTIC: (A) round (B) busy (C) huge (D) dangerous

_____ 3. VIGOROUS: (A) friendly (B) strong (C) scary (D) stiff

_____ 4. ACCOUNT: (A) report (B) discovery (C) number (D) journey

_____ 5. EXECUTE: (A) stop (B) leave (C) harm (D) kill

_____ 6. INTENTION: (A) secret (B) question (C) plan (D) nervousness

_____ 7. SUBSTANTIAL: (A) handy (B) solid (C) poor (D) different

_____ 8. CIRCULATE: (A) hide (B) find (C) spread (D) talk

_____ 9. QUALITY: (A) amount (B) excellence (C) price (D) decision

_____ 10. INCREDIBLE: (A) careless (B) wrong (C) lucky (D) unbelievable

Part B   Matching Definitions

Match each word on the left with its definition on the right. Write the letter of the definition in the blank.

_____ 11. inherit   a. barely enough or not enough

_____ 12. adverse   b. to enter by force in order to defeat

_____ 13. scanty   c. wild and violent; fierce

_____ 14. ferocious   d. what happens, or will happen, to a person or group

_____ 15. expedition   e. a person of high rank; one with a title, such as a duke

_____ 16. fate   f. to win; triumph; be greater in force

_____ 17. invade   g. something one is trying to get or achieve; goal

_____ 18. noble   h. to get or have after someone dies

_____ 19. prevail   i. acting against one's desires or interests; unfavorable

_____ 20. objective   j. a journey made for a particular purpose

UNIT 10 Test Yourself

Part A Applying Meaning

Write the letter of the best answer.

_____ 1. To <u>petrify</u> someone is to make that person unable to
a. move.   b. hear.   c. see.   d. understand.

_____ 2. Soldiers who <u>besiege</u> a town are trying to
a. bomb it.   b. capture it.   c. protect it.   d. escape from it.

_____ 3. Which of the following <u>accommodates</u> cars?
a. drivers   b. highways   c. tires   d. gasoline

_____ 4. Water will <u>permeate</u>
a. thirst.   b. a glass.   c. a sponge.   d. an umbrella.

_____ 5. Something that <u>smolders</u> is
a. coal.   b. a match.   c. a candle.   d. lightning.

_____ 6. An example of <u>domestic</u> work is
a. studying.   b. manufacturing.   c. ironing.   d. building houses.

_____ 7. If a chair is <u>available</u> for you, you can
a. see it.   b. sit in it.   c. sell it.   d. lift and move it.

_____ 8. You would <u>discount</u> someone's description of events if you thought it was
a. untrue.   b. amusing.   c. correct.   d. worth repeating.

Part B Synonyms

Write the letter of the word that is closest in meaning to the capitalized word.

_____ 9. DEMOLISH: (A) repair   (B) wreck   (C) threaten   (D) decrease

_____ 10. PLACID: (A) sharp   (B) flat   (C) calm   (D) hidden

_____ 11. HUMILIATE: (A) amuse   (B) punish   (C) scare   (D) embarrass

_____ 12. CONGREGATE: (A) gather   (B) pray   (C) listen   (D) agree

_____ 13. OPTION: (A) entrance   (B) sight   (C) argument   (D) choice

_____ 14. INCIDENT: (A) plan   (B) mistake   (C) event   (D) danger

_____ 15. INDUCE: (A) decide   (B) persuade   (C) understand   (D) discourage

_____ 16. MEAGER: (A) main   (B) bad   (C) small   (D) willing

_____ 17. MORALE: (A) idea   (B) enthusiasm   (C) success   (D) goodness

_____ 18. HESITATION: (A) pity   (B) sorrow   (C) habit   (D) pause

_____ 19. MIRACULOUS: (A) strange   (B) extraordinary   (C) pretend   (D) beautiful

_____ 20. OBVIOUS: (A) apparent   (B) correct   (C) needed   (D) normal

---

Score Yourself!   *The answers are on page 268.*   Number correct: _____   Part A: _____   Part B: _____

UNIT 11 Test Yourself

Part A   Matching Definitions

Match each word on the left with its definition on the right. Write the letter of the definition in the blank.

_____ 1. appoint   a. useful; realistic

_____ 2. token   b. agreement in feeling

_____ 3. snipe   c. to attack from a hiding place

_____ 4. parallel   d. to exchange letters

_____ 5. campaign   e. to name to an office or other position

_____ 6. percussion   f. the hitting of one object against another

_____ 7. institution   g. a series of actions meant to achieve a goal

_____ 8. practical   h. having only the appearance of; slight

_____ 9. sympathy   i. a longstanding custom or practice

_____ 10. correspond   j. going in the same direction, equally far apart forever

Part B   Recognizing Meaning

Write the letter of the word or phrase that is closest in meaning to the word or words in italics.

_____ 11. to speak *bitterly*
    a. loudly   c. carelessly
    b. with hatred   d. with humor

_____ 12. to *dispose of* a problem
    a. get rid of   c. think about
    b. result from   d. quarrel over

_____ 13. a *mortal* fear
    a. slight   c. foolish
    b. common   d. very strong

_____ 14. a dining room *suite*
    a. bouquet   c. hanging lamp
    b. large table   d. set of furniture

_____ 15. to decide to *resign*
    a. finish   c. try hard
    b. quit a job   d. start over

_____ 16. to *wage* a war
    a. win   c. carry on
    b. avoid   d. try to end

_____ 17. a brief *engagement*
    a. battle   c. summary
    b. period   d. love story

_____ 18. to have *repercussions*
    a. effects   c. enemies
    b. answers   d. disagreements

_____ 19. to *oust* their leader
    a. choose   c. follow
    b. force out   d. agree with

_____ 20. to show some *decency*
    a. pride   c. strong feeling
    b. ability   d. proper behavior

Score Yourself!   *The answers are on page 268*   Number correct: _____   Part A: _____   Part B: _____

UNIT 13 Test Yourself

Part A   Recognizing Meaning

Write the letter of the word or phrase that is closest in meaning to the word in italics.

_____ 1. our *uncommonly* good students
    a. famously   c. somewhat
    b. especially   d. supposedly

_____ 2. to view the *terrain*
    a. land   c. arrangement
    b. building   d. recent change

_____ 3. a *dismal* tone of voice
    a. angry   c. gloomy
    b. joking   d. unreasonable

_____ 4. to be *unmindful*
    a. stupid   c. relaxed
    b. careless   d. unexpected

_____ 5. your *previous* letter
    a. rude   c. expected
    b. earlier   d. overly long

_____ 6. the *duly* elected mayor
    a. properly   c. recently
    b. popularly   d. illegally

_____ 7. to have *ample* clothing
    a. beautiful   c. very stylish
    b. expensive   d. plentiful

_____ 8. the *geologist's* work
    a. jeweler's   c. earth scientist's
    b. stonecutter's d. plant scientist's

Part B   Matching Definitions

Match each word on the left with its definition on the right. Write the letter of the definition in the blank.

_____ 9. contrary   a. clear and unmistakable; precise; exact

_____ 10. consult   b. to ask the advice of

_____ 11. focus   c. to name to a position; establish by law

_____ 12. unheralded   d. in an organized, orderly manner

_____ 13. anonymity   e. opposite or opposed

_____ 14. definite   f. with a set goal in mind

_____ 15. engineer   g. to concentrate; give one's full attention to

_____ 16. systematically   h. having to do with more than one country

_____ 17. graduate   i. one trained in the use of science to meet everyday needs

_____ 18. international   j. not expected or announced

_____ 19. ordain   k. one who has completed a course of study

_____ 20. purposefully   l. the state of not having one's name made known

---

Score Yourself!   *The answers are on page 268.*   Number correct: _____   Part A: _____   Part B: _____

UNIT 14 Test Yourself

Part A Applying Meaning

Write the letter of the best answer.

_____ 1. An example of a <u>social</u> problem is a
    a. tornado.   b. plane crash.   c. forest fire.   d. lack of housing.

_____ 2. Judges are expected to <u>enforce</u>
    a. crimes.   b. the law.   c. prisons.   d. the police.

_____ 3. Someone interested in <u>politics</u> would be sure to pay attention to
    a. elections.   b. new movies.   c. sports.   d. good manners.

_____ 4. People have a <u>civic</u> responsibility to pay their
    a. taxes.   b. grocery bills.   c. employees.   d. rent.

_____ 5. You would expect a <u>cultured</u> person to have a lot of
    a. money.   b. knowledge.   c. duties.   d. free time.

_____ 6. A person could show a <u>dedication</u> to learning by
    a. being intelligent.   b. skipping class.   c. studying.   d. cheating on a test.

_____ 7. It is considered a sign of <u>respect</u> to
    a. yawn.   b. giggle.   c. bow.   d. blush.

_____ 8. You <u>persevere</u> when you keep working at something that is
    a. fun.   b. difficult.   c. foolish.   d. dangerous.

Part B Recognizing Meaning

Write the letter of the word or phrase that is closest in meaning to the word or words
in italics.

_____ 9. to show your *dedication*
    a. anger   c. ability
    b. devotion   d. sense of humor

_____ 10. Joe *versus* Janet
    a. after   c. against
    b. before   d. in addition to

_____ 11. a cheerful *attitude*
    a. look   c. place
    b. remark   d. way of feeling

_____ 12. to *ignite* our interest
    a. spark   c. notice
    b. approve of   d. guess about

_____ 13. a needed *reform*
    a. answer   c. description
    b. beginning   d. improvement

_____ 14. decide on a *policy*
    a. purchase   c. plan of action
    b. leader   d. location

_____ 15. a mighty *endeavor*
    a. effort   c. contest
    b. triumph   d. good chance

_____ 16. a *legitimate* worry
    a. deep   c. reasonable
    b. selfish   d. long-lasting

_____ 17. a clear *obligation*
    a. purpose   c. view
    b. mistake   d. responsibility

_____ 18. to show *discipline*
    a. self-control   c. high hopes
    b. friendliness   d. great ability

_____ 19. to *uphold* a decision
    a. argue with   c. support
    b. make known   d. understand

_____ 20. her *concern for* wildlife
    a. knowledge of   c. connection with
    b. skill with   d. interest in

Score Yourself!   *The answers are on page 268.*   Number correct: _____ Part A: _____ Part B: _____

UNIT 15 Test Yourself

Part A Matching Definitions

Match each word on the left with its definition on the right. Write the letter of the definition in the blank.

_____ 1. veteran   a. a place of safety

_____ 2. bewitch   b. to argue against; deny the truth of

_____ 3. contradict   c. able to move or to be moved

_____ 4. resent   d. to set apart from others

_____ 5. mobile   e. one who is in a contest against another

_____ 6. isolate   f. to put someone or something under a spell

_____ 7. competitor   g. to make certain

_____ 8. haven   h. one with much experience in a certain area

_____ 9. violate   i. to break or not pay attention to [a rule]

_____ 10. insure   j. to feel deep hurt or anger toward someone

Part B Synonyms

Write the letter of the word that is closest in meaning to the capitalized word.

_____ 11. SKIRMISH: (A) motion   (B) fight   (C) comment   (D) disturbance

_____ 12. TRANSMIT: (A) send   (B) change   (C) lift   (D) harm

_____ 13. COMPEL: (A) appreciate (B) force   (C) frighten   (D) speak

_____ 14. DECREASE: (A) reduce   (B) bend   (C) break   (D) sadden

_____ 15. PROCLAIM: (A) support   (B) end   (C) damage   (D) announce

_____ 16. APPAREL: (A) work   (B) protection (C) clothing   (D) tool

_____ 17. LODGE: (A) dwell   (B) sleep   (C) grow   (D) communicate

_____ 18. LOATHE: (A) misplace (B) fear   (C) despise   (D) notice

_____ 19. TOXIC: (A) strong   (B) poisonous (C) heavy   (D) frightening

_____ 20. CONSIDERABLE: (A) careful   (B) polite   (C) difficult   (D) large

Score Yourself!

Unit 1	Unit 2	Unit 3	Unit 5	Unit 6	Unit 7
Part A	*Part A*	*Part A*	*Part A*	*Part A*	*Part A*
1. c	1. c	1. e	1. A	1. a	1. f
2. b	2. d	2. d	2. D	2. d	2. l
3. a	3. d	3. c	3. B	3. c	3. b
4. d	4. b	4. b	4. C	4. a	4. d
5. a	5. b	5. l	5. B	5. b	5. e
6. c	*Part B*	6. n	6. A	6. b	6. a
7. a	6. C	7. f	7. D	7. d	7. j
8. d	7. D	8. j	8. C	8. b	8. c
9. b	8. A	9. i	9. B	9. b	9. k
10. c	9. A	10. g	10. C	10. c	10. i
Part B	10. B	11. m	*Part B*	11. b	11. g
11. d	11. C	12. o	11. c	12. d	12. h
12. a	12. B	13. h	12. a	13. a	*Part B*
13. h	13. D	14. a	13. b	14. d	13. b
14. c	14. A	15. k	14. c	*Part B*	14. d
15. f	15. A	*Part B*	15. b	15. b	15. b
16. g	16. D	16. b	16. d	16. a	16. d
17. e	17. B	17. a	17. a	17. a	17. b
18. i	18. C	18. c	18. b	18. c	18. a
19. j	19. D	19. a	19. d	19. c	19. c
20. b	20. D	20. d	20. c	20. b	20. d

Unit 9	Unit 10	Unit 11	Unit 13	Unit 14	Unit 15
Part A	*Part A*	*Part A*	*Part A*	*Part A*	*Part A*
1. A	1. a	1. e	1. b	1. d	1. h
2. C	2. b	2. h	2. a	2. b	2. f
3. B	3. b	3. c	3. c	3. a	3. b
4. A	4. c	4. j	4. b	4. a	4. j
5. D	5. a	5. g	5. b	5. b	5. c
6. C	6. c	6. f	6. a	6. c	6. d
7. B	7. b	7. i	7. d	7. c	7. e
8. C	8. a	8. a	8. c	8. b	8. a
9. B	*Part B*	9. b	*Part B*	*Part B*	9. i
10. D	9. B	10. d	9. e	9. b	10. g
Part B	10. C	*Part B*	10. b	10. c	*Part B*
11. h	11. D	11. b	11. g	11. d	11. B
12. i	12. A	12. a	12. j	12. a	12. A
13. a	13. D	13. d	13. l	13. d	13. B
14. c	14. C	14. d	14. a	14. c	14. A
15. j	15. B	15. b	15. i	15. a	15. D
16. d	16. C	16. c	16. d	16. c	16. C
17. b	17. B	17. a	17. k	17. d	17. A
18. e	18. D	18. a	18. h	18. a	18. C
19. f	19. B	19. b	19. c	19. c	19. B
20. g	20. A	20. d	20. f	20. d	20. D

Acknowledgments

- Curtis Brown Ltd.: For "Grandma and the Sea Gull" by Louise Dickinson Rich; copyright © 1943 by Louise Dickinson Rich.
- Harper & Row, Publishers: For an excerpt from *Sleep and Dreams* by Dr. Alvin and Virginia Silverstein; copyright © 1974 by Alvin and Virginia B. Silverstein.
- Rand McNally & Co.: For an adaptation from *Indian Legends of American Scenes* by Marion E. Gridley; copyright © 1939 Marion E. Gridley.
- Random House, Inc.: For an excerpt from *The Story of the Thirteen Colonies* by Clifford Lindsey Alderman; copyright © 1966 by Clifford Lindsey Alderman.
- Sherbourne Press: For an excerpt from "What Is Water Witching?" by Howard V. Chambers; published in *Dowsing, Water Witches and Divining Rods*; copyright © 1969 by Sherbourne Press.
- Franklin Watts, Inc.: For "Whales Shaped Like a Fish, But Not a Fish," from *Whales* by Helen Hoke and Valerie Pitt; copyright © 1973 by Helen Hoke and Valerie Pitt.

Every effort has been made to trace the ownership of all copyrighted material and to obtain permission.

Cover Art

Rippled Surface, 1950, M.C. ESCHER. National Gallery of Art, Washington, D.C., Cornelius Van S. Roosevelt Collection.

Photographs/Illustrations

- Cirrus Clouds, National Center for Atmospheric Research/National Science Foundation. p. 17
- Cumulus Clouds, © 1973 Russ Kinne/Comstock. p. 17
- Nimbus Clouds, National Center for Atmospheric Research/National Science Foundation. p. 17
- Stratus Clouds, National Center for Atmospheric Research/National Science Foundation. p. 17
- *Friends from Frolix 8*, JIM BURNS. p. 27
- Courtesy American Farriers Journal. p. 38
- © Elizabeth Crews. p.73
- From "A Book on Casino Craps," by C. IONESCU TULCEA © 1981 Litton Educational Publishing, Inc. Used by permission of the publisher, Van Nostrand Reinhold Co./A Division of Simon and Schuster, New York. p. 77
- *Sleeplessness*, JEFFREY FISHER. p. 84
- *The Trial of John Smith*, 1913, C.Y. TURNER. The Bettmann Archive, New York. p. 115
- North Wind Picture Archives. p. 127
- *Interior*, FISKE BOYD. Print Collection, Miriam and Ira D. Wallach Division of Art, Prints and Photographs, The New York Public Library, Astor, Lenox and Tilden Foundations. p. 139
- © Grafton Marshall Smith/The Image Bank. p.163
- UPI/Bettmann News Photos. p. 175
- *Strike*, TAYLOR OUGHTON. p. 186

Personal Vocabulary Log

Use the following pages to keep track of the unfamiliar words you encounter in your reading. Write brief definitions and pronunciations for each word. This will make the words part of your permanent vocabulary.

_____

_____

_____

_____

_____

_____

_____

_____

_____

_____

_____

_____

_____

_____

_____

_____

_____

_____

_____

_____

_____

_____

_____

Personal Vocabulary Log

Personal Vocabulary Log

Personal Vocabulary Log

Personal Vocabulary Log